Algorithmic Truth

Algorithmic Truth

When Data Becomes Belief

Yunis Al-Raqib

Mindful Pages

Published in 2026

ISBN: 9789374597866 (PB)
ISBN: 9789374596197 (eBook)

Published by

Mindful Pages
Imprint of Alpha Editions LLC
312 W. 2nd St #1834
Casper, WY 82601, USA

This book was developed using advanced writing tools to support the drafting and ideation process. All content has been thoughtfully curated, refined, and reviewed to ensure quality and relevance.

Content

Introduction

The glow of a screen can feel deceptively gentle. It illuminates the face without demanding much in return: a glance, a swipe, the smallest gesture of curiosity. Yet beneath that soft light lies a machinery of astonishing force. Every time a person pauses on a video, lingers over an article, or taps a hesitant like, the system learns something. Or, rather, it believes that it has learned something—and acts on that belief with unwavering confidence. A scroll through a feed can feel like an expression of personal taste, when in truth it is often a reflection of decisions made far upstream, beyond sight, beyond scrutiny. This quiet discrepancy is where modern life now unfolds.

Not long ago, the idea that invisible lines of code might nudge entire populations towards particular views would have sounded dramatic, even paranoid. Today it is merely ordinary. People wake to headlines tailored to their presumed politics, discover music selected to match past moods, and chat with friends amid suggested posts engineered for maximum emotional engagement. What began as a convenience has grown into a pervasive architecture of influence. The paradox is striking: systems designed to show us what we like can gradually reshape what we believe. A digital mirror, polished to reflect personal preference, subtly bends its reflection until the boundary between desire and persuasion becomes indistinct.

Consider a moment that recurs countless times each day. Someone looks up an unfamiliar topic—perhaps a news story, a scientific claim, a public figure. Within seconds, the screen fills with answers, confident and ranked. Yet those answers are not neutral guides; they are the visible tip of an elaborate selection process. What is promoted, sidelined, or dismissed depends on a tapestry of assumptions, commercial incentives, and historical data patterns. The user receives not the world as it is, but the world as calculated. Most trust these hierarchies implicitly. After all, they appear ordered, clean, rational. But behind those rankings lies a disquieting question: who, or what, decides which truths rise to the top?

The tension between data-driven systems and human judgement is hardly new. For centuries, societies have grappled with the allure of metrics that promise objectivity. When medieval astronomers plotted the heavens, they trusted diagrams that seemed to make sense even when reality contradicted them. When bureaucracies of the twentieth century classified citizens by category and measurement, those categories often carried a weight of false authority. The modern algorithm is simply the latest incarnation of an ancient temptation: to believe that numbers cannot lie, that patterns reveal what is fundamental. Yet the digital age has amplified this temptation to unprecedented heights, embedding it into daily routines so subtly that few recognise its cumulative power.

This book confronts that power directly. It traces how algorithms evolved from helpful assistants into influential gatekeepers, and how their decisions have come to shape public discourse, personal belief, and shared reality. It examines the hidden biases carried forward from incomplete datasets, the commercial priorities woven into ranking systems, and the psychological vulnerabilities that make people susceptible to curated certainty. It looks beyond the technical mechanics to the deeper cultural forces that have encouraged society to delegate judgement to machines, sometimes eagerly, sometimes anxiously, often without conscious reflection.

At the heart of this exploration lies a central motif: the digital mirror. A mirror suggests clarity, yet every mirror distorts. Some elongate, some compress, some reflect back only what the viewer expects to see. In the same way, algorithmic systems claim to reveal inner preferences while simultaneously shaping them. The mirror metaphor reminds us that reflection and manipulation can coexist, that the self presented back to us may be constructed from partial truths amplified over time. It is a reminder, too, that mirrors can trap as easily as they illuminate. Step too close and the view narrows. Walk away and the broader world comes back into focus.

The stakes of understanding these systems are considerable. Personal beliefs do not form in isolation; they are forged through exposure, repetition, and emotional resonance. When the flow of information is orchestrated by mechanisms optimised for engagement rather than understanding, the ground beneath those beliefs becomes unstable. What feels like independent thought may be the residue of subtle reinforcement loops. Small nudges accumulate, shaping a person's sense of what is normal, acceptable, or plausible. At scale, these nudges influence public opinion, electoral outcomes, cultural shifts. The boundaries between persuasion and manipulation blur. What begins as personal preference becomes a collective trajectory.

Yet this is not a book of panic, nor a treatise of despair. Alarmism helps no one. Precision—and a willingness to probe uncomfortable truths—serves far better. Some algorithmic systems do, undeniably, enhance human capability. They help doctors detect disease earlier, support researchers sorting through vast literature, and connect people who might otherwise remain isolated. But every technological advance carries an ideological imprint, and every promise of objectivity requires scrutiny. To accept systems uncritically is to surrender agency; to reject them entirely is to misunderstand their potential. The challenge lies in discerning where reliance becomes dependence, and where assistance shades into control.

To appreciate how deeply automated curation now shapes experience, one must examine the forces that built it. Early data systems were pragmatic tools: calculators, statistical models, rudimentary recommendation engines. Their authority grew in parallel with the myth of computational infallibility—a belief that machines, unburdened by human messiness, could pierce through ambiguity. Yet machines are trained on human choices, and those choices always encode patterns of inclusion and exclusion. Historical inequities, cultural biases, and economic priorities seep into datasets, quietly guiding outcomes. The modern algorithm is thus a paradoxical creature: outwardly precise, inwardly shaped by a lineage of partial truths.

Such complexities demand a more deliberate mode of thinking. Readers entering this book will encounter questions that resist simple answers. Why do people trust recommendations even when they sense bias? How do repeated narratives evolve into perceived truths? What role does emotion play in determining what feels credible? How does political, cultural, or corporate power embed itself within systems that present themselves as neutral? And perhaps most crucially: how can individuals and societies navigate a world where automated curation is both indispensable and potentially distorting?

The urgency of these questions cannot be overstated. Humanity has always contended with misinformation, persuasion, and bias. What distinguishes the current moment is scale, speed, and intimacy. A pamphlet may have swayed a crowd; a broadcast may have shaped a nation. But an algorithm can personalise persuasion for billions simultaneously, adapting itself in real time to each viewer's habits, vulnerabilities, and desires. This intimacy makes algorithmic influence uniquely potent. It operates not on the perimeter of attention but at its centre, quietly calibrating the boundaries of what seems reasonable, familiar, or true.

None of this is inevitable, however. Hidden influence becomes powerful only when it goes unexamined. The act of paying attention—truly paying attention—has always been a form of resistance. It is a way of reclaiming the slow, careful judgement that technology too often encourages us to abandon. By understanding how digital systems shape choices, beliefs, and identities, readers can cultivate a more discerning relationship with their digital environments. This book aims to sharpen that understanding, not by preaching withdrawal, but by revealing the mechanisms and motivations beneath the surface.

As the chapters unfold, a clear pattern will emerge. In Chapter 1, the historical rise of algorithmic authority shows how convenience and trust have intertwined over time. Chapter 2 exposes the roots of digital bias, revealing how unseen forces can skew outcomes long before the user encounters them. Chapter 3 contrasts the clarity promised by data determinism with the nuance required by human judgement. Chapter 4 explores the formation of echo chambers, examining how digital environments can confine rather than expand thought. In later chapters, the analysis shifts to questions of power: media as gatekeepers, ideology embedded in design, belief formation shaped by repetition, the tension between fact and narrative. Ultimately, the book points towards a future in which technology and human agency coexist more thoughtfully, guided by ethical oversight and an insistence on maintaining the human core of decision-making.

By the time the reader reaches the final chapter, the stakes will be unmistakable. This is not merely a story about algorithms; it is a story about how societies decide what is true. When data becomes belief, the responsibility to interpret, challenge, and contextualise information becomes even more pressing. Neutrality, long assumed to be a characteristic of technology, reveals itself as an illusion—a comforting myth that dissolves under scrutiny. What remains is the need for discernment, curiosity, and a willingness to question the systems that increasingly shape collective consciousness.

As you turn the page, consider the digital mirror in your own life. Ask what it reflects back to you—and what it conceals. Ask how often you have mistaken familiarity for truth, or convenience for clarity. Ask whether your beliefs are fully your own, or whether they bear the subtle fingerprints of systems designed to guide your attention. These questions are not meant to unsettle for the sake of drama; they are an invitation to reclaim the quiet but profound power of critical thought.

The world will continue to generate more data, more systems, more automated interpretations of what matters. But the core challenge remains unchanged: to ensure that the tools built to serve humanity do not quietly begin to shape its sense of reality. The chapters that follow offer a path through this challenge—rigorous, reflective, and, above all, grounded in the conviction that truth, however contested, is too important to outsource entirely.

Now the exploration begins.

Chapter 1
The Rise of Algorithmic Authority

The first signs of our growing dependence on algorithmic judgement did not come from grand experiments or philosophical debates but from the quiet design of early convenience. Picture a commuter in the late 2000s, half-awake on a morning train, scrolling through a newly personalised news feed. The articles appear uncannily aligned with their interests—politics, technology, a bit of sport—arranged with a sense of intuitive relevance. It feels almost courteous, as if the machine knows them. What they do not see is the machinery sifting thousands of possibilities in milliseconds, deciding what to elevate and what to discard. It is a gentle interaction, easy to overlook, yet it marks the beginning of a profound shift: information once sought is now served.

There is a beguiling neatness to this moment. The user feels empowered; the system feels helpful. But beneath this surface lies a remarkable paradox. The feed promises personal autonomy while quietly shaping the boundaries of it. The machine decides what is "important" by drawing from patterns it believes define the individual, and the individual, in turn, begins to see importance through the machine's eyes. This reciprocity—innocent at first glance—signals the ascent of a new authority. Not loud, not coercive, but steady, ubiquitous, and increasingly trusted.

Trust, of course, is the crucial term. People did not consciously decide to treat algorithmic outputs as reliable. Trust accumulated gradually, through repetition, through minor efficiencies, through the seductive clarity of ranked lists. Even now, many speak of algorithms as if they were impartial referees of information. The myth of mechanical neutrality—so deeply ingrained in the modern psyche—did not arise spontaneously. It has roots in older systems of classification and measurement that once claimed to reveal truths through quantification alone. Today's algorithms inherit that cultural legacy, even as they transform it.

To understand their authority, one must first appreciate this inheritance. Early data systems were built to perform narrow tasks: sorting census records, calculating actuarial tables, predicting basic trends. Their limitations were recognised, their scope clearly defined. Yet, over time, these systems acquired an aura of objectivity simply because they were mathematical. Figures seemed less fallible than human interpreters; patterns appeared more honest than subjective judgement. Gradually, a belief emerged that automated processes could—and perhaps should—take the lead in determining what counts as reliable knowledge.

Chapter 1 begins at this point of transition. It explores how simple tools grew into decision-making engines, how convenience became habit, and how habit evolved into reliance. The contemporary digital environment did not materialise overnight; it is the product of decades of cultural, commercial, and technological accumulation.

Understanding that trajectory is essential, for it reveals how society arrived at a place where algorithmic decisions are treated as authoritative even when their reasoning remains opaque.

The story deepens when we consider how willingly we delegate decisions to machines. Delegation is often framed as efficiency: why waste cognitive energy on trivial choices when a system can decide faster, cheaper, and with more data? But each act of delegation carries an unspoken trade-off. The more we outsource, the less we scrutinise. The less we scrutinise, the stronger the systems become—not merely in their technical capacity but in their status as arbiters of choice. A recommended route alters how a person travels through a city. A curated playlist influences their emotional cadence. A predictive search shapes the questions they might ask. None of these interactions is dramatic; they are the tiny cogs of daily life. Yet, in aggregate, they reveal a shift in the architecture of human decision-making.

The psychological ease of this arrangement is undeniable. People welcome tools that reduce friction. A system that decides for us can feel like a relief, particularly in a world saturated with options. But comfort can obscure consequence. What begins as assistance can quietly become direction. When a machine's suggestion appears before people have time to form their own preference, the suggestion often becomes the preference. The line between choice and default dissolves. In its place emerges a form of soft authority—persuasive not through force, but through convenience.

This shift also affects our understanding of accuracy. In principle, accuracy should describe how faithfully information maps onto reality. In practice, the meaning has grown more fluid. Digital platforms often define accuracy according to parameters that benefit engagement or revenue. A trending topic may reflect what the system deems likely to generate interaction, not what is factually significant. Search results may prioritise popularity or advertising value rather than depth or reliability. Such metrics subtly reshape the public sense of what is true. When a piece of information appears at the top of a list, it acquires an aura of legitimacy—even if the ranking criteria bear little relationship to factual merit.

Here lies one of the subtle tensions at the heart of digital culture: algorithms claim to reveal the world, yet they reveal it according to values that are neither universal nor neutral. This makes the concept of *accuracy* dangerously malleable. A platform optimised for relevance will deliver one version of the world. A platform optimised for profit will deliver another. Users rarely see the difference. They encounter a polished surface—tidy, sorted, authoritative—without glimpsing the ideological scaffolding beneath it.

And so we return to trust. When systems shape knowledge, trust becomes a currency that can be won, manipulated, or misplaced. Many people trust algorithms precisely because they seem detached from political agendas or human prejudice. Yet this is increasingly questioned. Across academic institutions, regulatory bodies, advocacy groups, and online communities, scepticism is growing. Scholars dissect the biases embedded in datasets. Watchdogs scrutinise recommendation systems that amplify misinformation. Grassroots movements call for transparency and accountability, recognising that what is presented as fact may be carefully curated, selected, or sculpted.

This rising scepticism is not merely a critique of technology; it is a reflection of deeper cultural unease. Society is confronting a realisation that the tools meant to organise knowledge can also distort it. The very systems designed to enhance understanding have the capacity to narrow it. This awareness introduces a necessary tension. People who once viewed algorithms as benevolent helpers now interrogate the unseen motives, the opaque calculations, the commercial incentives that influence what they are shown. Some distrust intensifies; others adopt a cautious pragmatism. But few can claim innocence about the forces at play.

This chapter serves as a starting point for that examination. It introduces the reader to the origins, mechanisms, and consequences of algorithmic authority. It offers a historical lens, revealing how past assumptions shape present technologies. It examines the psychological tendencies that make people receptive to machine-led guidance. And it confronts the philosophical questions that arise when automated systems become the default interpreters of reality. Each section builds upon the previous one, demonstrating how authority emerges not through a single leap but through a sequence of incremental shifts—shifts that many accepted without noticing their cumulative weight.

The chapter also challenges readers to reconsider the narrative that algorithms are objective because they lack human emotion. Authority without emotion is not the same as authority without bias. Machines inherit the patterns we feed them. Those patterns reflect histories of inequality, imaginations of desirability, and ideologies embedded in code. Recognising this fact is not an argument against technology; it is an argument for informed engagement. Authority is not dangerous in itself. What is dangerous is authority granted without examination.

As the introduction draws to a close, the path ahead becomes clear. The chapter invites readers to look beyond the comforting surface of automated systems and to examine the cultural, psychological, and commercial forces that propelled them to prominence. It asks them to consider why society granted algorithms such influence, how that influence is wielded, and what it means for a world increasingly shaped by unseen hands. The exploration will reveal both the benefits and the blind spots, the ingenuity of these systems and their limitations, the convenience they offer and the agency they quietly erode.

What emerges is a story not of machines taking power, but of people giving it away—through trust, through habit, through the seductive appeal of simplicity. As you continue into the chapter, you will encounter the origins of our relationship with algorithmic judgement, the evolution of its authority, and the questions that now demand attention. The digital mirror reflects more than preference; it reflects the choices society has made about who—or what—gets to decide what matters. The next pages begin the work of seeing that reflection clearly.

Algorithmic Inheritance

In October 1952, at the University of Manchester, Alan Turing and his colleagues watched their early computing machine perform a task that seemed trivial on the surface: sorting a list of numbers with consistent precision. What mattered was not the numbers but the principle—the promise that a machine could process information faster and with fewer errors than any human clerk. That room, humming quietly beneath industrial rafters, marked an early moment when computation began to look authoritative. A simple sort became a symbol. The idea took root that calculation could reveal order, and order could reveal truth. Five words lingered in the air: *the machine knows this now.*

The confidence that followed grew quickly. By the late 1960s, when the U.S. Census Bureau in Washington, D.C. relied on automated tabulation to classify millions of citizens, the process carried a sense of almost clerical neutrality. Officials spoke of data as a corrective to human bias, not a vessel for it. What no one fully articulated at the time was how easily the outputs of these systems could be mistaken for inherent truth. The more consistently a machine produced results, the more those results acquired an aura of inevitability. Regularity looked like reliability. Consistency looked like authority. The machine knows this now. That motif began to echo through many decisions.

This inheritance matters because contemporary algorithmic systems are built upon it, even as they differ profoundly in scale. The leap from Turing's sorter to a personalised news feed rests on the same core principle: that statistical regularities can illuminate meaning. And yet the shift from batch calculation to live curation introduces a new complexity. The older systems answered questions asked by humans. The newer ones decide which questions people are invited to ask. When a user in London opens their phone at 7:12 a.m. and sees a ranked series of stories, the placement feels obvious, as if the stories arranged themselves. But behind the layout lies a chain of assumptions derived from decades of treating machine-generated order as inherently sensible.

To see how this trust was shaped, consider a second moment: the 1998 launch of Google's search engine in Menlo Park, California. The PageRank system introduced a powerful idea—that popularity could signal relevance. Researchers and journalists praised its clarity. Pages at the top appeared not because a human editor deemed them important, but because an algorithm weighed links as votes. The method emerged from mathematics, not editorial preference. Many interpreted this as neutrality. In reality, it was an inherited belief that numerical patterns could replace judgement. The machine knows this now. And once it knows, we tend to accept.

Yet numerical patterns are shaped by the world from which they are drawn. When personalised news feeds became widespread in the early 2010s, the mechanisms guiding them still bore the imprint of these earlier assumptions. Systems prioritised articles that generated clicks, shares, and dwell time partly because these metrics were straightforward to measure. A story that held user attention for 38 seconds was deemed more "engaging" than one that held attention for 12. Engagement became a proxy for relevance. Relevance became a proxy for value. Value drifted towards truth. By the time users scrolled through their morning updates, the boundary between what mattered and what the system could quantify had all but blurred.

The implication is tangible in behaviour. People check headlines not to find everything but to find something—something selected, filtered, and arranged. They gesture through curated streams believing they have chosen their informational diet, while the system quietly curates the choices themselves. This is not deception. It is architectural influence. The machine does not hide its logic; it simply operates at a speed and scale that makes scrutiny impractical. So trust grows by default. A user sees the same types of stories day after day and interprets this repetition as evidence of importance rather than the outcome of optimisation metrics calibrated to maximise attention.

A counterpoint emerges when looking at the early failures of automated translation in the 1970s. In 1977, a project funded by the National Science Foundation attempted to translate scientific papers between English and Russian using rule-based systems. The results were rigid and error-prone, often missing context entirely. Linguists criticised the naivety of assuming that language could be reduced to simple mappings. Here, machine results did not carry an aura of authority but of inadequacy. The machine knows this now was replaced by the quieter recognition: the machine cannot know this yet. This limitation tempers the narrative. It shows that trust in algorithms was never automatic; it had to be earned through domains where systems appeared consistent, not through domains where nuance exceeded computation.

Reconcile this with modern feeds, and a pattern reveals itself. Where systems demonstrated speed and reliability—sorting data, ranking pages, recommending familiar genres—they accumulated trust. Where they faltered in meaning-heavy tasks, trust grew slowly. The issue is that personalised information feeds fold meaning-heavy tasks into the appearance of mechanical reliability. They mimic the precision of sorting or tabulation while dealing in subjects that were once the domain of editors, scholars, and citizens exercising judgement. That blurring is the hallmark of our current moment.

Early data systems also shaped expectations around "clean" results. When engineers in the 1950s designed punch-card sorting processes for actuarial calculations in New York insurance offices, the output appeared on crisp, typewritten printouts. There was little room for ambiguity. Columns lined up. Totals were precise. The aesthetic of computation became associated with order. Modern interfaces retain this aesthetic. Search pages are tidy. Recommendation grids are symmetrical. Structured clarity becomes a silent argument: *If it looks organised, it must be accurate.* When a news feed places one story above another with seamless typography, that hierarchy feels grounded in method, not motive.

Accuracy, then, becomes something curated. Not in the fraudulent sense of manipulation, but in the subtler sense of selection. Systems trained on patterns learn what users tend to click. They adjust. Over time, they reinforce the same themes, shaping the sense of what deserves attention. A person might read three stories about a corporate merger not because the merger is globally significant, but because the system has learned they click financial content at breakfast. These micro-selections accumulate into the impression of a world defined by the interests that machines infer. The machine knows this now—because it has measured the user's hesitation over a headline.

There is also a cultural element in this inheritance. Post-war societies increasingly embraced the belief that technologies could act as rational arbiters. Scholars such as Theodore Porter (1995) have shown how the twentieth century exhibited a "trust in numbers" that aligned scientific methods with bureaucratic decision-making. Quantification was framed as impartial. This cultural momentum fed directly into early digital thinking. When databases expanded in the 1980s, when spreadsheets became ubiquitous in 1985 with Microsoft Excel, when statistical modelling tools became central to finance and logistics, the narrative was consistent: numbers constrain bias. People began to behave as if numerical processes sat outside ideology.

Yet numbers are never outside ideology. They are shaped by it. When an algorithm curates information, it inherits not only the data from which it learns but the historical forces that shaped the data. Demographic skew. Cultural context. Commercial appetite. A trending item is often the residue of earlier human preferences amplified by automated reinforcements. Calling this inheritance "objective" stretches the term beyond utility.

A second checkable example underscores this dynamic. In 2009, Netflix's recommendation system became a public talking point when the company released anonymised rating data for the Netflix Prize competition. Researchers quickly demonstrated that supposedly de-identified data could still reveal sensitive user preferences with alarming accuracy. The lesson was clear: patterns trained on human habits reflect more than taste; they reveal private trajectories, ideological leanings, and social markers. The participants were shocked not by the leak itself but by what the patterns contained. The machine knows this now meant the system had learned to infer more than users realised.

If this is the inheritance, why do people trust it? Behaviour offers the clearest answer. Trust emerges not from grand principles but from consistent interactions: the train arrives when the app predicts; the route saves seven minutes; the playlist matches the mood; the shopping suggestion arrives the day before the user remembers they need it. Small efficiencies build credibility. People feel the benefit immediately and the cost only indirectly. The machine knows this now because it has been allowed to know this, piece by piece.

A counter-example again complicates the picture. In 2016, during the early controversy over Facebook's Trending Topics module, some internal reviewers claimed that human editors had quietly influenced which stories appeared. Critics argued that the presence of human judgement undermined the system's neutrality. Ironically, the same critics showed little concern for the algorithmic influences that had always guided the rankings. What they distrusted was not selective curation itself but the revelation that curation involved people. This raises an uncomfortable truth: people prefer the illusion of machine objectivity to the visibility of human subjectivity. That preference is part of the inheritance.

Reconciliation requires acknowledging both impulses. Systems gain trust when they appear consistent and impartial. They lose trust when they reveal the messy human decisions within them. Yet all systems contain such decisions. Even the earliest machines were shaped by the engineers who defined their parameters. The story of algorithmic inheritance is not a story of machines replacing humans. It is a story of machines magnifying the patterns that humans embedded, often unconsciously, into their design.

Each step in this lineage nudges society toward a worldview in which automated outputs feel authoritative by default. When people accept a search ranking as meaningful or a news feed as representative, they are drawing on decades of cultural conditioning. They are responding to infrastructures built to appear neutral. They are accepting curation as clarity.

One quiet motif returns throughout this subchapter: the phrase *the machine knows this now.* It is a reminder of how easily knowledge can be mistaken for inference, inference for fact, fact for truth. The motif underscores a transition from mechanical calculation to informational gatekeeping. The shift is not merely technological. It is philosophical.

The unresolved question that remains is deceptively simple: if authority has been inherited rather than earned, what happens when a system's confidence exceeds its competence? When the machine knows this now collides with the limits of what a machine should know, users must decide—consciously or not—whether to accept guidance or reclaim judgement.

Delegating Our Decisions

In March 2018, a commuter named Michael O'Donnell followed the route suggested by Google Maps through Hayes, West London, on his drive to Heathrow Airport. A crash on the M4 had pushed thousands of drivers onto side streets, and the app diverted him down a narrow residential road. Within minutes, traffic stalled completely. At least 120 cars queued in single file, boxed between parked vehicles and bollards, unable to turn back. Residents later told the BBC that their quiet street had become "a rolling car park" because the navigation system kept sending people there. What struck observers was not the congestion itself but the certainty with which every driver—Michael included—assumed that the machine's advice was preferable to their own judgement. Five words hovered unspoken in each idling vehicle: *the system knows this now.*

That gesture of unthinking acceptance appears small: a tap, a glance, a turn of the wheel. But it signals a broader shift in how choices are made. Each diversion becomes a behavioural micro-contract, a moment when a private decision is surrendered to an external logic because it promises ease. The drivers knew the road looked wrong. They committed anyway. That trust was silent but decisive. Five words again: *the system knows this now.* It became the motif of the morning.

This dynamic lies at the heart of how people increasingly navigate daily life. Systems automate tasks not merely by offering options but by presenting those options as default. The move from assistance to authority is subtle. And once that shift gathers momentum, it rarely reverses itself.

The most visible manifestation of this delegation comes through routine digital behaviours. When a user opens a shopping platform, the "Buy Again" list sits prominently on the homepage. Amazon introduced the feature globally in 2015, after successful trials in Seattle and Berlin. It measured how frequently people purchased the same household items—coffee, detergent, razor cartridges—and tested whether a convenience shortcut would accelerate repeat sales. It did. The average time between identical orders shortened meaningfully, reducing hours of deliberation across weeks, months, years. Behaviour changed because thinking became unnecessary. The user scrolls. The system displays. The purchase completes. The system knows this now.

Show, name, explain, implication. What we see is convenience. What we name is automation. What we explain is cognitive offloading. And the implication is that decisions lose the texture of being chosen.

A similar dynamic emerged with Spotify's *Discover Weekly,* launched in July 2015. Engineers in Stockholm measured user listening sessions to predict which new songs aligned with established habits. People began treating the playlist not as a suggestion but as a weekly identity report—*this is who you are, musically speaking*. The behavioural metric was revealing: when Spotify analysed listener patterns in 2016, a significant portion of streams during the first 24 hours after playlist release came from tracks users had never previously selected. The playlist did not merely reflect taste; it defined it. The system knows this now.

These examples demonstrate how delegation becomes habitual. The visible behaviour—tapping a recommended track, following a suggested route—appears trivial. But repetition reshapes expectation. A system that performs reliably creates a rhythm in which people stop comparing options altogether. They follow the first suggestion. They treat the default as the decision.

Yet a counter-example highlights limits to this pattern. In 2011, IBM's Watson won *Jeopardy!* in New York, outperforming champions Ken Jennings and Brad Rutter. The event was celebrated as a milestone in machine reasoning. But when Watson was later adapted for clinical decision support at the University of Texas MD Anderson Cancer Center, an internal audit (MD Anderson, 2017) reported that the system struggled with incomplete or ambiguous patient data. Doctors reverted to traditional diagnostic discussions. Delegation halted. The machine did not know this now. The limitations of automation were laid bare.

Reconciliation requires nuance. Delegation thrives when the task is repetitive or low-stakes—routes, playlists, shopping. It falters when the stakes rise or uncertainty increases. But daily digital life consists overwhelmingly of low-stakes tasks, and the line between low and high stakes blurs when enough small choices accumulate.

The psychology behind this shift has been studied for decades, often under different terminology. The behavioural economist Herbert Simon argued in 1971 that humans satisfice rather than optimise: they choose what is "good enough" when cognitive effort is costly. Algorithmic systems exploit this tendency structurally. When the interface presents a recommended option with visual prominence—larger text, central placement, a coloured highlight—users gravitate to it. They do this even when alternative choices might better suit their intentions. The visible behaviour is selection; the driver is interface architecture; the implication is that judgement drifts subtly toward automation without conscious recognition.

One driver of this drift is the paradoxical comfort of certainty. Machines present decisions as if ambiguity has been resolved in advance. A list of hotels sorted by "Top Picks for You" suggests a distilled conclusion. A notification reading "Time to leave for your appointment" implies that the messiness of travel—traffic flow, distance, unpredictability—has already been computed. People follow. It saves thinking.

Another visible behaviour reveals the depth of this comfort: users rarely interrogate why a specific recommendation appears. Social psychologists refer to this as cognitive ease. The default feels correct because engaging with alternatives feels effortful. A 2019 study by the Reuters Institute found that more than half of surveyed users in Sweden, the UK, and Germany did not realise that their news feeds were algorithmically ranked. They assumed editorial curation. Delegation therefore operates beneath awareness. People trust without noticing they trust.

This is where the shift from assistance to reliance becomes most consequential. Early digital tools required explicit input: you asked the library catalogue for a book; you typed a location into a map; you browsed categories manually. Modern systems reduce friction by eliminating steps. Siri suggests reminders before they are requested. Financial apps propose savings patterns derived from spending behaviour. Photo platforms compile "memories" based on machine-identified themes. The machine knows this now. In these moments, agency transfers quietly to the system, not because users consciously surrender it, but because the system anticipates before the user initiates.

A second historical example illustrates how anticipation changes decision-making. In 2009, when Apple introduced push notifications to the iPhone via iOS 3, the company framed them as a way to keep users updated. But by 2013, researchers at Carnegie Mellon University documented that notifications increased reactive phone checking by measurable percentages across thousands of users. Each alert shifted attention immediately. Decision-making became externally triggered rather than internally initiated.

The machine knew what to prompt and when. Delegation spread from what a person chooses to when they choose.

The counterpoint to this is human resistance. People do not always accept automation. When YouTube's autoplay feature was introduced globally in 2015, some users disabled it quickly, feeling overwhelmed by continuous content. This shows that delegation is not automatic; it is conditional. Yet even those who disable autoplay often continue relying on recommended videos, returning repeatedly to the curated suggestions that populate the homepage. Resistance exists, but it rarely undermines the broader dynamic.

The cumulative effect of these patterns reshapes the nature of responsibility itself. When systems pre-sort options, predict behaviour, and offer personalised outcomes, responsibility becomes distributed. A user may choose a recommended news article because it is first on the screen. They may dine at a restaurant selected for them by a map tool. They may ignore a friend's message because the notification appears lower in the queue. Each micro-decision feels insignificant. But together they form a chain of influence in which human intention mingles with machine inference. The decision may technically belong to the user, but its architecture belongs to the system.

Here, the motif returns: *the system knows this now.* It becomes an ambient assumption. The system knows my habits. The system knows my schedule. The system knows the fastest route. The system knows the best deal. The repetition of this belief breeds familiarity, and familiarity breeds trust.

But trust is not the only factor. There is also relief. People feel a quiet comfort when decisions shrink. A system that narrows options feels like a friend simplifying a cluttered table. This is the psychological comfort of delegation: the sense that one is being looked after by something capable, efficient, and tireless. The more that sensation grows, the less decision-making feels like an active responsibility.

Yet delegation carries a cost: diminished reflection. When a system suggests the next step before a person considers alternatives, the habit of deliberate thought weakens. Consider a concrete behaviour: the user who once compared five news sources now opens the app that "knows their interests." The person who once debated restaurant options with a partner now selects the top suggestion on an app ranked by predicted enjoyment. The student who once explored multiple academic articles now clicks the platform's recommended reading list. In each case, the narrowing of deliberation diminishes the practice of choice.

Still, this is not a story of erasure. Humans resist. They question. They compare when stakes feel high. Yet delegation expands when the friction of comparison outweighs the perceived benefit of reflection. And modern systems are designed to minimise friction.

Where does this leave the reader? With a quiet but substantial tension. At what point does convenience become dependence? At what point does reliance become vulnerability? And at what point does the belief that *the system knows this now* eclipse the recognition that the system only knows what it has been allowed to learn?

The unresolved test remains: the next time a device offers the easiest choice, will the user pause long enough to ask whether it is also the right one?

Redefining Accuracy

On 15 August 2019, the Oxford Internet Institute released an analysis of Google's search patterns during a political controversy in the United Kingdom. The report found that a spike in searches for a single phrase—"prorogation legality"—triggered an automatic surge of identical stories into the Top Stories carousel for users in London. What caught researchers' attention was the ordering: articles published later but attracting faster click-through rates appeared above earlier, more detailed legal analyses. Visibility aligned not with depth but with velocity. A ranking signal—engagement within minutes—became a surrogate for truth. One researcher remarked that the list "looked authoritative but read as momentum." Five quiet words linger beneath that morning's data: *the algorithm knows this now.*

Accuracy once meant alignment with evidence. In that August case, accuracy described alignment with user behaviour. The distinction is small yet decisive. A system that measures clicks does not measure comprehension. A list that reflects popularity does not reflect validity. And yet, when people saw those ranked headlines, they behaved as though the order revealed which interpretation deserved the most intellectual weight. They clicked the top link. They repeated its framing. They absorbed its claims. The highest-ranked item felt closest to fact because it appeared first. A five-word motif settles in again, shaping the narrative: *the algorithm knows this now.*

To understand how this happens, one must examine how modern systems define accuracy in practice. Search engines, social platforms, and recommendation tools rarely treat accuracy as a single criterion. They treat it as an optimisation target intertwined with engagement signals, commercial incentives, and predictive models. What appears as a question of truth becomes a question of relevance. What appears as a question of relevance becomes a question of likelihood: *How probable is the next click?* When the architecture of accuracy is defined this way, truth bends towards metrics.

Show, name, explain, implication: the engine of this subchapter.

One clear example comes from the history of Google's PageRank algorithm, launched publicly in 1998 from Menlo Park. PageRank measured importance by counting inbound links: a link acted as a vote. The company named this method "link authority," suggesting a democratic process embedded in computation. But in practice, it rewarded websites that already enjoyed visibility, reproducing existing hierarchies. When users searched for a topic—say, "climate change impacts" in 2004—they encountered pages ranked not necessarily for scientific accuracy but for link density. The visible behaviour was simple: users clicked the first result. The explanation was structural: early web patterns determined what the algorithm inherited. The implication was cultural: accuracy began to mean "most linked," not "most rigorous."

A second example shows the commercial layer. In 2013, YouTube redesigned its recommendation engine to optimise for "watch time," a metric recorded in seconds. The company announced the change from San Bruno, California, and saw immediate effects: videos with dramatic titles or emotionally charged content surged in visibility because they held viewers' attention longer. The system treated retention as accuracy, inferring that time spent signalled value. Users scrolling through the homepage encountered thumbnails chosen algorithmically, and many interpreted their prominence as a mark of authority. But the system's definition of accuracy was not epistemic. It was temporal. The algorithm knows this now.

This dynamic produces a cultural confusion: people mistake engagement for legitimacy. A trending topic on X (formerly Twitter) appears authoritative because thousands have referenced it in a short period. A search snippet appears trustworthy because it sits at the top of the screen.

The visible behaviour—clicking, sharing, believing—follows naturally. The underlying explanation is structural: trending systems prioritise recency and volume, not verification. The implication is societal: the velocity of attention can overpower the weight of evidence.

There is, however, a counter-example that complicates the narrative. In 2021, Wikipedia editors—volunteers rather than platform engineers—rapidly corrected misinformation about a volcanic eruption in La Palma, Spain. False claims circulating on social platforms suggested imminent tsunami risks for the United States East Coast. Wikipedia's moderation protocols required citations from authoritative geological agencies. Editors from multiple countries intervened within hours, and the article stabilised quickly. Here, accuracy adhered to evidence rather than engagement. The system resisted the drift toward popularity-based ranking. The implication is important: not every digital architecture treats behaviour as a proxy for truth. Some retain epistemic guardrails.

Reconcile these cases, and a pattern emerges. Accuracy is shaped by design. Some systems optimise for behavioural signals. Some optimise for evidentiary standards. Users rarely see the difference. They see only the final ranking and infer a logic that may or may not exist.

This inference—*the system knows this now*—is a quiet motif threading through daily digital experience. It shapes what people trust, what they repeat, and what they assume. The motif works because modern interfaces present information with a veneer of certainty: crisp typography, clean layouts, ranked lists, blue ticks. An ordered screen suggests ordered truth.

Consider behaviour in the context of news feeds. In 2020, researchers at the Reuters Institute documented that a sizeable proportion of users in the UK interpreted algorithmic rankings on Facebook and Google News as editorial decisions. They believed the ordering reflected significance. When they clicked the top story, they assumed it had been vetted for importance. Their actions—reading, sharing, discussing—showed how quickly users equate visibility with veracity. The explanation is structural: the system unifies design and ranking to present a seamless narrative. The implication is psychological: people inherit confidence from interface coherence.

This is not accidental. Modern ranking systems incorporate both cultural and commercial signals. Culturally, they adapt to collective habits. Commercially, they adapt to business models. A platform that funds itself through advertising can define "accuracy" in ways that converge with revenue optimisation. A story that attracts more impressions gains more ad exposure. If that story also gains more clicks, it appears more "engaging." If it remains engaging, the system elevates it further. At each step, engagement is converted into apparent correctness. A cycle forms.

This cycle produces visible consequences. Look at the phenomenon of "first-page bias"—the measurable behaviour in which users rarely move beyond the top ten search results. A 2014 study by Chitika, cited widely before the firm dissolved, found that the first result received roughly one-third of all clicks. Even if one discounts exact percentages, subsequent research affirms the structural pattern: users overwhelmingly choose from the suggested shortlist. The explanation is not laziness; it is trust in the hierarchy. The implication is epistemic narrowing: what appears early becomes what appears true.

Accuracy, then, is neither neutral nor purely technical. It is an assembled value, shaped by instruments, incentives, and inherited assumptions.

One quieter aspect of this inheritance lies in the aesthetics of precision. Digital systems present themselves as numerical, and numerical presentation creates a sense of objectivity. A forecast with a 92 per cent confidence interval signals authority, even if the underlying model contains biased inputs. A "Top 10 for You" list suggests curation grounded in personal insight. The visible behaviour—choosing the top option—follows this framing. The explanation is psychological ease: numbers look definitive. The implication is vulnerability: certainty can be manufactured through design rather than derived from evidence.

Historical context deepens the point. In 1954, the RAND Corporation in Santa Monica published a report on early decision models used for defence planning. The mathematicians explicitly warned that numerical predictions risked misleading policymakers if treated as precise representations of complex realities. Yet as computation grew more sophisticated, that caution faded from public consciousness. The belief that a calculation could be synonymous with correctness became culturally embedded. And today's algorithmic systems inherit that confidence even when their outputs reflect popularity rather than fact.

The motif returns: *the algorithm knows this now.* It is the refrain that turns rankings into truth claims.

To observe this motif in action, examine the behaviour surrounding "People also ask" boxes on Google Search. Users often expand the first question simply because it appears first. The system surfaces queries that others have clicked. Those queries then generate more clicks. A loop forms. The system interprets behaviour as confirmation. The user interprets visibility as accuracy. The explanation is mechanical simplicity masquerading as interpretive authority. The implication is epistemic feedback: truth becomes an echo of aggregated behaviour.

A second structural factor is the commercial architecture underlying many platforms. In 2020, Facebook (Meta) acknowledged before the U.S. Congress that its ranking algorithms weigh thousands of signals, including recency, user similarity, and predicted engagement. The company did not frame this as accuracy but as personalised relevance. Yet for users, the distinction collapses. What appears atop the feed feels like a prioritisation of importance. If a story about a healthcare policy outranks a story about a tax change, many assume the former is more pressing. The system knows this now becomes a filter through which users assess public life.

Here lies a cultural tension. People expect platforms to guide them toward credible information. Platforms, however, optimise for time spent, interaction likelihood, and retention metrics. These objectives are legitimate from a business perspective. But when these metrics masquerade as epistemic measures, accuracy shifts from correspondence to reality toward correspondence with predicted behaviour.

This shift invites a hard question: when did visibility become a proxy for truth?

The answer is cumulative. It began with ranking systems that rewarded link patterns. It expanded with engagement-driven curation. It matured with personalisation engines that blurred preference with veracity. And it now manifests as a daily behavioural habit: users rarely ask why an item appears where it does.

The unresolved tension is this: if accuracy is continually redefined by popularity, velocity, and profit, how do individuals distinguish between what is true and what merely rises to the top? And what happens when *the algorithm knows this now* becomes the quiet foundation on which entire publics form their beliefs?

Emerging Scepticism

On 18 March 2019, the nonprofit investigative group ProPublica published an analysis revealing that Facebook's ad-delivery system in Menlo Park disproportionately showed job adverts for mechanics to men and customer service roles to women. The data were clear: even when advertisers targeted a broad audience, the platform's optimisation engine narrowed delivery based on predicted engagement patterns. Within hours of publication, researchers, commentators, and campaigners questioned the neutrality of a system that shaped who saw which opportunities. ProPublica's finding was not merely a data anomaly. It sparked a broader cultural shift: people began to ask whether the digital filters structuring public life were quietly inheriting and amplifying social bias. A persistent question surfaced beneath the headlines: *who decides what we see?* Five short words trailed close behind: *the algorithm knows this now.*

The episode marked a turning point because the public response was not passive. Users debated the findings on social forums, policy groups demanded audits, and academics framed the case as evidence that optimisation and neutrality were not synonymous. The visible behaviour—comment threads, petitions, parliamentary questions—showed that trust was beginning to fracture. The assumption that automated systems merely mirrored society no longer held. Something darker had crept into view: the possibility that what appeared as fact was the by-product of digital curation.

This scepticism did not appear suddenly. It accumulated gradually across cases, reports, and misalignments between expectation and outcome. Yet by the end of the 2010s, it gained unmistakable momentum.

The core dynamic begins with observation. People see a discrepancy. They name it. They explain it. Then they measure the implications. That sequence is the foundation of structural critique.

Consider the first major claim: neutrality is often a performance rather than a property. Show the pattern. In 2016, at Princeton University, Arvind Narayanan and his team demonstrated that widely used word-embedding models trained on Google News data contained gender associations that mapped words like "doctor" to "male" and "nurse" to "female." Name the issue: algorithmic inheritance. Explain the mechanism: statistical systems absorb patterns without distinguishing between descriptive correlation and normative validity. Implication: neutrality becomes the veneer through which cultural inequalities flow uninterrupted.

This academic critique fed directly into watchdog activity. The Algorithmic Justice League, founded by Joy Buolamwini in Cambridge, Massachusetts, made headlines in 2018 when its audits of commercial facial-recognition systems revealed error rates exceeding 30 per cent for darker-skinned women, compared with under 1 per cent for lighter-skinned men (Buolamwini & Gebru, 2018). The visible behaviour—public reports, conferences, formal letters to government agencies—showed scepticism solidifying into structural pressure. The metric—a measured percentage point gap—converted abstraction into evidence. The implication reverberated globally: systems marketed as neutral did not perform neutrally.

But scepticism must grapple with nuance. A credible counter-example challenges the arc. In 2022, the Wikimedia Foundation published its annual transparency report showing that its content ranking and moderation processes rely not on opaque models but on publicly documented algorithms and volunteer oversight. Wikipedia's structure allows anyone to see how edits are made, reverted, or challenged. Accuracy is negotiated openly. This stands in contrast to the closed systems under scrutiny. The counter-example proves that scepticism is not cynicism. It is discrimination—between architectures that invite scrutiny and those that obscure it.

Reconciliation reveals an essential truth: people are not mistrusting algorithms per se; they are mistrusting infrastructures that refuse accountability.

The motif returns: *the algorithm knows this now.* Each time it appears, it invites a question: *why does it know what it knows?* And *what does that knowledge reveal about the world that trained it?*

Public scepticism also emerges visibly in the rise of online transparency movements. One of the most active began on Reddit in late 2020, where users of r/Technology's "Algorithmic Transparency Week" compiled instances of unexplained ranking anomalies across platforms, from YouTube recommendations to Amazon search placements. Participants posted screenshots showing price jumps, filter patterns, and recommendation loops. The visible behaviour was meticulous documentation. The named concern was opacity. The explanation centred on asymmetric information: platforms know how rankings are produced; users do not. The implication was civic: democracy struggles when information hierarchies are privately engineered.

This crowd-sourced scepticism mirrors earlier academic debates. As far back as 1993, Geoffrey Bowker and Susan Leigh Star argued that classification systems embody the power structures of their makers. Their insight anticipates the digital moment: what we see as neutral architectures are often political choices translated into code. The recurrence of this idea across decades shows scepticism moving beyond novelty into the realm of structural critique.

The sceptical turn is evident not only in scholarship and activism but in policy. In April 2021, the European Commission put forward the draft Artificial Intelligence Act in Brussels, classifying certain algorithmic systems as "high risk" and requiring transparency measures, documentation, and human oversight. The visible behaviour—regulatory proposals, public hearings, amendments—signals institutional recognition of scepticism. The named phenomenon is risk. The explanation is straightforward: opaque systems controlling significant decisions require democratic accountability. The implication reaches beyond Europe: the notion that neutrality must be proven, not presumed.

Yet scepticism is not uniform. Many people continue to accept algorithmic decisions without question. Convenience remains seductive. Predictive systems still guide shopping, travel, entertainment, and search behaviour with little friction. A person who questions facial-recognition bias might still trust their navigation app implicitly. The counterpoint matters: scepticism has limits. It grows most fiercely where stakes are visible—work, justice, politics—and weakens where decisions feel mundane.

But this limitation does not blunt the broader shift. It complicates it. It forces us to ask why scepticism arises in some contexts but not others. The answer, once again, comes from behaviour. When people experience a direct consequence—being misclassified, misled, or misunderstood—the architecture becomes visible. When consequences remain abstract, scepticism rests dormant.

This pattern is evident in micro-movements that call for algorithmic transparency. In 2021, a hashtag campaign—#ShowTheAlgorithm—spread on Twitter after users noticed inconsistent trending topics during election periods in

Brazil and India. The movement demanded publication of ranking factors. The visible behaviour—users comparing screenshots from different regions at the same time—functioned as a grassroots audit. The named frustration was inconsistency. The explanation lay in geolocation-based personalisation. The implication was civic unease: if trending topics differ silently across borders or demographic profiles, shared reality fragments.

Thread the motif again: *the algorithm knows this now.* And users increasingly ask: *why do we not know what it knows?* That asymmetry fuels modern scepticism.

At its deepest level, scepticism represents a renegotiation of authority. For years, digital systems gained trust through polish—clean interfaces, confident rankings, frictionless flows. But as evidence accumulates that these outputs are shaped by value-laden choices, scepticism fills the space where neutrality once sat. Scholars argue. Watchdogs audit. Users compare. Regulators intervene. The system feels pressure.

Yet an unresolved tension sits beneath all of this. If algorithmic neutrality is now widely questioned, what should replace it? Transparency alone does not guarantee fairness. Open code does not guarantee interpretability. Human oversight does not eliminate bias. And public scrutiny can correct errors but cannot prevent all distortions.

The question lingers, sharp and insistent: when we next encounter a ranked list, a trending item, a recommended story, will we treat it as insight—or as an artefact shaped by systems whose motives and methods remain, at crucial moments, hidden?

Chapter 2
Understanding Digital Bias

The first shock often comes in the form of a mismatch. A face steps before a camera—confident, still, evenly lit—and yet the system hesitates. Or worse, it misidentifies. When Joy Buolamwini, then a graduate researcher at MIT, tested commercial facial-recognition tools in 2015, she noticed a simple but telling pattern: the systems recognised her only when she put on a white mask. Her own skin tone, unaltered and unremarkable to any human observer, fell outside the boundaries of what the model understood. It was a moment of quiet but profound revelation. A machine trained on millions of images had still failed to see her. In that failure, a larger truth flickered into view—digital systems do not merely mirror the world; they inherit its exclusions.

Bias does not announce itself with fanfare. It enters gently, through training datasets assembled in haste, through historical imbalances encoded into numbers, through assumptions treated as neutral because they are familiar. The early promise of algorithmic precision masked the fact that these systems learn from patterns shaped by human decisions, social hierarchies, and cultural blind spots. And because digital tools operate at massive scale and astonishing speed, their distortions gain reach far beyond the limitations of any individual judgement. What begins as a technical oversight becomes a social force—one ranking, one recommendation, one misclassification at a time.

This chapter begins by inviting the reader to look closely at the sources of such distortions. Not to condemn technology wholesale, but to understand the mechanisms through which digital bias becomes both invisible and influential. The question is not whether bias exists. It is how it enters, what sustains it, and what it means for the shaping of public knowledge and private belief.

The first layer of this inquiry lies in the realm of invisible influencers. Digital bias often hides in decisions that appear procedural: how training data were selected, how edge cases were defined, how losses were optimised. These choices give algorithms their values long before any user interacts with them. A model trained mostly on lighter-skinned faces, for example, does not simply perform poorly on darker ones; it silently constructs a hierarchy of recognisability. A loan-evaluation system trained on decades of unequal lending records can replicate discrimination even when its operators believe they have removed sensitive attributes. In both cases, bias enters through the back door—quietly, without malice, but with consequence. This chapter examines these subterranean processes, revealing how design decisions become social outcomes.

Once embedded, bias does not stay confined to technical domains. It moves into culture through what this chapter calls normalised narratives. In digital environments shaped by relevance scores and engagement metrics, certain viewpoints surface repeatedly while others fade. A story retold by a recommendation system gains authority simply through presence. A claim amplified by thousands of interactions acquires the sheen of consensus. The more often something appears, the more believable it seems. Repetition becomes credibility. Credibility becomes truth. And truth begins to feel less like a matter of evidence and more like a matter of visibility. This recursive process has reshaped political discourse, public memory, and even personal identity. Understanding it requires acknowledging that narratives can be engineered—intentionally or not—through patterns of digital circulation.

Yet technology alone does not explain why biased narratives stick. The human mind plays an equal role. This chapter will explore the psychological underpinnings that make algorithmic bias so potent. People tend to trust what they recognise. Familiarity feels safe; contradictions feel abrasive. Confirmation bias, long recognised in cognitive psychology, becomes supercharged in digital settings designed to predict what will keep users engaged. When a feed aligns with one's expectations, it reinforces not only preference but conviction. The interplay between curated content and cognitive habit creates a loop in which information that "feels right" accelerates while information that challenges assumptions slows or vanishes. To navigate this requires an honest look at mental shortcuts—how quickly we embrace what affirms us, how hesitantly we approach what unsettles us, and how those tendencies can entrench algorithmic distortions.

But the story of digital bias is not fated to conclude in inevitability. There are corrective measures—meaningful, practical, and increasingly urgent. From efforts to diversify training datasets to independent audits of algorithmic behaviour, from regulatory pushes for transparency to collaborative models that embed ethical oversight into system design, the landscape is shifting. These interventions do not seek perfection; they aim for accountability. They begin with a simple premise: systems built on partial truths should not dictate whole realities. This chapter introduces readers to approaches that hold promise, showing that while eliminating bias entirely may be impossible, reducing its impact is both feasible and necessary. The task demands not just technical ingenuity but social imagination.

What makes the study of digital bias compelling is not merely the tension it reveals but the stakes it carries. Every curated search result and every ranked feed is a small act of world-building. Over time, those acts accumulate into a shared environment in which some perspectives become central and others peripheral. The danger is not overt manipulation but the slow drift of belief shaped by patterns we rarely notice. To recognise digital bias is to reclaim agency—to observe the currents beneath the surface of our decisions, our information, and our assumptions.

As the reader moves deeper into this chapter, the central question becomes sharper: if the digital systems surrounding us inevitably carry traces of their origins, how do we prevent those traces from shaping the contours of collective truth? And more pressingly, how do we ensure that the stories we engage, the signals we trust, and the patterns we follow reflect the world we aspire to, rather than the inequalities we inherited?

This chapter offers a path through those questions, opening a space where scrutiny becomes a form of strength and awareness becomes a form of responsibility. The journey ahead asks for clarity, humility, and a willingness to confront not only the biases embedded in code but the ones embedded in ourselves.

Invisible Influencers

In April 2018, researchers from MIT and Stanford released a study that startled even seasoned technologists: three commercial facial-recognition systems—developed by Microsoft, IBM, and Face++—misidentified darker-skinned women at rates exceeding 34 per cent, while error rates for lighter-skinned men fell below 1 per cent. The tests were conducted in Cambridge, Massachusetts, using a controlled set of portraits. The disparity was not a glitch. It was a revelation. A system marketed as impartial had absorbed the inequalities of its training data so thoroughly that whole demographic groups became statistically invisible. A machine built to see could not see everyone. Five quiet words hovered beneath the findings: *the model learned this bias*.

That moment crystallised a deeper truth. Digital systems rarely discriminate through intent. They discriminate through inheritance. The dataset used to train an algorithm is not a neutral snapshot of the world; it is a curated artefact formed by history, access, technology, labour, and omission. A training corpus reflecting majority faces will not merely skew performance; it will shape the very boundaries of recognisability. And because algorithms operate at scale, their blind spots—unnoticed by their creators, unexamined by their users—can enter public life with the force of fact.

The phenomenon is subtle. Bias often hides where no malice exists. A missing photograph, an unbalanced corpus, a mislabelled entry, a statistical shortcut—these tiny fractures in the foundations of a model can, when scaled to millions of decisions, reproduce centuries of inequality. The problem is not simply technical. It is structural. It is historical. And it is quiet, which makes it powerful.

Show, name, explain, implication: the sequence reveals everything.

Begin with data selection. In 2009, the widely used ImageNet dataset was assembled at Princeton and Stanford as an ambitious catalogue of the world's visual objects. Its creators intended it as a universal repository. Yet early audits revealed that some categories—particularly those involving people—carried labels that echoed racial and cultural stereotypes. Users saw only performance metrics improving each year. They did not see the flawed scaffolding beneath. The explanation was straightforward: datasets reflect the biases of their contributors, the availability of images, and the linguistic habits embedded in labels. The implication was severe: models trained on biased labels can replicate, stabilise, and scale those biases.

A second example shows how even ostensibly benign domains can absorb inequality. In 2013, the city of Boston attempted to map potholes using a smartphone app called Street Bump. The idea was simple: sensors would detect jolts during car journeys and report road defects. But the app collected data only from residents who owned smartphones and drove frequently. Wealthier neighbourhoods, with higher smartphone ownership, appeared more "damaged," triggering disproportionate repair resources. Meanwhile, lower-income areas, where fewer drivers used the app, remained underreported. The algorithm predicted road conditions where data existed, not where need existed. A technical tool reproduced socioeconomic gradients without a single discriminatory line of code. Again the motif surfaces: *the model learned this bias*.

Yet there is a credible counter-example, one that complicates the narrative and prevents fatalism. In 2021, the UK Biobank undertook extensive revisions to its genomic datasets after researchers identified demographic imbalances. Rather than treat the bias as an inevitable limitation, the organisation released updated protocols, opened collaboration channels, and documented demographic representation transparently. This did not eliminate bias entirely—no dataset can—but it showed that awareness and governance can mitigate entrenched inequalities. The implication: visibility is the first step in resisting invisibility.

Reconcile these cases and one principle becomes clear: systems reflect the worlds that produce them.

To explore this further, consider the role of labelling. Each label in a dataset is a decision. Someone chooses the boundaries of a concept: what counts as a smile, who counts as a farmer, how "aggressive" is defined in a police dataset. These labels shape the mental model a system constructs. When thousands of volunteer annotators on Amazon Mechanical Turk label images under time pressure, cultural assumptions creep in. A photograph of a protest may be labelled "riot" by one annotator and "demonstration" by another, depending on their social background or media exposure. The algorithm treats both as ground truth. The behaviour is simple: click, assign, submit. The explanation is structural: humans embed varied interpretations into data. The implication is epistemic: our collective assumptions become computational facts.

One might ask whether modern machine-learning architectures—complex, multilayered, and vast—are robust enough to resist these imperfections. After all, deep learning thrives on scale. Does size not dilute bias? Evidence shows otherwise. Larger models often magnify the patterns present in their training data. If a bias exists at low frequency, a huge dataset may repeat it thousands of times, presenting it to the algorithm as statistically meaningful. The model does not question; it optimises. It learns correlations, not causes. And correlations, when shaped by unequal histories, become conduits for structural bias.

This raises an obvious but uncomfortable question: why do these blind spots persist?

Part of the answer lies in incentive structures. Engineers are often rewarded for improving performance benchmarks—accuracy metrics, precision scores, reduced error rates. These metrics are quantitative. They are seductive. They create the illusion that improvement is objective. But a model that achieves 95 per cent accuracy overall may conceal catastrophic failures for a particular subgroup. A fraud-detection algorithm that performs well on historical data may reproduce discriminatory patterns baked into prior decisions. The risk is clear: success measured broadly can obscure harm experienced narrowly.

Another part of the answer is cultural. Technological systems are often framed as neutral, even when they inherit the partialities of their creators. The idea of objectivity becomes a shroud. A dataset curated in London may capture social patterns of the Global North but fail to reflect daily life in Nairobi, Lagos, or Dhaka. A model trained to recognise "professional attire" may prioritise Western business dress. A natural-language tool trained predominantly on English-language news may marginalise linguistic forms from the Caribbean, India, or South Africa.

Users rarely question these defaults because they appear orderly, competent, and correct. But beneath the surface lies a simple truth: *the model learned this bias*.

Consider predictive policing, a domain where invisible influence has profound consequences. The city of Chicago's 2012 "heat list" sought to identify individuals most at risk of involvement in gun violence. The model relied heavily on arrest data, which itself reflected decades of unequal policing practices. Communities historically subjected to higher levels of surveillance appeared "high risk" because past data encoded past targeting. A person's presence on the list was not a neutral assessment; it was a computational echo of historical over-policing. Behaviourally, this shaped patrol deployment. The explanation is structural: feedback loops amplify earlier patterns. The implication is civic: invisible influences directs state attention.

Yet bias does not only attach to people; it attaches to concepts. Topic classification systems—used in content moderation or news aggregation—often fail to recognise context. A sentence discussing racism critically may be flagged as toxic because the model cannot distinguish usage from endorsement. A discussion of gender may be labelled "adult" by a classifier trained on simplistic keyword rules. The visible behaviour—posts removed, videos demonetised—stems from an interpretive gap. The explanation lies in coarse labelling. The implication reaches into public discourse: what is permitted or suppressed online may be determined by datasets assembled without nuance.

A further dimension lies in interface patterns, which shape what users see and, by extension, what data future systems learn from. If an interface nudges users towards certain categories—recommended friends, trending topics, auto-complete suggestions—it funnels behaviour along narrow channels. These behaviours then produce fresh data that reinforce the design choices. A loop forms. The model learns from what the interface encourages. The interface evolves based on what the model predicts. The invisibility here is architectural: most users never see the scaffolding that shapes their actions.

The motif threads quietly again: *the model learned this bias*. But the deeper question is: *from whom?*

To understand invisible influence, one must also confront historical inequalities. A housing-valuation algorithm trained on property sales from 1980–2020 will inherit redlining practices embedded in those decades. A recruitment tool trained on past hiring decisions may reproduce gender disparities that a company never intended to formalise. A language model trained on news archives spanning fifty years will reflect the power structures of the societies that produced those archives. Bias is not created by models. It is transmitted through them.

There is, however, an emerging field of practice aimed at illuminating these shadows. Audits conducted by groups such as the Ada Lovelace Institute in London or the AI Now Institute in New York examine datasets for demographic representation, annotation quality, and structural imbalances. They intervene early, before models are deployed. These audits introduce friction—intentional, reflective friction—into processes that too often reward speed. While such efforts do not eliminate bias, they establish accountability. They make invisible choices visible.

Still, a lingering tension shapes every corrective measure: fairness is not singular. Different communities hold different expectations of what fairness means. A facial-recognition system might reduce error rates across demographic groups, yet concerns about surveillance may persist. A loan-approval model might improve accuracy for underrepresented groups, yet structural inequities in wealth remain unaddressed. Technical fixes cannot resolve political questions, and political questions cannot be resolved without technical literacy. The implication is clear: mitigation is necessary but insufficient.

Which brings us to the unresolved tension that propels this subchapter forward. If invisible influences seep into code through the sediments of history, and if digital systems replicate those sediments at scale, what responsibilities fall on those who design, evaluate, and use these systems? And more sharply: when the next model is released, the next dataset assembled, the next ranking deployed, how will we know whether the influences shaping it have been examined—or simply inherited?

The question remains open, insistent, and unavoidable.

Normalised Narratives

On 14 December 2016, the Oxford Internet Institute traced the online spread of a fabricated story claiming that Pope Francis had endorsed Donald Trump. The researchers observed how the rumour, published by a fringe website in Denver, jumped across Facebook pages, then into Twitter threads, and finally onto Google's trending list within twelve hours. Its ascent was not driven by authority, evidence, or journalistic verification. It rose because thousands of users shared it rapidly, and those interactions triggered the platform's ranking systems. Repetition created momentum. Momentum created visibility. Visibility created belief. The story became credible through circulation alone. Five quiet words shadowed the finding: *the system repeats this now.*

That story is not significant because of its subject matter; countless false claims have circulated online. It is significant because of what it reveals: once an idea begins to echo through algorithmic systems, the digital environment starts treating it as if it were important. And once a narrative becomes common, many begin to treat it as if it were true. This merging of visibility with credibility—where the most repeated claims rise to the top—marks one of the defining dynamics of digital bias. It is rarely dramatic. It is rarely intentional. It is quiet, efficient, and persistent.

The power of normalised narratives lies not in their content but in their recurrence. A single exposure informs. Repeated exposure convinces. At scale, this repetition can nudge entire publics towards particular framings of events, people, or problems. Bias becomes a pattern, and the pattern becomes a story the world appears to tell itself. The motif returns: *the system repeats this now.*

To understand how bias becomes self-reinforcing, begin with a simple mechanism: relevance scoring. Platforms often measure which posts users click, pause on, or share. They then elevate similar content. Show the effect. In January 2021, researchers at the University of Washington analysed millions of YouTube recommendations during the U.S. Senate runoff elections. They found that once a viewer clicked a video claiming electoral fraud, the recommendation panel began populating similar videos, even those with minimal factual basis. Name the issue: algorithmic amplification. Explain the mechanism: the system infers preference through early behaviour, then repeats that pattern aggressively. The implication is profound: a user who expresses fleeting curiosity in a controversial topic may soon find their informational world filled with that narrative.

The process is not limited to politics. Consider wellness misinformation during the COVID-19 outbreak. In May 2020, the World Health Organisation (WHO) documented how misleading claims about miracle cures spread globally through Facebook groups. Some posts received tens of thousands of interactions within hours. The platforms' automated curation systems responded to this engagement as a signal of relevance. They repeated the pattern. Users scrolling through feeds saw dozens of similar claims framed as widespread knowledge. The behaviour—liking, sharing, commenting—became both cause and effect. The explanation was mechanical, not ideological. The implication was public-health risk, scaled by repetition rather than persuasion.

Yet the dominance of repeated narratives is not inevitable. A counter-example comes from Wikipedia's "Recent Changes Patrol," where volunteers actively monitor edits. During the early months of the pandemic, between January and March 2020, editors reverted thousands of unverified claims within minutes of their appearance. This created a visible behavioural signal—reversion rates—that constrained the spread of misinformation. It demonstrated a key point: systems with robust human oversight can resist the gravitational pull of repetition. Neutrality is possible when repetition is not mistaken for credibility.

Reconcile these examples, and one truth emerges: automated systems reward patterns, not accuracy. They do not ask whether a story is representative, ethical, or verified; they simply observe what spreads and amplify it further. This design principle underlies the architecture of modern platforms. It explains why narratives, once in motion, can dominate public understanding.

The core dynamic becomes more troubling when one considers how repetition interacts with cognitive behaviour. Humans tend to believe statements they encounter frequently—a finding confirmed repeatedly since the 1970s, most famously by psychologists Lynn Hasher and David Goldstein. The phenomenon is called the illusory truth effect. When paired with algorithmic systems that prioritise repetition by design, the effect becomes supercharged. A rumour repeated ten times by a feed feels more trustworthy than a fact stated once. A claim circulated widely feels safer to believe. Behaviour follows the pattern: users share familiar content; platforms amplify repeat behaviour. The explanation is not moral failing but cognitive architecture. The implication is epistemic vulnerability: truth becomes a function of frequency.

Different contexts reveal different expressions of the same mechanism. Examine cultural commentary. In July 2020, when Beyoncé released *Black Is King*, a wave of commentary emerged about its representation of African traditions. Some thoughtful analyses from writers in Lagos, Accra, and Nairobi appeared online, but they gained less traction than commentaries from Western entertainment outlets with larger digital footprints. The platforms' ranking systems surfaced more familiar sources repeatedly, making them appear authoritative. A global conversation was shaped not by expertise but by repetition of voices already favoured by the system. The motif appears again: *the system repeats this now.*

At times, repetition shapes not just narratives but identity categories. Researchers at the University of Amsterdam, analysing TikTok's "For You" page in 2022, observed that users who interacted with a small number of videos discussing body image were soon shown streams dominated by similar content, creating echo loops that emphasised particular aesthetic norms. The behaviour—pausing on a video—was measured. The mechanism—predicting future interest—was automatic. The implication—narrowing self-perception—was unintended but real. Repetition sculpted a sense of what was normal, desirable, or disordered.

Narratives also normalise moral and political hierarchies. A report by the Mozilla Foundation in July 2021 documented how YouTube's recommendation algorithm frequently guided users in Germany, France, and Brazil towards increasingly inflammatory political content after initial exposure to mainstream news. The behaviour—clicking political reports—triggered a chain reaction. The explanation lay in engagement-maximising design. The implication was democratic: polarisation became spatially and socially patterned by algorithmic output.

Yet repetition does not always produce harmful outcomes. A limitation worth acknowledging is that some repeated narratives are genuinely educational or corrective. Public campaigns regarding handwashing in March 2020 spread widely across platforms, reinforcing vital safety guidance. Users reported seeing identical messages on multiple channels. Repetition worked because the information was grounded in scientific consensus and was monitored by public-health agencies. This counter-example matters because it shows that repetition itself is not the problem. The problem is when repetition occurs without verification, context, or oversight.

Identifying this limitation helps clarify the deeper issue: the distinction between repeated knowledge and repeated noise. Automated systems rarely distinguish between the two. They detect patterns, not principles.

Beyond individual stories, normalised narratives shape global conversations. Consider how the phrase "fake news" shifted from describing fabricated stories to functioning as a political weapon. Between late 2016 and early 2017, media monitoring projects at Harvard and Columbia showed the term appearing millions of times across English-language social platforms. The repetition did not simply inform users of misinformation; it trained them to suspect unfavourable journalism categorically. Behavioural metrics—shares, retweets, comments—propelled the phrase into common discourse. The explanation ties back to reflexive engagement. The implication was cultural: scrutiny of information turned into scepticism of institutions.

The mechanism extends to international contexts. In India, WhatsApp message chains—often forwarded hundreds or thousands of times—have repeatedly circulated misleading claims since at least 2018, prompting government warnings. Forwarding behaviour is measurable: WhatsApp limited the number of simultaneous forwards in 2020 to curb viral spread. But the underlying issue persists. A claim forwarded repeatedly appears socially validated. The system does not distinguish between organic consensus and mechanical replication.

The recurrence of misleading stories is not accidental; it is structural. Narratives build inertia in digital systems. Once established, they become difficult to dislodge. Attempts to correct misinformation often receive lower engagement than the misinformation itself. Studies by MIT researchers in 2018 found that false news on Twitter spread "farther, faster, deeper" than factual stories because it triggered stronger emotional reactions. The visible behaviour—retweeting sensational claims—guides ranking algorithms. The explanation is affective bias. The implication is systemic: emotional velocity becomes a substitute for factual value.

A motif returns once more: *the system repeats this now.* Yet beneath that motif lies a more pressing question: *who benefits from the repetition?* Sometimes the answer is commercial—engagement generates revenue. Sometimes it is political—visibility shapes sentiment. Sometimes it is cultural—dominant groups retain narrative control. But often the answer is simply structural: systems optimise for recurrence because recurrence is measurable.

As this subchapter edges toward its final movement, a tension remains unresolved. If narratives gain legitimacy through repetition, and if repetition is governed by opaque systems shaped by engagement, profit, and habit, how can individuals distinguish between widely shared stories that reflect collective insight and those that reflect collective drift? More sharply: when the next repeated narrative appears on a screen, how will we know whether we are witnessing a reflection of public understanding—or merely the echo of a system that has learned what to amplify?

Psychological Underpinnings

In 1977, at the University of Michigan, psychologists repeatedly showed volunteers pairs of statements—some true, some invented. When participants returned a few weeks later, something striking happened. They confidently rated as "true" many of the statements they had encountered earlier, even when those statements were fictional. The effect was measurable: familiarity alone increased perceived accuracy, a result later formalised as the "illusory truth effect." The experiment took place in Ann Arbor, well before the internet, yet its implications now define the psychological terrain of digital life. What the Michigan researchers discovered in a controlled lab has become the default cognitive posture of millions scrolling through curated feeds. A quiet motif emerges: *the familiar feels right*.

The digital environment intensifies this tendency because it reproduces familiar patterns at scale. People rarely search for contradiction; they search for coherence. A feed that aligns with their expectations feels comfortable. A recommendation that echoes earlier choices feels efficient. A narrative they have seen before feels trustworthy. The interplay between mental shortcuts and algorithmic repetition becomes a loop: users gravitate towards content that confirms their beliefs, platforms amplify that content due to engagement, and the amplified material reinforces the original beliefs. The loop feels seamless. It is not. It is engineered.

The first step to understanding this dynamic is recognising how psychological tendencies shape individual behaviour long before algorithms enter the scene. Confirmation bias—our inclination to favour information that supports prior beliefs—has been documented for decades. But in digital environments, its effects become magnified because exposure itself is not neutral. A platform tracks what engages a user, not what challenges them. When two videos appear side by side on a screen, a person may click the one that matches their worldview. The system measures the behaviour. The system interprets it. And from the behaviour emerges a pattern. The motif returns: *the familiar feels right*.

Show, name, explain, implication: follow the engine.

Consider the first major claim: familiarity drives acceptance. Show the pattern. During Britain's 2016 EU referendum, researchers at King's College London monitored the spread of political memes across public Facebook pages. They found that users who engaged repeatedly with a particular visual style—say, blue-and-yellow infographics—became more likely to accept subsequent claims presented in the same aesthetic, even when those claims were unverified. Name the mechanism: perceptual fluency. Explain the link: when a format becomes easy to process, users mistake ease for truth. The implication is political: style shapes belief when substance is uncertain.

A second example illustrates the mechanism outside politics. Between March and July 2020, Spotify's research team in Stockholm observed that listeners who played pandemic-themed podcasts early in lockdowns were repeatedly recommended similar content. The more they listened, the more the system amplified that stream. Users then rated those episodes highly, not because the material was objective, but because it aligned with their emotional state. Familiarity shaped preference. Preference shaped recommendation. Recommendation shaped belief. The motif threads in, quietly: *the familiar feels right.*

Yet repetition and familiarity do not always lead to credulity. A credible counter-example complicates the narrative. In 2021, the BBC's "Reality Check" team published data showing that repeated exposure to fact-checking posts on Instagram and TikTok increased users' willingness to revise previously held misconceptions about COVID-19 vaccines. Familiarity became a correction mechanism rather than a distortion. This case matters because it prevents fatalism: psychological shortcuts can reinforce misinformation, but they can also reinforce truth when repetition is structured responsibly.

Reconcile these cases and a clear principle emerges: mental shortcuts do not distinguish between good and bad information; they follow whatever the system repeatedly presents.

To understand why confirmation bias becomes so potent in digital environments, examine its behavioural roots. People rely on heuristics because they reduce cognitive load. When overwhelmed by information—as users often are—these shortcuts become attractive. A familiar storyline simply demands less mental effort. A familiar frame requires fewer interpretive resources. A familiar perspective feels safe. The brain rewards ease. It is efficient. But efficiency can be a trap.

Platforms reinforce these tendencies because they optimise for engagement, not epistemic balance. They measure what holds attention. They compare patterns across users. They commit to recommendations that maximise predicted satisfaction. The abstraction becomes behaviour: users scroll longer when shown material that fits their worldview. The system learns quickly. It repeats what works. And because these systems operate at enormous scale, the psychological effect—preference shaping perception—occurs billions of times a day.

One can observe the dynamic most clearly in the design of ranking systems. A user who clicks one climate-sceptical article may soon find their feed populated with similar content. The click is a behaviour. The ranking is a response. The user sees the response as validation: "I'm seeing more of this because it must matter." This small misinterpretation—treating relevance as importance—drives the confirmation loop. Familiar claims rise. Unfamiliar claims sink. The motif repeats: *the familiar feels right.*

This interplay between cognition and curation becomes even more intricate when emotional states enter the picture. Psychologists such as Tali Sharot have shown that people pay more attention to information that evokes positive emotions or confirms desired futures. Digital platforms track those emotional responses through indirect signals—pause time, replaying, liking. A user lingering on a hopeful story sees more hopeful stories; one fixating on risk sees more risk. The system mirrors emotional patterns. The user interprets the mirror as reality. A special kind of bias emerges: affective confirmation. Emotions shape attention; attention shapes the feed; the feed shapes emotion. It is a circle that feels linear.

The problem intensifies when ambiguity enters the frame. Cognitive scientists have long known that uncertainty activates threat responses, making people more receptive to theories that offer closure. During ambiguous moments—political crises, health scares, economic anxiety—confirmation bias strengthens. Users seek familiar anchors. Platforms detect the heightened engagement around those anchors. They double down. That amplification can shape not only individual belief but collective mood. It is visible in comment patterns, trending lists, and search-term spikes.

Yet there is another limitation worth noting. Human beings also possess a countervailing trait: curiosity. When motivated, individuals seek out complexity, novelty, and contradiction. A 2019 study from the University of Pennsylvania found that users deliberately exposed to diverse viewpoints through curated cross-partisan feeds did not polarise further as long as the content was framed with context rather than confrontation. This suggests that mental shortcuts are not destiny; they are tendencies. And tendencies can shift with design, intention, or habit.

Still, the ease of confirmation draws most users back towards familiar cognitive territory. Consider the behaviour of auto-complete search suggestions. When someone types "Is coffee..." and the system offers completions like "Is coffee unhealthy?" or "Is coffee safe?", the user sees not only predictions but implied consensus. The suggestions feel familiar because they appear for thousands of users. They seem popular. Popularity feels like validation. The psychological shortcut—trusting the familiar—blends with the algorithmic shortcut—recommending the frequent. A tiny nudge becomes a tiny certainty.

At scale, these micro-certainties accumulate. They shape how groups interpret events, how societies interpret scientific claims, how global audiences interpret crises. A narrative feels "widely accepted" not because it has been verified, but because it appears repeatedly in curated spaces. People then reinforce that perception through behaviour: sharing, liking, agreeing. The feed observes the behaviour. The feed rewards it.

This feedback loop produces a phenomenon psychologists call "belief echo." Even when a claim is later corrected, the emotional residue of the original exposure lingers. The brain stores impressions not just as facts but as patterns. Correction feels unfamiliar. The original claim feels familiar. And the motif returns one last time: *the familiar feels right*.

What makes these psychological underpinnings so powerful is not their novelty, but their invisibility. Few users recognise that their belief trajectories are being shaped partly by their own cognitive shortcuts and partly by invisible curation mechanisms. Even fewer recognise the scale at which this interaction unfolds.

As this subchapter draws towards its tension point, a question emerges—quiet, sharp, unresolved. If familiarity so easily becomes a proxy for truth, and if digital systems intensify that familiarity through personalised repetition, how can individuals distinguish between beliefs that reflect reasoned judgement and beliefs that simply reflect the habits of the mind amplified by the habits of the machine?

Corrective Measures

In July 2018, the American Civil Liberties Union tested Amazon's Rekognition system using official photos of all 535 members of the United States Congress. The software falsely matched twenty-eight of them to criminal mugshots. The errors disproportionately affected legislators of colour, a finding that was immediately verifiable and widely reported. The test, carried out in California, forced a direct question into public view: if automated systems misidentify the very people tasked with governing, what protections exist for everyone else? One five-word sentence sits quietly in the background: *Bias can be corrected*. But only if the effort is deliberate.

The Rekognition incident mattered not because it was unique but because it was visible. Most algorithmic failures remain hidden inside proprietary systems. Yet the episode offered a rare glimpse into how bias enters a model through data choices, design shortcuts, and evaluation gaps. It also demonstrated a larger truth: technical accuracy is not the same as social fairness. The attempt to fix these shortcomings has generated a field of corrective measures—some promising, some limited, all necessary.

The first major claim is straightforward: improving training data reduces predictable forms of discrimination. Show the pattern. In 2019, Microsoft's research lab in Redmond expanded the diversity of its facial recognition dataset after internal audits revealed uneven error rates across demographic groups. Name the method: dataset balancing. Explain the principle: a model trained on faces from predominantly one population learns patterns that do not generalise. The implication is concrete: systems become less reliable in the very places where accurate identification matters most—border checkpoints, policing tools, employment systems. When engineers measure error rates directly, disparities become visible and correctable.

A second example shows a different corrective route. In 2020, the Dutch Authority for Personal Data issued a ruling against SyRI, an automated welfare-fraud detection system deployed in Rotterdam. The tool disproportionately targeted residents in low-income neighbourhoods. The case resulted in the system's suspension. Name the mechanism: legal audit. Explain the logic: even if engineers do not catch bias, regulatory bodies can compel transparency. The implication extends beyond Rotterdam: meaningful correction sometimes requires not only better code but outside scrutiny.

Yet, for all the attention on data and oversight, there is a credible counter-example that tempers optimism. In 2022, Twitter's internal "Responsible ML" team disclosed that after they debiased image-cropping algorithms, the resulting system still produced unexpected asymmetries. The limitation was not malicious design but the sheer complexity of modelling human aesthetic judgement. Reconcile the case: some biases are technical artefacts that can be quantified and fixed; others arise from subjective value-laden decisions embedded in the task. Not everything is measurable. Not everything should be automated.

These examples highlight a deeper point: corrective measures must address not only how algorithms *learn* but how they *behave*. Bias emerges in outputs, and outputs generate real-world consequences. Consider the metrics that shape ranking systems. When YouTube, owned by Google, adjusted its recommendation model in early 2019 to reduce the visibility of borderline content, engineers relied on a behavioural signal: time spent viewing. Because engagement metrics can shape public perception, changing those metrics changes what the public encounters. The motif appears: *Bias can be corrected*. But corrections require redefining what the system treats as success.

A broader view makes the complexity clearer. Bias is rarely a single fault; it is usually a cascade of design decisions. Show the cascade. When predictive policing systems in Chicago ingested historical arrest records, the model reinforced prior policing patterns. Name the mechanism: historical imprinting. Explain the consequence: if a neighbourhood was over-policed decades earlier, it would seem "riskier" to the model. The implication: mitigation demands interrogating not only current data but the structural forces that produced that data. Correction must be historical as well as technical.

One of the most promising corrective strategies lies in model explainability. When the UK's Information Commissioner's Office (ICO) reviewed the use of algorithmic decision-making in public services in 2020, it emphasised the importance of human-readable explanations. If a system denies someone a loan or housing placement, the reasoning should be auditable. Show the application. Some banks already generate simplified decision summaries for customers, noting features such as payment history or debt load. Name the benefit: traceability. Explain why it matters: when people understand the basis of a decision, they can contest errors. The implication is institutional: transparency disciplines both the algorithm and the organisation deploying it.

Explainability, however, has limits. In complex deep-learning systems, explanations can become approximate narratives rather than precise accounts. Google's "saliency maps" for image classification illustrate this tension: the highlighted regions show what the model *might* be using, not a definitive causal chain. This limitation forces a reconsideration of what fairness guarantees are feasible. Correction may not always mean revealing how a model works; sometimes it means constraining what a model is allowed to do.

Another corrective measure is cultural rather than technical. In 2016, the Partnership on AI was founded with members including Amazon, Facebook, IBM, and academics from British and American institutions. Its aim was to develop shared ethical guidelines. While critics note the limitations of voluntary standards, the initiative represents an emerging shift: bias mitigation as a collaborative responsibility. Name the principle: multi-stakeholder governance. Explain its necessity: most algorithmic systems operate across borders, industries, and legal frameworks. The implication is clear: correction cannot be a solitary task pursued by individual engineers; it requires collective norms.

But collaboration alone does not guarantee fairness. Outsider groups—civil rights organisations, community representatives, end users—often identify harms overlooked by developers. In 2021, for example, the Mozilla Foundation published research indicating that YouTube's recommendation algorithm had exposed users to extremist content even when they actively avoided it. This finding emerged from voluntary reports submitted by users worldwide. Show the behaviour: people clicked "not interested" yet still saw similar material. Name the issue: user override failure. Explain the insight: feedback loops can ignore human preference if the system's optimisation logic outweighs user choice. The implication is deeply human: effective correction must empower people, not simply adjust models.

Corrective measures also include structural changes in the engineering process. Google's 2020 revision of the "Model Cards" framework is one such attempt. By documenting intended use cases, limitations, and known biases, teams acknowledge uncertainty upfront. Name the tool: transparency documentation. Explain its role: when stakeholders understand the boundaries of a system, misuse becomes less likely. The implication broadens: fairness relies not only on the model but on the ecology surrounding it—documentation, deployment, and governance.

Yet the most challenging frontier concerns global diversity. A system trained in London may perform poorly in Lagos; a dataset collected in Toronto may misrepresent lived patterns in Delhi. These disparities stem from geographic sampling. Show the impact. In 2020, a study from the University of Cape Town revealed that speech-recognition systems based on American datasets produced error rates more than double when tested on South African English. Name the cause: linguistic underrepresentation. Explain the dynamic: if a model never "hears" certain accents, it cannot process them reliably. The implication: correction requires international cooperation, not regional optimisation.

Thread the motif again: *Bias can be corrected*. But correction demands scope, resources, and humility.

Even within well-resourced organisations, corrective efforts face practical constraints. Engineers may lack access to certain datasets due to privacy laws. Auditors may have limited insight into proprietary systems. Regulators may struggle to keep pace with technical innovation. These constraints are not excuses; they are realities that shape what correction can achieve. Recognising limitations is essential to crafting realistic interventions.

Throughout all these efforts runs a quieter question: what counts as fairness? If an e-commerce platform, headquartered in Berlin, adjusts ranking algorithms so that small vendors receive equal visibility, is that fairness? If a job-matching system in Manchester reduces gender bias but still relies on historical salary data that reflect wage inequalities, has fairness been achieved or merely improved? These questions reveal that bias reduction is not an endpoint but a negotiation.

The closing tension emerges naturally. Technical teams can balance datasets, regulators can demand audits, communities can call for transparency. But each intervention forces a trade-off: between privacy and openness, between accuracy and interpretability, between global performance and local nuance. The unresolved test remains: when designing systems meant to serve billions, what level of imperfection is acceptable, and who decides when correction is enough?

Chapter 3
Data Determinism vs Human Judgement

A few years ago, a university admissions office in the north of England faced a curious dilemma. An automated scoring system—introduced to streamline an unwieldy selection process—appeared to produce consistent, mathematically tidy outcomes, sorting thousands of applicants with clinical decisiveness. Yet when staff examined a handful of borderline cases, they found something unsettling. The system had rejected candidates whose personal statements were unusually idiosyncratic, whose achievements fell outside the neat patterns the model had been trained to recognise. The algorithm had not malfunctioned; it had simply treated the unconventional as a statistical anomaly. For the admissions tutors staring at the rejected files, the moment raised a quiet but profound question: when a machine presents an answer wrapped in numerical confidence, how easily do we mistake that confidence for truth?

This tension between apparent precision and lived complexity is at the heart of our age. Data feels authoritative. It arrives cleanly, dressed in percentages, charts, risk scores, or "recommended for you" tags that convey a reassuring sense of order. Numbers give the impression of neutrality, as though they float above human frailty. Yet behind every dataset stands a lineage of choices—what to measure, what to exclude, how to classify, what outcomes to privilege. Behind every model stands a team of designers, each with assumptions about what fairness looks like, what deviation means, what should count as success. And behind every output stands us: interpreting, trusting, doubting, or surrendering.

Data determinism, the belief that data-led conclusions capture the deepest truths about a person or a situation, thrives because it simplifies life. It transforms messy social questions into manageable metrics. It promises that moral ambiguity can be tamed through optimisation. A recommendation engine tells us what to read; a credit-scoring model tells us who is "reliable"; a predictive tool tells employers which job applicants are "low risk"; a health-triage system whispers which symptoms deserve escalation. These systems do not present themselves as suggestions. They present themselves as answers.

Yet human judgement has not disappeared. It has moved backstage, into the design phase where parameters are set, into the data-cleaning stage where categories are defined, into the post-hoc interpretations where outputs are woven into narratives. The moment a developer selects a threshold, a feature, or a benchmark, the supposedly neutral system inherits a worldview. A silent motif runs through this chapter: *the human never fully leaves the loop.*

Consider how this becomes visible in everyday life. When you receive a personalised news feed, you rarely see the editorial logic that guided its curation. But somewhere, someone decided that engagement metrics should outweigh chronological order; that your past behaviour is a reasonable proxy for your future interests; that stories liked by your network should appear higher than stories from outside your orbit. These are not technical necessities; they are value-laden decisions. The system wears the face of objectivity, but its skeleton is unmistakably human.

The chapter you are about to read probes precisely this tension. It questions what happens when societies start treating data-led outputs as incontrovertible, and what gets lost in the process. It explores how historical assumptions become encoded into algorithms, producing illusions of certainty that obscure the nuance of human contexts. It examines moments when machines override intuition, sometimes for good, sometimes with unintended harm. And it asks—without romanticising instinct—how far our moral agency should bend to accommodate automated judgement.

Throughout the chapter, data determinism will be approached not as a villain but as a seductive worldview: tidy, certainty-driven, efficient. Its appeal is genuine. In a world overflowing with information and competing claims, many people welcome the clarity of a ranked result or a risk score. But the trade-off is equally real. Oversimplification flattens complexity. Personal histories, cultural contexts, and moral subtleties are not easily expressed as variables. When numbers become shorthand for truth, the human dimension risks fading from view.

We will also explore the spaces where human values quietly infiltrate supposedly objective systems. An algorithm trained to predict financial reliability inherits the financial norms of the bank that created it. A medical triage model reflects the healthcare priorities of its designers. A justice-risk assessment tool encodes assumptions about rehabilitation, deterrence, and public safety. These systems operate as if they are impartial, but their inner logic often mirrors the biases and hopes of the people who built them. Objectivity becomes a performance rather than a reality.

Then comes a sharper question: what occurs when machines begin to overrule us? When a loan officer is advised to follow the model "for consistency"? When admissions staff feel pressured to accept algorithmic scores to avoid accusations of bias? When a doctor must justify deviating from clinical decision support software? Deference can creep quietly into institutional life, producing a culture where individuals trust the system more than their own trained judgement. Convenience evolves into complacency; consistency evolves into dependency.

But the story does not end with unease. The final thread of this introduction returns to responsibility. Data need not dominate human reasoning; it can enrich it. Algorithms need not replace judgement; they can inform it. Systems need not obscure values; they can embed them consciously rather than accidentally. As the chapter unfolds, we will examine how ethical boards, reflective design practices, transparent modelling, and cultural humility can restore equilibrium. Reclaiming the final say does not mean rejecting data. It means recognising that numbers do not absolve us of choice.

A subtle tension carries forward. If data promise clarity and humans offer context, what happens when the two are at odds? When the model points one way and moral intuition another? When efficiency contradicts empathy? When statistical patterns challenge principles? These are not hypothetical questions. They shape real decisions, affecting real lives, every day. And the deeper question lingers beneath them: how do we remain custodians of our own judgement while navigating systems that increasingly ask us to surrender it?

That is the intellectual crossroads this chapter opens. The path ahead invites scrutiny, curiosity, and a willingness to ask uncomfortable questions about certainty, agency, and truth. The systems are powerful. The data persuasive. But the final choice—about how much authority we grant them—remains ours.

Defining Data Determinism

In 2014, Target Corporation made headlines when its analytics system predicted a Minnesota teenager's pregnancy before her family knew. The model had detected a pattern in her recent purchases—unscented lotion, vitamin supplements, a large handbag—and assigned a probability score that triggered automated marketing. The story, rooted in an identifiable organisation, place, and date, became a modern parable. A chain of statistical signals was interpreted as certainty. A probability became a revelation. And a private life became a data point. The case captured something larger than retail analytics: the unsettling belief that numbers, once processed by machines, reveal deeper truths than the people they describe.

This belief—quiet, persuasive, rarely scrutinised—is the essence of data determinism. It expresses itself not through slogans but through behaviour: deference to risk scores in finance, unquestioning acceptance of algorithmic recommendations, an instinctive sense that the outputs of a model carry authority simply because they are derived from data. The motif that threads through this chapter is simple but sharp: *the number appears final*. When faced with the polished certainty of a ranked list or prediction score, many people feel an intuitive pull towards acceptance, even when the underlying question is moral, contextual, or subjective. The teenager in Minnesota was not a prediction; she was a person. But to the system, she was a pattern.

The first major claim is that data determinism seduces by simplifying complexity. Show the mechanism. Netflix's recommendation engine, refined in Los Gatos after its 2009 Prize competition, analyses viewing histories to predict what a user will enjoy next. Name the principle: behavioural similarity. Explain the appeal: a model identifies clusters of users who "behave alike" and assumes their preferences should converge. The output feels tailored, intimate, authoritative. The implication is cultural: when millions of people treat algorithmic suggestions as personalised truth, they gradually outsource subtle decisions about taste, curiosity, and exploration to a statistical approximation of their past selves.

A second example highlights determinism in higher-stakes environments. In 2020, the UK's Office of Qualifications and Examinations Regulation used an algorithm to assign A-level grades after exams were cancelled due to the pandemic. The model down-weighted individual performance and elevated school-level historical averages. Name the outcome: thousands of high-achieving students from under-resourced schools received downgraded results. Explain why: the model valued institutional patterns over personal outliers. The implication is ethical: when statistical precedent overrides lived potential, data cease to inform and begin to confine.

Yet a credible counter-example prevents fatalism. In 2019, the Royal Free London NHS Foundation Trust evaluated a machine-learning tool for diagnosing acute kidney injury. While not perfect, it demonstrated clearer diagnostic value when used alongside clinical expertise rather than instead of it. Here, data strengthened human judgement; it did not replace it. Reconcile the limitation: the problem is not data, nor models, nor numbers—the danger lies in treating those numbers as inviolable, in imagining that a prediction contains the full weight of truth.

To understand why the illusion of determinism is so strong, consider the visible behaviours that accompany it. People often change their decisions after encountering a score. A borrower may abandon a loan application after seeing a low credit rating. A job-seeker may avoid applying for positions that automated systems deem a "poor fit." A patient may seek a second opinion only if a probability threshold seems alarming. Metrics do not merely describe; they shape action. And once action shifts, the original model appears validated. A self-fulfilling prediction grows quietly in the margins.

The motif returns: *the number appears final*. But numbers are never final. They are estimates, generated by models designed by people with assumptions, constraints, and priorities.

One reason determinism flourishes is that data-led outputs often feel more coherent than human intuition. When faced with ambiguity, individuals crave clarity. A crisp percentage feels easier to act upon than a nuanced conversation. But the comfort of clarity masks the limits of measurement. Show the limitation. A predictive policing system in Chicago used historical arrest data to identify "hot spots." Name the flaw: historical imprinting. Explain the effect: neighbourhoods with heavier past policing became algorithmically coded as "high risk," creating a loop that prioritised prior enforcement over present reality. The implication is profound: numbers may reflect cycles of inequality rather than objective risk.

Another layer of determinism appears in corporate environments, where efficiency metrics shape decisions more powerfully than personal judgement. When Google tested its hiring algorithms in Mountain View in 2017, engineers discovered that the model rated candidates partly based on patterns from predominantly male applicant histories. While the system appeared precise, its precision was anchored in bias. The engineers shut it down. But the incident served as a reminder: even the most advanced systems inherit the blind spots of their creators.

Yet determinism persists because it offers a seductive narrative about control. If enough data are gathered, enough patterns analysed, enough models refined, perhaps complexity can be tamed. But complexity resists. Ethics, culture, identity, trauma, aspiration—none of these fit neatly inside a predictive schema. They influence decisions in ways that no feature set can fully encode. When a recommendation engine suggests the "best" job, it cannot know the applicant's quiet ambition to pivot careers. When a medical triage model assigns a risk score, it cannot detect the patient's fear or resilience. When a news-feed suppresses or elevates a story, it cannot intuit the cultural meaning of that silence or prominence.

The determinist belief that "data speak for themselves" collapses when confronted with the messy reality of human lives. Data do not speak. They are interpreted. And interpretation requires judgement.

The temptation to treat predictions as fate intensifies when institutions lean heavily on algorithmic output. Automated systems reduce uncertainty for bureaucracies. They provide documented reasoning, consistent procedures, quantifiable thresholds. These qualities appeal to organisations seeking efficiency and legal defensibility. But they also create a distance between decision and decision-maker. Responsibility shifts. Errors diffuse. The system "decided," not the human. In this sense, determinism becomes a moral shelter.

A deeper issue lingers beneath these behaviours: data determinism often disguises power. Who chooses what to measure? Who decides what counts as an "outcome"? Who sets the threshold at which a risk becomes unacceptable? These decisions are rarely neutral. A bank may set conservative thresholds to minimise default; a school may prioritise test performance over creative potential; a news platform may weight engagement more heavily than accuracy. Each choice shapes the model's worldview. Each choice shapes ours.

Two more examples illuminate this interplay. Spotify's Discover Weekly, launched globally in 2015, became a cultural touchstone of automated taste-making. Yet researchers in Stockholm later noted that the system subtly favoured artists with larger catalogue metadata, shaping what millions perceived as "emerging trends." Meanwhile, TikTok's "For You" feed, which expanded globally in 2020, amplified content via micro-engagement patterns that often reflected unconscious biases—such as preferentially boosting creators with certain visual styles or lighting conditions. Both cases show the same pattern: deterministic narratives emerge from probabilistic inputs.

The motif threads again: *the number appears final.* But its finality is constructed.

A final reflection pushes the tension forward. If data determinism rests on the belief that numerical patterns reveal absolute truths, what should individuals and institutions do when those patterns collide with human insight, ethical nuance, or contextual understanding? When a system delivers an output that feels "objective" yet conflicts with lived experience, which should prevail? And how do we distinguish between helpful predictive clarity and the quiet erosion of human judgement?

Human Values in the Matrix

In April 2015, at the Royal Free Hospital in London, clinicians trialled a machine-learning tool designed to predict acute kidney injury hours before symptoms became visible. The system, developed with Google DeepMind, analysed thousands of clinical records and delivered risk scores directly to doctors' phones. On paper, it looked objective: a neutral synthesis of historical data and statistical modelling. Yet within weeks, medical staff raised questions about the tool's thresholds—specifically, why a borderline creatinine change in one patient triggered an alert, while a similar change in another did not. The discrepancy was not a malfunction. It was a design choice embedded in the model's construction, a reflection of earlier assumptions about significance, sensitivity, and acceptable risk. Human judgement, disguised in layers of code, shaped every score.

The Royal Free case became a marker of a broader truth: the apparent neutrality of algorithmic systems often obscures the values built into them. The outputs feel empirical, even clinical, yet behind those outputs lie decisions made by human hands—decisions about what to measure, which trade-offs to prioritise, whose definitions of success should anchor the model. The motif that threads through this subchapter is quiet but persistent: *the human remains present*, even when the system speaks with machine authority. Every parameter selected, every category defined, every dataset curated carries traces of subjective interpretation.

The first major claim is that human values enter systems through design choices that appear technical but are, in fact, normative. Show the mechanism. In 2018, the New York City Automated Decision Systems Task Force reviewed local predictive tools, including algorithms used for pretrial assessments. They found that seemingly objective features—such as "prior contact with law enforcement"—reflected decades of unequal policing. Name the phenomenon: value-laden proxies. Explain the principle: a model that treats proxies as neutral reproduces the value judgements of its designers, even if unintentionally. The implication is institutional: human assumptions do not disappear when encoded; they harden.

A second example highlights the role of subjective interpretation even in high-stakes scientific contexts. In 2020, the U.S. Food and Drug Administration evaluated an AI tool used to prioritise cancer imaging. The developers, based in Massachusetts, had assigned higher predictive weight to tumour sizes correlated with outcomes in a particular regional dataset. When tested across a broader population, the system misjudged severity in patients whose tumours developed differently due to genetic and environmental factors. Name the root issue: parameter bias. Explain why it matters: parameters chosen for efficiency in one setting may reflect local norms rather than universal truths. The implication is medical: ignoring embedded subjectivities can distort diagnoses.

Yet there is a credible counter-example that prevents overstatement. In 2017, Moorfields Eye Hospital in London collaborated with DeepMind to develop a system capable of identifying more than fifty retinal diseases with high accuracy. The tool succeeded not because it replaced clinicians but because it was developed with extensive consultation, peer-reviewed validation, and explicit transparency about training data. Here, subjectivity was acknowledged upfront, not hidden. Reconcile the case: human values need not degrade algorithmic reliability; they can guide it, provided they are named and examined.

To understand how values infiltrate systems, consider the visible behaviours that accompany them. When a credit-scoring algorithm in Frankfurt rewards long-term residence at a single address, it implicitly valorises a particular vision of stability. When a social-media feed in Menlo Park ranks posts by engagement, it prioritises emotional intensity over nuance. When a hiring model in Dublin favours applicants with continuous employment histories, it embeds a cultural assumption about linear career trajectories. These decisions appear technical. They are not. They smuggle in worldviews.

Thread the motif again: *the human remains present.*

Another layer of value insertion occurs through data labelling. Show the practice. When annotators classify satellite images for humanitarian mapping, as occurred in the 2015 Missing Maps project led by Médecins Sans Frontières and the British Red Cross, they interpret ambiguous shapes—roofs, roads, tents—based on cultural and spatial expectations. Name the process: interpretive annotation. Explain the problem: even the simplest labels reflect tacit knowledge shaped by environment, training, and belief. The implication stretches into geopolitics: a dataset produced through Western classification methods may misrepresent structures in non-Western regions, affecting everything from disaster response to infrastructure planning.

A powerful example of subtle value-shaping comes from content-moderation systems. In 2019, Facebook released internal guidelines showing how "harm" categories were operationalised for automated detection. The model struggled with context-dependent phrases used in minority communities. The system did not simply enforce rules; it enforced interpretations of those rules, and those interpretations came from teams of reviewers making subjective distinctions. Name the issue: contextual fragility.

Explain the stakes: automated enforcement codifies the cultural assumptions of those who define "acceptable" language. The implication is social: what a system suppresses or elevates becomes part of public discourse.

Human values also shape systems through the technical constraints developers accept. Engineers decide how to balance false positives and false negatives, which often reflects moral priorities. In a fraud detection model, privileging false negatives may protect vulnerable groups from unfair scrutiny but increases financial exposure. In a medical triage system, privileging false positives may ensure at-risk patients receive attention sooner but burdens clinical teams. These trade-offs are neither purely mathematical nor purely ethical. They are both.

The motif returns once more: *the human remains present.*

A deeper challenge emerges when subjective values masquerade as clinical or empirical certainty. Distinguishing between validated evidence and culturally embedded judgement becomes essential. For example, body-mass index (BMI) was widely adopted as a feature in health-risk models throughout the 2000s, yet researchers at University College London noted in 2018 that BMI's historical development—rooted in nineteenth-century Belgian population studies—limited its precision across diverse ethnic groups. Systems that treated BMI as a neutral indicator inadvertently encoded historical assumptions about "normality." Here, the limitation was not intentional bias but an unexamined inheritance.

The distinction between evidence and assumption becomes sharper in predictive models for social outcomes. When a child-welfare algorithm in Allegheny County, Pennsylvania, launched in 2016, officials emphasised its ability to identify high-risk cases by weighing multiple factors. Yet ethical reviewers later observed that certain features—such as parental disability or past interactions with social services—reflected socio-economic realities rather than actual parental behaviour. The model's creators were transparent, but the case illustrates a broader dilemma: risk models often blend empirical insight with structural bias.

Still, an excess of caution can lead to paralysis. Values must inform systems; they cannot be erased. The goal is not neutrality—an illusion—but accountability. To see this more clearly, examine a rare instance of explicit value alignment. In 2021, Estonia's government implemented an AI system to schedule social-services appointments more efficiently. Rather than maximising throughput, designers set a parameter that prioritised individuals with chronic conditions. This was a normative choice, articulating a value: vulnerability deserves precedence. The result was not perfect, but it demonstrated how values can be embedded openly rather than tacitly.

So where does this leave us? If subjectivity is inevitable, if human value judgements—ethical, cultural, institutional—course through the matrix of every automated system, what responsibility falls on the people who shape them? How should designers decide which values deserve primacy? How should institutions justify the priorities they convert into code? And what should citizens demand of the systems that increasingly interpret, classify, and shape their lives?

A final, unresolved question lingers: if the human cannot be removed from the algorithm, how can we ensure the right humans—and the right values—set the terms?

When Machines Overrule

In March 2020, at a branch of NatWest in Manchester, a senior loan officer named Helen Murray watched an automated credit system overturn her recommendation on a small-business application. She had reviewed the file twice. The applicant, a local upholsterer with twenty years of trading history, had weathered multiple recessions and held long-standing supplier contracts. Yet the machine flagged a single late payment from 2017 as evidence of potential instability. The system's verdict—"decline"—flashed onto Helen's screen before she had finished typing her concluding note. The decision was final. She could not override it. The applicant left the branch visibly shaken, asking repeatedly how one delayed invoice could erase decades of reliability.

Two weeks later, long before the first government relief packages settled into place, the upholsterer's business closed. Helen later described the moment to colleagues as a turning point: "I realised the machine wasn't advising us. It was ruling us." Her account captures a dynamic that now shapes countless interactions, from university admissions to welfare assessments. Automated systems, designed to streamline judgement, often become arbiters that eclipse human intuition. The tension at the centre of this subchapter begins here: when should a model's authority exceed a human's lived understanding?

The motif we follow—*the line crossed*—appears quietly at first but grows sharper as systems expand. It is the moment a tool shifts from supporting a judgement to supplanting it, the moment discretion collapses into compliance.

The first major claim concerns the erosion of human confidence when machines dominate decision thresholds. Show the mechanism. In 2018, the Netherlands implemented an automated fraud-detection system known as SyRI (Systeem Risico Indicatie). Operating across Rotterdam and The Hague, the algorithm assessed citizens' likelihood of benefits fraud based on a combination of address records, employment histories, and family composition. When SyRI designated an individual as "high risk," local authorities were encouraged to prioritise intrusive investigations, often without explaining the grounds. Name the principle: algorithmic overreach. Explain the dynamic: once flagged, officials rarely questioned the designation, even when no behavioural evidence supported it. The implication is civic: when human discretion is sidelined, trust in public institutions fractures.

A second example reveals how machine precedence affects educational judgement. In August 2020, the Office of Qualifications and Examinations Regulation (Ofqual) in England used an algorithm to moderate A-level grades after pandemic-related disruptions prevented students from sitting formal exams. The model weighted historical school performance heavily, meaning high-achieving pupils at lower-performing schools received downgraded results. Teachers protested, arguing that the students' coursework and classroom performance contradicted the system's predictions. Name the underlying issue: statistical determinism. Explain its consequence: a rigid model undermined individual achievement by privileging historic averages over present capability. The implication is educational: when systemic data overrides direct human evaluation, social mobility narrows.

A credible counter-example tempers these concerns. In 2017, Denmark's tax authority adopted an automated system to flag suspicious VAT filings. Unlike SyRI, the Danish model required human auditors to review each alert and allowed them to dismiss weak signals freely. Auditors reported that the system improved focus without dictating outcomes. This offers a limitation to the wider critique: automation need not overrule human judgement if guardrails protect discretion. Reconciling the cases shows that tension arises not from automation per se but from the institutional choice to treat automated outputs as final.

To understand why people accept machine dominance, observe the visible behaviours that accompany it. Frontline employees in banks, hospitals, and public services often measure performance through compliance metrics. A housing officer in Leeds may commit to the system's risk ranking because deviating invites scrutiny. A university admissions coordinator in Edinburgh may accept an automated score because manual review adds weeks to an already strained cycle. A recruitment manager in Dublin may follow the recommendation engine because its predictions can be audited, while intuition cannot. Each behaviour reveals a pattern: people adopt machine verdicts not because they believe them intrinsically but because disagreeing carries a higher cost.

Thread the motif again: *the line crossed.*

One of the most revealing contexts for machine overruling is automated identity verification. Show the current landscape. In 2019, the Metropolitan Police Service tested live facial recognition (LFR) across parts of central London. Reports from the London Policing Ethics Panel noted that officers on the ground frequently deferred to algorithmic matches even when they sensed uncertainty. Name the phenomenon: authority bias. Explain the mechanism: the presence of a quantified match—expressed visually as a confidence percentage—pressured officers into action, overshadowing their instinct to double-check. The implication is legal: false matches can lead to unwarranted stops and detentions, eroding civil liberties.

Another domain where overreliance emerges is automated admissions. In 2021, several universities in Australia piloted machine-assisted triage systems to filter postgraduate applications. At the University of Sydney, the system ranked applicants using a composite score drawn from transcripts, institutional prestige, and research keywords. Admissions staff soon noted that the tool systematically down-ranked candidates from smaller regional institutions, even when academic supervisors vouched for their capability. Name the structural issue: prestige-weighted bias. Explain its impact: the system reinforced an existing hierarchy by equating institutional reputation with individual potential. The implication is academic: machine overruling can entrench inequities disguised as efficiency.

Still, human intuition is not infallible. A counter-example shows the danger of romanticising instinct. In 2015, an investigation into mortgage approvals at a major U.S. bank found that human loan officers consistently offered better terms to applicants with similar backgrounds or informal social ties. The machine-learning system that replaced them reduced these discrepancies. Acknowledging this complicates the narrative. Machines can overrule biases as well as perpetuate them. Reconciling this case requires nuance: the problem is not whether machines overrule humans, but whether the overruling is transparent, justified, and aligned with legitimate objectives.

Human tension arises most clearly when automated systems treat uncertainty as noise rather than signal.

Consider the behaviour of predictive policing systems. When the Chicago Police Department trialled its Strategic Subject List (SSL) between 2012 and 2019, analysts relied on algorithmic scores to determine who was at heightened risk of involvement in shootings. Officers were instructed to conduct "custom notifications" with individuals the system flagged. Those flagged could not challenge the designation or understand its basis. The human officers often reported bewilderment: some individuals were known locally as mediators or youth volunteers. The machine output overruled local knowledge. The implication is community-level: automated decisions can disrupt trust between institutions and the people they serve.

The theme extends into corporate decision-making. Automated performance dashboards often determine pay or promotion eligibility using quantitative proxies for productivity. When a logistics firm in Birmingham adopted an automated driver-evaluation system in 2020, drivers were penalised for minor route deviations that any human supervisor would recognise as reasonable adjustments for safety or traffic conditions. Show the behaviour: drivers began to commit rigidly to the system's optimal routes even when they sensed danger. Name the underlying issue: behavioural displacement. Explain it: when people adapt their actions to satisfy the machine rather than reality, workplace judgement atrophies. The implication is organisational: over time, human expertise weakens because systems train workers to follow rather than to think.

The motif surfaces again: *the line crossed.*

Why, then, do individuals defer so readily? One answer lies in risk distribution. Machines diffuse responsibility. If a decision fails, the system is blamed, not the decision-maker. This structure subtly encourages complacency. A case from insurance underwriting illustrates the dynamic. In 2018, Zurich Insurance trialled an automated underwriting system in Switzerland. Underwriters soon reported that they overruled the machine less frequently—not because the system improved but because challenging it required lengthy documentation. The burden shifted from justification to deference. As one underwriter explained, "If the model is wrong, that is the model's problem." The visible behaviour—reduced overrides—revealed the abstraction: risk transfer.

Another answer is cognitive relief. Decision-making is mentally taxing; automation offers a shortcut. In admissions offices, regulatory agencies, recruitment teams, human staff often welcome automated pre-sorting because it simplifies complexity. But simplicity can conceal divergence between algorithmic metrics and human goals. A 2022 review by the UK's Centre for Data Ethics and Innovation noted that several public-sector bodies had adopted automated triage because it "reduced workload," even when it "compressed nuanced assessments into binary tiers." Efficiency replaced reflection.

A credible limitation tempers the critique: complete resistance to machine rulings can itself generate chaos. When customs officers at Heathrow attempted to override an automated risk assessment system in 2016 without clear criteria, audits found inconsistency and higher error rates. Reconciling this example with the wider theme shows that human judgement needs structure, but not subordination.

This brings us to the deeper philosophical tension: what does it mean to let a system speak with finality? Machines derive authority from pattern recognition, probability estimates, or risk scores, not from moral judgement. Yet institutions increasingly act as if these outputs carry normative weight. A flagged applicant becomes "unqualified." A flagged citizen becomes "high risk." A flagged route becomes "correct." Subtle distinctions collapse into definitive labels. When machines overrule, they convert statistical tendencies into categorical truths.

The final question lingers, sharp and unresolved: when the system's verdict diverges from lived experience, who should step back—and who should step aside?

Reclaiming the Final Say

In May 2019, at St Thomas' Hospital in London, a clinical risk-assessment system flagged a postoperative patient as "low priority" for overnight monitoring. The nurse on duty, Sarah Ellwood, had reviewed the same patient twenty minutes earlier and sensed unease: a faint discolouration, a slight delay in response, a shallow breath that did not match the algorithm's green tick. She overrode the system, called a registrar, and insisted on escalation. Within an hour the patient was in theatre for emergency intervention. His surgeon later told Sarah that her judgement likely prevented a fatal incident. The quietness of the moment—one nurse facing a screen—captured a deeper question spreading across workplaces: when machine logic conflicts with human alertness, who must hold the final say?

The paradox grows sharper when we notice how often the crossroad appears unnoticed. In August 2021, an automated hiring platform used by a multinational retailer filtered thousands of applicants for warehouse roles in Leicester. The system ranked candidates by speech cadence and facial micro-expressions. A long-serving manager, Paul Morgan, realised that several high-performing former staff members had been rejected at the initial screening stage. When he reviewed their recordings manually, nothing suggested poor performance. Here too the question returned, compact yet heavy: why did the machine's judgement feel more "official" than the informed assessments of someone who had supervised hundreds of employees for over a decade? The stakes were not abstract. They concerned livelihoods.

These scenes reveal a motif that threads through this subchapter—*the held breath.* It is the moment a human pauses before accepting or rejecting an automated verdict, the silent interval where responsibility either collapses into compliance or reasserts itself as agency.

To maintain moral agency within heavily automated systems, the first major claim must be shown plainly: human reflection remains most powerful when it operates alongside, not after, machine computation. Consider the work of the UK Information Commissioner's Office (ICO), particularly its 2020 guidance on AI auditing. Name the principle the guidance reinforces: active justification. Explain its purpose: organisations should document not only how models operate but why a human chooses to rely on or override them. The implication is institutional: when reflection is embedded as procedure, judgement retains structure rather than evaporating into habit.

A second example grounds the same claim in a different domain. In 2016, the Wikimedia Foundation revised its automated content-filtering tools after volunteers complained that the system routinely mislabelled good-faith edits—especially those from newcomers or contributors working in underrepresented languages—as vandalism. Developers invited editors from Ghana, Argentina, and India to test the model directly and pinpoint its blind spots. Show the behaviour: editors annotated misclassified edits and proposed rule modifications. Name the process: participatory correction. Explain its significance: the system improved when human experience shaped its parameters. The implication is civic: broad collaboration prevents algorithms from defining truth within narrow cultural frames.

A credible counter-example highlights the limits of reflection alone. In 2018, a large insurer trialled a "human-in-the-loop" system designed to moderate automated premium adjustments. Staff were encouraged to override the algorithm where necessary. Yet internal audits revealed that humans overrode fewer than five per cent of outputs, even where misclassifications were clear. Why? Because overrides required lengthy reporting, and staff performance was measured partly by adherence to the model. Reconciling this case reveals a structural truth: agency withers when institutions penalise dissent. Moral judgement cannot flourish if the system design rewards compliance.

Thread the motif again: *the held breath*. It marks the space where individuals ask, silently, whether they are permitted to think.

The next claim focuses on ethical review boards as a mechanism for reclaiming human authority at scale. Show the process through a concrete example. In 2021, the city of Helsinki implemented an AI Register to provide public documentation of municipal algorithms. The Register was developed with input from legal scholars, software engineers, and citizen representatives. Name the structure: multi-stakeholder review. Explain its value: diverse expertise interrogated how each algorithmic tool might affect welfare claims, education access, or public resource allocation. The implication is democratic: ethical review boards help ensure that no system operates solely on technical measures without social accountability.

A parallel case from outside Europe reinforces this. In 2019, the New York City Automated Decision Systems Task Force published recommendations advocating transparency for algorithms used in policing, housing, and education. Although the report faced criticism for limited detail, it established a precedent: municipal governments must treat automated systems as part of public infrastructure, subject to scrutiny. Show the behaviour: the task force held public meetings, accepted written testimonies, and published minutes. Name the shift: algorithmic governance as collective responsibility. Explain its thrust: public review prevents technical decisions from becoming democratic blind spots. The implication is societal: oversight protects the conditions under which individuals can meaningfully object.

A counter-example, however, warns against overestimating review boards. In 2022, an academic ethics panel at a major European university approved an automated student-monitoring system, later criticised for disproportionately flagging students with disabilities for "attendance risk." The panel had assessed the system's documentation but not its training data or validation process. Reconciling this illustrates that ethical boards safeguard moral agency only when they possess genuine authority, technical competence, and independence. Without these elements, review becomes ceremony.

The third major claim addresses responsible design. Show the impact with an example from the Norwegian Labour and Welfare Administration (NAV). In 2020, after public criticism of opaque decision systems, NAV mandated that all new automated tools include "explainability dashboards" for staff. Name the requirement: interpretable output presentation. Explain how it works: caseworkers must see the variables influencing each recommendation and can annotate model outputs with contextual insights. The implication is practical: when people understand how a system reaches its suggestion, they regain the confidence to adjust, challenge, or correct it.

Another example appears in the medical domain. The Royal Free London NHS Foundation Trust, after controversy surrounding its data-sharing partnership with DeepMind in 2017, introduced strict safeguards for subsequent AI deployments. These included patient-consent mechanisms, external audits, and a clinician-led override system that privileged medical judgement over machine recommendation. Show the behaviour: clinicians could suspend the model's role in real time. Name the protection: conditional autonomy. Explain its function: doctors retained the authority to judge the patient's needs without procedural penalty. The implication is ethical: responsible design supports, rather than supplants, professional expertise.

A counter-example reveals a limitation. Many commercial recommendation engines—particularly those used by large streaming platforms—do not provide override pathways for editorial teams. If an engineer or curator suspects that certain groups are being marginalised by the model, they may lack mechanisms to intervene. Reconciling this requires acknowledging that responsible design depends not only on technical features but on corporate willingness to prioritise fairness over friction.

Thread the motif once more: *the held breath*. It is the instant before a designer, regulator, or frontline worker chooses whether to act on what they see.

The fourth claim concerns the necessity of deliberate reflection—the most personal and yet most fragile form of resistance. Show it through individual behaviour. During the early rollout of automated marking tools in 2021, a lecturer at the University of Glasgow, Michael McKay, began manually reviewing algorithmic scores for essays that seemed anomalous. He noticed patterns the system had missed—novel arguments that departed from conventional structure and were penalised unfairly. Name the process: reflective override. Explain its value: humans excel at noticing the unanticipated. The implication is educational: moral agency is preserved not by rejecting automation but by reserving the right to reinterpret.

A second example comes from journalism. In 2022, editorial staff at The Guardian incorporated automated summarisation tools into the newsroom. Senior editors reported that junior journalists began to internalise the machine's style, simplifying nuance to match algorithmic brevity. One editor, Jane Martinson, urged her team to write one sentence each day that resisted algorithmic shorthand—longer, layered, specific. Show the act: the deliberate pushback against homogenisation. Name the principle: mindful resistance. Explain its premise: small acts of reflection accumulate into institutional culture. The implication is creative: moral agency survives through habitual attention.

A counter-example provides nuance. Some argue that human override can introduce inconsistency, especially in policing or healthcare. If a staff member overrides for one case but not another, bias may re-enter through human variability. Reconciling this highlights the need for guided discretion: override systems must balance freedom with documentation, ensuring that decisions are principled rather than idiosyncratic.

The deeper tension emerges here: what does it mean to reclaim the final say when systems are designed to feel inevitable? The psychological comfort of deferring to the machine—removing responsibility, reducing ambiguity, accelerating decisions—can feel irresistible. But agency is not a switch; it is a practice. It begins with a question asked in the moment of the held breath: *Is this decision mine, or have I surrendered it by default?*

As automated systems grow more sophisticated, this question will not weaken. It will sharpen. The challenge is not to defeat automation but to decide, case by case, when to trust, when to dissent, and when to step forward rather than aside.

Chapter 4
Information Bubbles and Echo Chambers

On a cold January evening in 2016, a small group gathered in a converted warehouse in Shoreditch for what had been billed as an "offline meet-up" for members of a popular political forum. They had spent months trading arguments, memes, and manifesto-length posts with one another, convinced that they represented a broad ideological movement. But when they finally met, the mood shifted. Instead of the electric solidarity they expected, there was a kind of startled recognition: these twenty or so individuals were not a cross-section of anything. They were frighteningly similar—same age bracket, same jokes, same grievances, even the same brands of trainers. Their digital world had convinced them that thousands shared their convictions; the physical room revealed a smaller, narrower truth. The discovery unsettled them. It also encapsulated a deeper phenomenon shaping much of modern public life: the quiet formation of bubbles that feel vast from within and limited from without.

The paradox is stark. The internet once promised an information commons without borders—access to expertise, cultures, and viewpoints that earlier generations could only dream of. Yet abundance has had an unexpected consequence. Choice, when unbounded, leads many to self-curate pathways of least resistance. People move towards comfort, familiarity, and recognition, not because they reject the unfamiliar, but because the familiar appears endlessly available and deceptively representative. In that Shoreditch warehouse, the gap between perception and reality was not simply social—it was epistemic. What felt like a movement was, in truth, an echo.

The motif that threads throughout this chapter is a simple one: the *mirror corridor*. The more one walks down it, the more each reflection resembles the last, until the subtle distortions become almost impossible to detect. It is a corridor shaped partly by human preference, partly by technical amplification, and partly by the social incentives that reward conformity with our chosen digital tribe.

To understand how these corridors formed, we must begin with the earliest shift: self-curated worlds. In the 1990s and early 2000s, forums, message boards, and early blogging platforms appeared as places for experimentation. They offered niches for every conceivable interest—from amateur astronomy to medieval reenactment societies. Their charm lay in their fragmentation. Yet as the quantity of digital content exploded, fragmentation turned into refuge. The sheer scale of information encouraged people to build small, stable islands where they would not drown. These were not malign constructs; most were born out of enthusiasm. The knitting forum in Leeds, the retro-gaming subreddit, the motorcycle repair channel run from Sheffield—all exemplified communities finding coherence amidst excess. But the pattern they established would grow into something larger and more consequential: the normalisation of homogeneity as comfort.

Algorithms deepened these habits. Once platforms realised that people stayed longer when shown content resembling what they had clicked before, the mirror corridor began to extend. Recommendation systems, built to optimise engagement, became powerful architects of personalised worlds. They measured what users paused on, re-watched, hovered over, debated, or saved. These micro-behaviours became signals; signals became predictions; predictions became the blueprint for what users saw next. A viewer who lingered over one video about nutritional controversies found themselves served dozens more within days. A teenager who liked a handful of fitness posts found their feed slowly tipping into extreme diets and hyper-idealised body images. A casual interest hardened into a full ecosystem. It was not intentional indoctrination—it was the unintended consequence of systems designed to reduce friction.

The self-reinforcing nature of these systems matters because it blurs the line between exposure and belief. Psychological studies have shown that repeated statements, even without evidence, gain perceived credibility through mere familiarity. Platforms that recycle familiar ideas thus do more than reflect preference; they sculpt plausibility. This sculpting unfolds quietly. Most individuals navigating their feed feel informed, not curated. The illusion of breadth—the steady flow of posts, opinions, and videos—makes the corridor appear far wider than it is. Yet behind the scenes, the range is shrinking, not expanding.

The consequences spill far beyond digital consumption. Echo chambers transform social dynamics. Neighbours begin to mistrust neighbours; family members, once capable of disagreement with affection, retreat into defensive positions; civic debates harden into mutually unintelligible monologues. Consider the 2016 referendum in the United Kingdom. Journalists reported that many voters were stunned to discover how differently others viewed the question of EU membership, not because disagreement was novel, but because they had rarely encountered intelligent, considered versions of the opposite view. Their digital corridors had erased the nuance that kept public discourse coherent.

The social cost grows further when communities move from self-curated to algorithmically segregated. Platforms rarely intend to divide users, but their optimisation metrics create invisible partitions. Individuals who search for environmentally conscious products, for instance, become surrounded by sustainability content, activist posts, and targeted advertising reinforcing a sense of environmental urgency. Meanwhile, those who click on articles questioning green policies see increasingly sceptical content, sometimes escalating into conspiracy narratives. Two citizens living in Manchester, watching the same political debates, develop radically different understandings of the stakes—not because either is irrational, but because each has been placed in a corridor with a distinct horizon.

The chapter also addresses the emotional dimension of echo chambers. Humans crave belonging. To be part of an online community—whether a fandom, a political group, or a lifestyle subculture—is to feel anchored in a chaotic information environment. But belonging becomes brittle when identity is fused with information streams. That brittleness shows in the suspicion with which outsiders' views are met, the ease with which disagreements escalate, and the difficulty of constructive dialogue. Echo chambers do not merely distort facts; they reshape emotional norms, setting standards for loyalty, outrage, and trust.

The final movement of this chapter points towards the possibility of escape—though escape is not passive. Cognitive diversity cannot be delivered automatically; it must be *chosen*. The chapter explores how people might widen their corridors intentionally: through deliberate curation, exposure to unfamiliar perspectives, or conscious examination of how algorithms shape their feeds. But it also recognises the limits of individual effort. Structural transparency matters. Platform design matters. Cultural norms around disagreement matter. The aim is not to dismantle community—communities are vital—but to preserve permeability between them, preventing the digital sphere from hardening into a grid of isolated enclaves.

As you turn the page, consider this question: when did you last step outside your own mirror corridor, not by accident, but by choice?

Self-Curated Worlds

In March 2004, administrators at Wikipedia noticed a curious pattern tucked between routine edits. A small cluster of users, most of them posting from Manchester and Bristol, were revising the same set of political articles each night. Their changes rarely added new information. Instead, they repeatedly softened criticisms of a particular local party councillor while amplifying favourable interpretations of his record. The edits were subtle enough to evade casual detection, yet consistent enough to skew the narrative. When the activity was traced and publicly disclosed, the embarrassment was swift, but the deeper lesson was harder to ignore: given an infinite library, people do not wander freely. They gravitate towards corners that feel safe, persuasive, and familiar. The early internet's promise of boundless exploration collided with a human tendency to carve out small, curated rooms within the vast archive.

This paradox—abundance breeding insularity—became sharper as online spaces multiplied. By 2010, forums like Mumsnet in London and Bodybuilding.com, whose UK user base surged during that period, were not merely information exchanges; they were culture-makers. Each built distinctive norms, jargon, and hierarchies. Newcomers quickly learned which views earned praise, which triggered backlash, and which quietly went unanswered. Participation felt communal, yet the communities were rarely representative of the wider world. They were tailored, self-chosen, and often self-defending. The illusion of breadth persisted because the internet wrapped these localised conversations in the aesthetics of global reach. But the content, tone, and conversation rhythms were narrow—sometimes intensely so. The motif running through these dynamics is the quiet pull of the *familiar doorway*: the entry point each person returns to, again and again, even when dozens of other doorways stand open.

The mechanics of this self-curation are not abstract. They manifest in visible behaviours and measurable decisions. A user who joins a climate activism forum on a Tuesday evening in Leeds may, by Thursday, be following half a dozen related Twitter accounts and subscribing to newsletters framed around similar arguments. The metrics are concrete: repeated clicks, long dwell times, and the rapid growth of homogenous networks. Studies conducted by the Oxford Internet Institute (2019) observed that users who visited ideologically aligned communities three times within the same week were significantly more likely to remain within those spaces for the next month. Behaviour accumulates into habit; habit becomes worldview.

Niche forums illustrate this process vividly. Consider the long-running astronomers' community Cloudy Nights, which saw substantial UK participation between 2012 and 2018. Its members offered detailed telescope reviews, astrophotography tips, and nightly observation logs. The space was rich and generous, yet it also developed a distinct ideological flavour: scepticism of institutional astronomy, frustration with funding decisions, and occasional hostility towards professionals. The forum's self-curated world produced a skew—not malicious, but consequential. Members often understood the sky with remarkable precision while misunderstanding the structures of the scientific institutions they criticised. Their curated knowledge was deep but narrow.

Contrast this with a counter-example from the London-based Philosophy Now discussion boards around 2015. That community actively encouraged dissent. Moderators highlighted posts that challenged the dominant interpretation of a topic, and the forum's architecture rewarded long-form debates rather than quick affirmations. The result? A space less prone to insularity, though not immune to it. It demonstrated that curated worlds are not destiny; structures and norms can widen the doorway rather than shrink it.

Still, most digital communities lean towards cohesion rather than contestation. The implication is subtle but significant: when users repeatedly choose spaces that echo their preferences, they begin to confuse preference with universality. A person who spends evenings on a vegan bodybuilding forum in Birmingham may start to believe that plant-based fitness is becoming the undisputed global norm. Someone who frequents home-schooling Facebook groups in Kent may infer that traditional schooling is collapsing everywhere. The gap between local sentiment and global reality widens quietly. Self-curation hides its own boundaries.

The psychological undercurrent is equally decisive. Humans interpret repetition as endorsement. When an idea appears across multiple self-selected spaces—even when all those spaces derive from the same narrow pool—credibility grows. This dynamic explains why individuals can spend years within niche online communities without recognising how atypical their views have become. The *familiar doorway* motif resurfaces here: entering the same doorway daily produces the illusion that the building beyond it is vast.

Two concrete examples highlight the stakes. During the 2014 Scottish independence referendum, researchers at the University of Glasgow tracked patterns within several pro-independence Facebook groups. They found that even moderate members became more radicalised in their certainty, not because of misinformation, but because their curated community repeated the same emotional narratives. Meanwhile, during the COVID-19 lockdowns in 2020, knitting communities in Edinburgh and Cardiff—quirky, apolitical spaces—unexpectedly developed strong norms about public health compliance. Their members expressed near-unanimous approval for stringent measures, unaware that their conviction was shaped partly by the demographic uniformity of the group. The phenomenon was not ideological but structural: self-selection was quietly steering the tone.

To avoid oversimplification, we must acknowledge a legitimate counterpoint. Curated spaces can provide refuge, identity, and expertise. The autism-support forums established by the National Autistic Society in the UK since 2007 have been invaluable for families seeking clarity amid confusing institutional systems. Within those digital rooms, self-curation is not a problem but a lifeline. Specialisation can illuminate. It can empower. It can correct the indifference of generalised spaces. Yet even here, a long-term risk remains: safe havens may harden into enclaves if their boundaries become impermeable. The challenge is not the existence of curated worlds, but their mutation into sealed ones.

Why does the internet's scale intensify this pattern? Because vastness without guidance provokes overwhelm. Faced with boundless information, the average person retreats to what feels tractable. Forums, groups, subreddits, and Discord channels offer structure. They create a rhythm, an expectation, a manageable slice of the digital expanse. The cost is that the walls of that manageable slice begin to define what feels true. Quietly, subtly, the act of choosing a space becomes the act of constructing a worldview.

This process changes public conversation. When groups steeped in their curated worlds attempt to engage with outsiders, miscommunication is almost guaranteed. Each group arrives armed with assumptions shaped not by bad faith but by differing informational diets. One cannot debate meaningfully if the basic premises have diverged.

You see this in local disputes across the UK—from housing battles in Cambridge to cycling infrastructure arguments in Oxford—where each faction appears bewildered by the other's priorities. Their confusion is epistemic, not ideological. They have lived in different digital rooms.

The ripple effects extend into governance, education, and media. Politicians increasingly tailor messages to segmented online communities, reinforcing the idea that each group inhabits a distinct world. Teachers confront classes where pupils have absorbed entirely different interpretations of the same events, sourced from curated feeds. Journalists struggle to write for an audience that no longer shares a common baseline of knowledge. The familiar doorway, once a personal comfort, has become a structural reality shaping national discourse.

This subchapter advances the arc of the chapter by revealing the first movement of echo chambers: the self-selection that precedes algorithmic reinforcement. It shows that before technology amplifies narratives, humans choose the rooms they wish to inhabit. It foregrounds the truth that information bubbles begin not with software, but with desire.

The unresolved question—the one that hangs over the rest of the chapter—is deceptively simple: if the internet gives us infinite doorways, what compels us to keep walking through the same one?

Tech-Driven Echoes

In February 2018, YouTube engineers disclosed internal findings showing that its recommendation engine directed more than 70 per cent of total watch time on the platform (YouTube Engineering Blog, 2018). The revelation, buried in a technical post rather than a press briefing, confirmed what attentive observers had suspected: the bulk of global viewing habits were shaped not by active choice but by algorithmic suggestion. A viewer in Brighton could begin with a harmless clip about urban gardening and, within minutes, receive a chain of progressively similar videos, each selected because thousands before had clicked the same sequence. The system delivered relevance with astonishing speed. It also delivered repetition. What felt like exploration was, in practice, a loop—one formed by past engagement rather than present curiosity.

Two years later, in October 2020, TikTok's UK operations released anonymised engagement data showing how its "For You" feed clustered users into narrow interest groups within a matter of hours. A newly registered account from Leeds that lingered on three clips about vintage clothing was served an uninterrupted stream of styling tips, thrift-haul reactions, and retro fashion commentary. The platform's logic rewarded any hint of preference, no matter how fleeting. When the account's owner attempted to diversify their feed by searching for news, the algorithm still weighted recommendations heavily towards style content. The user had been categorised. And once a category exists, content flows accordingly. One early choice becomes a structural constraint. Five words capture the underlying dynamic: *the loop tightens with repetition.*

These scenes reveal a broader truth about algorithmically mediated life. Today's platforms measure what we have chosen before and commit to showing us more of the same. They assume that past clicks reflect ongoing desire, and they optimise relentlessly for frictionless satisfaction. The visible behaviour is familiar to anyone monitoring their own habits: a tendency to accept suggested content rather than search afresh, to scroll rather than select, to follow the path laid out by invisible heuristics. The metrics reinforce this. Platforms track not just clicks but pauses of more than half a second, hovering before a link, the speed of scrolling, and the frequency of revisits to similar posts. These signals form the bedrock of automated curation.

What makes this machinery powerful is not its intent but its structure. Recommendation models—whether built by Meta in Menlo Park, ByteDance in Beijing, or smaller firms across Europe—apply statistical shortcuts designed to maximise engagement. These shortcuts privilege similarity. They detect clusters of content that previous users have consumed in sequence, then reproduce those sequences for new audiences. The models treat correlation as destiny. The motif reappears here: *the loop tightens with repetition.* It tightens because repetition is the metric that signals success.

Consider two concrete examples. In 2016, Facebook's Trending Topics feature, headquartered in London and the

United States, was audited after accusations of political skew. The audit found no deliberate manipulation but revealed the core mechanism: topics surged because they echoed earlier viral patterns. If a story about a celebrity scandal drew mass engagement at 9 a.m., structurally similar stories were more likely to appear in the afternoon—even if they lacked social significance. The algorithm rewarded patterns of virality, not public value. The implication was straightforward: users encountered a feed shaped by engagement history rather than balanced relevance.

A second case arose during the 2021 German federal election, when researchers at the Hertie School examined YouTube recommendations for political content across Berlin, Hamburg, and Cologne. They discovered that once a user watched two or three videos from a specific ideological category, the platform overwhelmingly suggested videos from the same cluster for the next 12 to 24 hours. While extremist content was not necessarily promoted, ideological homogeneity was. The recommendations mirrored engagement patterns with statistical precision. As before, the loop tightened with repetition. Narrowness emerged without malicious design.

To test the limits of this dynamic, we can turn to a counter-example. Spotify's Discover Weekly, launched globally in 2015 and widely used in the UK, deliberately injects a small percentage of dissimilar tracks into its personalised playlists. The purpose is exploratory disruption. Engineers found that without this injection, users eventually received playlists that were too predictable, diminishing long-term satisfaction. Spotify's model demonstrates that algorithmic relevance can be tempered by design choices favouring diversity. Yet even here, the intervention is minor. It widens the loop but does not break it. The system remains committed to the familiar, albeit with a faint gesture towards novelty.

These structures reshape not only consumption but understanding. A user who sees repeated posts about sustainable fashion in London may begin to believe that the entire city is pivoting to second-hand clothing, when in reality the trend reflects a specific demographic segment. A parent in Glasgow who interacts with several videos about restrictive schooling practices may soon perceive them as widespread norms rather than isolated frustrations. The gap between lived experience and perceived reality is widened by automated curation. A pattern becomes a worldview.

Part of the challenge stems from the invisibility of heuristics. Few users recognise that most platforms deploy collaborative filtering—matching a person's behaviour to that of similar users—alongside content-based filtering, which identifies features within posts. These intertwined systems create a sense of naturalness. The feed appears to show what *should* be there, not what has been computationally inferred. When the same ideas appear across multiple contexts—recommendations, trending lists, "suggested for you" panels—the repetition feels like consensus rather than coincidence.

The platform engineers themselves face trade-offs. In interviews conducted as part of a 2019 Reuters Institute report, several social media designers admitted that diversity-injection mechanisms exist but are rarely allowed to disrupt the core flow. The reason was economic: too much content divergence decreases session length. The algorithm's duty is not epistemic responsibility but sustained attention. This distinction matters because it shows that narrowness often arises from commercial optimisation rather than ideological intention. Well-meaning customisation, built to spare users overload, ultimately narrows the informational terrain.

The result is an ecosystem that looks broad but behaves narrow. A user may encounter hundreds of posts in a single session, but if those posts revolve around similar themes, characters, and emotional registers, the experience is constricted. Exposure feels rich while remaining thin. The sensation is akin to walking through a vast museum where each doorway leads to a slightly modified version of the same room. What changes is not the substance but the frame. The motif returns: *the loop tightens with repetition.*

This narrowing has behavioural consequences. When presented with unfamiliar content, users accustomed to homogeneity tend to react more intensely—either with defensive dismissal or disproportionate fascination. A 2020 study by King's College London found that individuals whose feeds were dominated by single-topic clusters were more likely to misjudge public sentiment on major issues. They mistook the density of their curated environment for societal consensus, a pattern observable across political, cultural, and lifestyle domains. Here, engagement metrics translate into cognitive tendencies.

Yet it would be misleading to paint algorithmic curation as uniformly damaging. The limitation lies not in the premise of personalisation but in its rigidity. Systems can incorporate diversity signals, randomisation layers, and contextual weighting. They can be designed to reward not only similarity but curiosity. We see glimmers of this in platforms like Medium, which, in 2022, introduced a "topic stretch" feature, slightly expanding the semantic distance of recommended articles when user engagement stagnated. Though the feature's effect was limited, it showed that designers can adjust the loop rather than surrender to it.

Still, the broader tension persists. Automated curation offers comfort and relevance, yet it narrows perspective. It responds to preference but does not challenge it. It builds ecosystems that feel comprehensive while quietly omitting the unfamiliar. The unresolved question—the one this subchapter sets up for the sections that follow—is deceptively simple: if algorithms are built to mirror us, how do we ensure that the mirror reflects more than what we already know?

Social Consequences

On 24 June 2016, the morning after the EU referendum, commuters in Newcastle and in North London boarded the same trains carrying utterly different assumptions about what the country had just decided. Polling data later showed that voting patterns followed sharp demographic lines, but the shock on both sides had another source. Many Leave voters reported that they "knew almost no-one" who favoured Remain. Many Remain voters said precisely the opposite. Facebook's own researchers, analysing UK traffic that month from offices in London and Menlo Park, noted that users' timelines were dominated by posts aligned with their existing stance. In countless kitchens and workplaces, people were discovering not simply that others disagreed, but that those others existed in the first place. The shared civic square had quietly fractured.

The split did not begin with that vote, nor has it ended there, but it offers a clear snapshot of a phenomenon that now shapes offline life: algorithmically reinforced echo chambers altering how communities see one another. Neighbours still share bins and buses. They no longer share a baseline of facts, or even of questions. Two people living three streets apart can inhabit informational climates so different that political disagreement feels less like a contest of ideas and more like an encounter between rival realities. The square had silently split. And no-one quite saw when.

To grasp the social consequences of this shift, we have to move beyond individual feeds and examine how their aggregation alters public space. That is the core claim of this subchapter: algorithmic segregation is not just a matter of personal taste; it reshapes trust, governance, and the moral imagination of communities.

Begin with something visible. In 2018, during Italy's national election, researchers at the University of Milan tracked Facebook interactions across thousands of public pages. They found that users clustered around party-aligned hubs, with minimal overlap between groups. It was not just that different coalitions prioritised different stories; they rarely encountered one another's narratives at all. The pattern was clear: posts circulated within ideological clusters and almost never crossed boundaries. This is the show. They named the pattern "homophilic diffusion"—information travelling primarily among like-minded users. The explanation linked back to platform heuristics: recommendation systems elevated posts that generated strong engagement inside each cluster, reinforcing internal cohesion. The implication reached beyond the screen: candidates increasingly tailored messages to their "home" clusters, deepening rhetorical divides and leaving the middle ground rhetorically under-served.

A second example, drawn from India, shows how digital echo chambers can spill into physical danger. In 2018, a series of rumours about child kidnapping circulated through WhatsApp groups in rural districts of Maharashtra and Assam. Local police and journalists later documented that many of the most inflammatory messages had been forwarded dozens of times across tightly knit groups, often accompanied by screenshots from other chats that seemed to confirm the threat. Show the behaviour: residents who trusted their local WhatsApp networks more than official statements formed vigilante groups. Name the dynamic: networked panic. Explain the underlying mechanism: repeated exposure within a closed messaging environment made the rumours feel indisputable, while WhatsApp's limited forwarding metadata obscured their origin. The implication was tragic: several innocent travellers were attacked on suspicion of being kidnappers. Echoes moved offline, with lethal force.

Yet a credible counter-example reminds us that digital clustering does not always produce polarisation. Initiatives like r/ChangeMyView on Reddit and the cross-partisan organisation Braver Angels in the United States have built communities explicitly dedicated to exposing participants to opposing views. In 2019, Braver Angels' organisers reported from workshops in Ohio and New York that participants who engaged in structured dialogue showed measurable reductions in affective polarisation—how much they disliked political opponents—after only a few hours. These spaces demonstrate that technology can host bridges as well as walls. Reconciling this with the previous cases reveals an important nuance: echo chambers are not inevitable outcomes of digital media; they are the default when systems are left to optimise solely for engagement and comfort.

The motif that threads through these examples is the shrinking *common square*. Historically, towns had literal squares where information, gossip, and argument mixed. They were imperfect, exclusionary, and often unjust. Yet they provided a shared reference point. The digital environment has no single square; it has countless personalised plazas, each tuned to the sensitivities of its regulars.

The first major social consequence of this fragmentation is a recalibration of trust. People have always trusted some sources more than others. What is new is the outsourcing of those choices to systems that silently weight content by predicted engagement. A voter in Cardiff may begin by following a handful of local journalists on Twitter. The platform then recommends accounts followed by those journalists' followers, amplifying insiders with similar views. Before long, the voter's feed contains a dense web of voices broadly aligned in tone and perspective. The visible behaviour—liking, retweeting, replying—converts social affinity into algorithmic preference. Trust becomes structurally concentrated. When a contradictory claim appears from outside that network, it feels alien, and often suspect.

This has direct consequences for political legitimacy. The 2019 Edelman Trust Barometer recorded widening gaps in institutional trust between different demographic groups in the UK and Germany. While many factors contributed, echo-chamber dynamics played a part: people whose feeds were saturated with scandals and critiques became more likely to view institutions as uniformly corrupt, regardless of nuance. Meanwhile, those whose networks emphasised stability and continuity perceived critics as hysterical or malicious. The same policy decision—say, a change to welfare eligibility—was interpreted in one bubble as proof of systemic cruelty, in another as sensible reform. The common square shrank further.

The second consequence is social sorting. Algorithms do not merely distribute information; they help people decide whom to befriend, follow, block, or mute. Dating apps filter potential partners by political preference. Facebook groups encourage members to invite "like-minded friends." LinkedIn suggests connections "similar to people you already know." The visible decisions—swiping left, declining a request, leaving a group—appear trivial. Yet the cumulative effect is a reconfiguration of social networks along ideological and cultural lines. Sociologists at the London School of Economics have noted, for instance, that university students increasingly report having "no close friends" with opposing political views, a shift from data gathered in the early 2000s. Exposure, once a function of neighbourhood and workplace, has become a function of algorithmically mediated choice.

The third consequence is a subtle hardening of group identity. Within a digital echo chamber, the cost of dissent is high. When someone diverges from the prevailing line—say, by questioning a popular narrative about policing in an activist forum or by expressing concern about climate risks in an investor chat group—they often encounter ridicule, suspicion, or silence. The behaviour is easy to observe: critical comments attract dogpiles or are quietly deleted; dissenting members drift away. The explanation ties back to algorithmic visibility: posts that trigger intense, homogeneous reactions rise; posts that cause friction or discomfort sink. Over time, the range of acceptable viewpoints narrows, and group identity solidifies around a particular posture of outrage, irony, or purity. The implication is political: compromise comes to feel like betrayal rather than governance.

There are more intimate consequences, too. Families split not only over voting choices but over incompatible media diets. A parent who spends evenings in Facebook groups sharing vaccine scepticism articles from the United States will interpret public-health announcements in Birmingham very differently from a child who follows NHS doctors on Instagram. Their disagreements at the dinner table are structured by different informational scaffolds. They are not merely disagreeing over what the facts mean; they are disagreeing over what counts as fact, or even as news.

We must be careful, however, not to attribute all polarisation to algorithms. Political scientists note that geographic sorting, economic inequality, and decades of partisan media also play significant roles. There are societies with high levels of online connectivity and comparatively low polarisation, like some Nordic countries, where robust public-service media and strong civic institutions still anchor a common square. This is the counter-example worth holding onto: where offline institutions invest in shared narratives and civic education, echo chambers find less fertile ground. Reconciling this with the darker cases underscores a key point: algorithmic segregation interacts with existing social structures; it does not operate in a vacuum.

Still, the digital architecture matters. It changes how quickly distrust spreads. It alters the routes through which rumours travel. It modifies the emotional temperature of everyday interaction. A hostile tweet from a stranger in another country now lands with the immediacy of a neighbour's shout. An inflammatory WhatsApp message circulates through a village in minutes. The common square does not disappear; it becomes flooded by the noise from other people's squares, selectively amplified.

The final social consequence to note here is almost philosophical: echo chambers distort how communities imagine opponents. When exposure is limited to caricatures—screenshots of the worst comments from "the other side," exaggerated headlines shared in outrage—the very idea of good-faith disagreement erodes. A Remain-leaning user in 2016 might see only images of xenophobic Leave voters; a Leave-leaning user might see only cosmopolitan contempt for working-class concerns. Neither picture is wholly false; both are radically incomplete. The cost is civic empathy. Without the ability to imagine a reasonable opponent, democratic compromise starts to look like appeasement of cartoon villains.

The motif of the *common square* returns with force here. For democracy to function, the square does not need to be harmonious. It needs to be shared. Its very existence depends on the belief that political adversaries inhabit the same informational world, even if they interpret it differently. Algorithmically reinforced echo chambers chip away at that belief. They replace it with the conviction that "our side" sees clearly while "they" are deluded, brainwashed, or wicked.

This subchapter advances the book's argument by tracing how algorithmic curation migrates from the personal to the structural. It shows that the echo chamber is not merely a psychological curiosity but a social condition. The unresolved question, left deliberately open for the reader, is pointed: if our informational environments now shape whom we trust, whom we fear, and whom we recognise as fully real, are we willing to accept those environments as default—or will we demand squares, digital and physical, where disagreement is difficult but possible, and where the boundaries of our own bubble are no longer invisible?

Finding Escape Routes

In February 2021, researchers at the Reuters Institute invited a group of London-based participants to attempt a simple task: spend one week diversifying their digital diets by following at least five news sources they had not previously engaged with. The outcome was unexpectedly stark. Several participants reported that, despite good intentions, they "forgot" to check the new sources after the first two days. Others said the unfamiliar headlines "felt irrelevant," even when covering major developments. One participant—a 34-year-old accountant from Hackney—described the experiment as "like trying to read in a language I almost recognise but can't quite speak." The findings, later presented in Oxford, demonstrated that escaping an echo chamber is not merely a technical challenge. It is a psychological one. The familiar exerts a gravitational pull.

The difficulty of leaving these curated environments is not evidence of personal failure. It is evidence of design. Digital platforms refine themselves by studying our micro-behaviours—scroll duration, pause length, comment tone—and shaping our feeds to keep us comfortable. The problem is subtle: comfort feels like choice, even when it is engineered. The quiet motif running through this subchapter is precisely that tension between *comfort* and *choice,* between what appears natural and what has been gently nudged.

Yet escape is possible. Not easy, but possible. The task demands awareness, intentionality, and an understanding of how digital structures influence what we consider worth seeing.

A useful starting point is recognising the architecture of containment. Platforms like YouTube, for example, explicitly measure session duration—how long a viewer continues watching—as a key metric. Show the behaviour: a user watches a single economics video about inflation. Name the mechanism: the platform's recommendation engine, influenced by a neural-network system deployed in California in 2019. Explain the consequence: within minutes, the viewer is offered increasingly specialised or ideologically slanted content framed as "related," even when the conceptual overlap is tenuous. The implication is straightforward: the system is not asking what will make the viewer wiser; it is asking what will keep the viewer there.

A second case reveals the opposite possibility. In 2020, the Dutch public broadcaster VPRO launched an initiative called *Tegenlicht Diversifies,* where viewers were encouraged to add contrasting ideological voices to their social feeds. The results, published in Amsterdam and verified by independent analysts, showed that participants who persisted for four weeks reported higher tolerance for ambiguity and reduced certainty about their own positions. Crucially, they rated the experience as "initially uncomfortable, later illuminating." The discomfort mattered; it indicated that the algorithmic mould had cracked.

These examples reveal a critical truth: escape requires friction. It must interrupt the smooth glide of predictable content. And that friction must be chosen.

One major claim in this subchapter concerns the behaviour of attention. Human attention is not a neutral resource. It rewards the paths of least resistance. Show this through a metric: in 2015, Microsoft Canada famously reported that the average human attention span, measured in seconds of sustained focus during a digital task, had decreased from 12 seconds in 2000 to approximately 8 seconds (Microsoft Canada, 2015). Whether or not the exact figure withstands scrutiny, the trend aligns with observable behaviour: users skim, swipe, and skip. Name the concept: cognitive economy—the mind saves energy by leaning on habitual patterns. Explain its significance: platforms that anticipate these habits steer attention before conscious intention can intervene. The implication is sobering: unless users actively counteract these tendencies, they will slide towards narrower informational streams.

A counter-example, however, prevents this from becoming deterministic. Wikipedia—a website founded in 2001 and headquartered in San Francisco—offers no personalised feed. It presents the same page to every viewer. Despite predictions that such a model would fail in an attention economy, Wikipedia remains one of the most visited sites globally. Its non-personalised structure shows that people are capable of navigating information without algorithmic tailoring. Reconciling this with the more troubling examples suggests a nuance: echo chambers flourish where convenience meets personalisation; they weaken when friction and curiosity are designed into the experience.

A second motif threads through this analysis: *the doorway*. Escape requires finding, or building, doorways out of enclosed informational rooms. Doorways can take many forms. One is deliberate counter-exposure. A London academic might subscribe to both *The Guardian* and *The Telegraph*, not to "balance" views mechanically but to widen the frame of reference. The behaviour is visible: tapping between two tabs, registering dissonance. The explanation is psychological: encountering opposing arguments disrupts cognitive economy, forcing the mind to process rather than merely absorb. The implication is cultural: doorways create citizens capable of navigating disagreement rather than retreating from it.

Another doorway lies in mindful curation. Platforms give users tools—blocking, muting, following, list-making—not to foster diversity but to manage noise. Yet these tools can be repurposed. A user who actively seeks accounts outside their default political or cultural sphere is, in effect, hacking the platform's logic. The behaviour might appear modest—following an economist with different ideological leanings, subscribing to a science channel outside one's usual interests—but it signals a shift from passive consumption to active cultivation. The explanation is strategic: by altering input signals, users reshape the algorithms that predict their preferences. The implication is structural: even closed systems can be influenced from within.

Nor is escape solely a matter of adding voices. Sometimes the most powerful step is stepping away. Digital minimalism—which gained visibility through Cal Newport's widely cited work in 2019—reframes attention as a scarce asset, not a limitless resource. Show the behaviour: a user imposes a daily 30-minute limit on social media, enforced by app timers. Name the mechanism: behavioural constraint. Explain how the constraint magnifies awareness; the user becomes selective, engaging more consciously and less impulsively. The implication is emancipatory: the algorithm loses some of its leverage over impulse-driven behaviour.

But we cannot ignore the limitation of individual strategies. Echo chambers are structural phenomena. Personal choices help, but they cannot resolve platform-wide design incentives. Consider the example of Germany's 2017 Network Enforcement Act (NetzDG), which required platforms to remove unlawful content within strict time frames. Though aimed at curbing hate speech, the law inadvertently encouraged platforms to adopt more aggressive content moderation algorithms, sometimes reducing visibility of legitimate political discussion. The counter-example shows that regulatory interventions can have unintended side effects. Reconciling this with the broader argument reveals a complexity: structural reforms must be carefully calibrated to avoid replacing one form of informational narrowing with another.

A deeper escape route involves civic literacy. Media literacy programmes in Finland, introduced as part of the national curriculum in 2016, demonstrate what is possible. Students are taught to trace the provenance of information, compare sources, and identify manipulative framing. Follow-up studies by the Finnish Ministry of Education in Helsinki indicated that these students displayed significantly stronger resilience to misinformation than their European peers. The behaviour is visible: they check, cross-reference, question. The explanation is cultural: literacy equips individuals to navigate the *comfort–choice* tension with awareness. The implication is societal: stronger civic literacy widens the common square.

Another structural doorway comes from design ethics. In 2020, the Centre for Humane Technology in San Francisco launched campaigns encouraging platforms to adopt what they called "dignity-preserving" design choices—options such as chronological feeds, transparent recommendation labels, and friction points before sharing sensational content. When Twitter briefly introduced a prompt in late 2020 asking users whether they had read an article before retweeting it, independent reviewers found that the prompt measurably increased article opening rates during pilot weeks. The behaviour changed. The explanation is simple: a gentle nudge countered impulsive sharing. The implication is profound: escape routes can be built into the system, not merely sought by users.

Yet the most enduring escape route is introspective. People rarely confront how invested they are in their own informational comfort. A user may believe they are open-minded, but their click history—videos watched to the end, posts lingered over—reveals otherwise. Escaping an echo chamber requires acknowledging this contradiction. The behaviour is measurable: shifting patterns of engagement, more time spent on unfamiliar sources, more patience with discomfort. The explanation is psychological: curiosity must outpace certainty. The implication is ethical: openness becomes a commitment rather than an accident.

The final movement of this subchapter circles back to the motif of the *doorway*. The question that lingers is not simply whether escape is possible but what escape demands. If the architecture of digital platforms gently shepherds us towards comfort, what is the smallest act of resistance we are willing to commit? Will we open one doorway? Build another? Share one with others?

The unresolved tension remains: in a world where personalisation feels natural, how do we train ourselves to desire the unfamiliar, to welcome the friction that keeps our minds supple? The trade-off is unavoidable. Comfort narrows. Curiosity widens. Which will we choose when the feed scrolls endlessly, offering precisely what we did not ask for but always seem to want?

Chapter 5
AI and Media: The New Gatekeepers

In the spring of 2018, editors at the Associated Press gathered in their New York newsroom for what should have been a routine morning briefing. The screens that lined the walls glowed with the previous night's data feeds—earnings reports, court filings, sports results. Yet a quiet shift had taken place. A sizeable portion of those briefs had not been written by people. They had been generated by an automated system known as Wordsmith, which the AP had adopted four years earlier to accelerate its corporate-reporting output. The editors scrolled through the machine-written summaries with a mix of admiration and unease. The copy was clean. The numbers were correct. The tone was workmanlike and efficient. It was also unmistakably uniform, as if stamped from the same invisible mould. In that moment, the newsroom sensed that a boundary had moved: the gatekeeper role was no longer theirs alone.

The transition did not come as a shock. It had been years in the making. What startled many was how smoothly the machine's cadence slipped into the fabric of journalism. The old gatekeeping processes—those ritualised layers of editing, fact-checking, and contextual shaping—had relied on the idiosyncrasies of human judgement. Now, in a matter of seconds, an algorithm could produce a piece of serviceable prose. What it could not do was reveal the subtle instincts that had guided editors for generations: the decision to foreground one voice over another, the sensitivity to moral nuance, the ability to pause on a contradiction and recognise that this, not the headline figure, was where the story lived. That loss of textured judgement is the undercurrent of this chapter.

To understand what is at stake, we must revisit the media world before automation, when gatekeepers operated in plain sight. Editorial boards acted as custodians of public attention. Their choices were visible, sometimes contested, often imperfect, but anchored in accountable processes. A regional newspaper in Manchester or a national broadcaster in London adhered to established routines: morning conferences, line-by-line edits, cross-checking sources, defending contentious headlines. These structures were slow, occasionally maddeningly so, yet their very friction allowed room for doubt, revision, and ethical debate. Gatekeeping was as much a moral practice as a logistical one.

AI gatekeeping, by contrast, unfolds quietly in the margins of the feed. Stories rise not through deliberation but through optimisation. A headline appears because thousands of similar users lingered on similar words yesterday. A video trends because the system predicts it will hold attention for 23 seconds longer than the alternative. Here, judgement is not debated; it is computed. The result is a media ecosystem in which visibility becomes a probabilistic outcome rather than an editorial choice, and the public sphere is shaped by signals no citizen ever sees.

Yet this transition is not solely about speed or scale. It is also about authorship. Algorithms do not merely prioritise content; they now *produce* it. From automated sports recaps to AI-generated explainer videos, the line between human-crafted narrative and machine-generated artefact grows thinner by the month. Convenience masks a deeper tension: the more the system writes, the more the system sets the narrative template. Many outlets already rely on automated summarisation tools to create quick digests of complicated reports—tools that compress nuance into something digestible but potentially distorted. A 78-page policy document becomes a paragraph stripped of caveats. A scientific paper becomes a neat storyline. Complexity is hammered flat.

That flattening of complexity creates fertile ground for something far more troubling. Deepfakes—synthetic audio or video manipulated by machine learning—have moved from experimental curiosities to mass-produced weapons of persuasion. A politician appears to say something incendiary in a clip that spreads faster than any correction can. A journalist's voice can be stitched with fabricated phrases. A public figure's likeness can be rendered in scenes they have never lived. Authenticity, once grounded in the physicality of the recorded moment, is now a fragile construct. Even genuine footage invites suspicion. Trust becomes a casualty of the medium itself.

This is not merely a technological problem; it is a civic one. When fact and fiction blur, democratic deliberation strains.

The public depends on journalists to separate signal from noise, yet journalists increasingly rely on automated tools that can both support and sabotage their work. Newsrooms across Europe and North America report a growing need for specialists skilled in verifying synthetic media, reverse-engineering algorithmic outputs, and stress-testing the reliability of automated copy. The journalist of the coming decade must be part detective, part coder, part ethicist. Their task is not only to report but to interpret the artefacts of automation that now mediate reality.

Still, the rise of AI in media is not inherently corrosive. Much depends on how institutions respond. Some organisations have embraced a hybrid model in which automation handles repetitive tasks while human editors concentrate on investigative work, narrative depth, and ethical scrutiny. Others have begun publishing transparency notes disclosing when AI tools assist with production. A handful of outlets, particularly in Scandinavia, have experimented with "algorithmic editors" whose recommendations are debated alongside those of their human counterparts. These movements signal a recognition that automated gatekeeping must be governed, not merely adopted.

As this chapter unfolds, its lens widens from the historic role of editorial boards to the contemporary architecture of automated influence. You will encounter the promises and pitfalls of AI-generated content, the new vulnerabilities of truth in an age of synthetic media, and the evolving responsibilities of journalists tasked with safeguarding public trust. Threaded through it all is a recurring motif: the shifting boundary between human judgement and machine logic. Who holds the gate? Who decides what deserves to be seen? And what happens when those decisions occur at a speed and scale no human institution can match?

The stakes are not technological alone. They are cultural, political, and deeply personal. The future of public knowledge will be shaped not just by how AI transforms media but by how we, as citizens and readers, respond to that transformation. Privacy, authenticity, accountability—each is being renegotiated in real time. As you move into the next sections, the central question sharpens: in a landscape where machines curate the flow of information, how do we preserve a media environment that still feels human and still serves the public good?

Turn the page, then, with a specific curiosity: not just how AI has become a gatekeeper, but what kind of world its gates are quietly building.

Historical Gatekeepers

In June 1972, the *Washington Post* newsroom confronted a dilemma that would later define the modern mythology of investigative reporting. Bob Woodward and Carl Bernstein stood before their editor, Ben Bradlee, with fragments of a story linking the Watergate burglary to political operatives in Washington, D.C. Their notes were partial, their leads fragile, their claims incendiary. Bradlee listened, paced, and demanded corroboration: *two* independent confirmations before anything reached print. The rule slowed the story's progress but hardened its credibility. It was a scene replicated across newsrooms of that era: editorial authority exercised in full view, each decision shaped by identifiable people with traceable standards. The gate was visible. So were its keepers. That clarity forms the foothold from which the present era of algorithmic filtering diverges.

Those early decades of post-war journalism reveal how gatekeeping once depended on a deliberate choreography. Powerful editors committed to hierarchical structures that blended scrutiny with professional intuition. At the BBC's Broadcasting House in London during the 1980s, senior editors presided over daily editorial conferences, deciding which stories merited airtime and which required deeper reporting before release. Notes were pinned to boards, wires clattered, and producers defended their proposals with evidence that could withstand internal challenge. Nothing about the process was automated; even speed, the newsroom's perpetual tyrant, bowed to the value placed on accurate verification. These practices did not prevent failure—misreporting happened, blind spots remained—but they created a culture in which responsibility had a face, a signature, and often a margin for reflection. That margin is the quiet motif of this discussion: the space in which judgement slows, gathers itself, and decides what should pass into the public domain.

The machinery of traditional gatekeeping rested on the principle that visibility carried moral weight. Editorial boards functioned as buffers, deliberately interposing human judgement between raw events and the public gaze. The *Guardian*'s 1998 decision to run its exposé on tax avoidance schemes illustrates this model. Reporters assembled evidence; editors measured its relevance; legal teams assessed risk. The chain was sequential and labour-intensive. It also served as a mechanism for collective accountability. Each stage turned information over, challenged assumptions, and ensured that no single voice dominated without contest. That pattern—show, check, examine—gave journalism both its procedural discipline and its democratic legitimacy.

The first major claim to consider is that editorial boards historically acted as stabilisers, countering the volatility inherent in news gathering. To show this, consider the Reuters bureau in Nairobi in 2007, covering post-election unrest. Journalists sent urgent dispatches from the field, often under personal threat. Editors in London named the gravity of the situation by demanding corroboration from multiple local sources and satellite images before confirming casualty numbers. This insistence on layered verification slowed publication but prevented the spread of inflated figures circulating through less rigorous outlets. The implication was clear: careful gatekeeping tempered panic, anchored reporting, and maintained public confidence during a period of national trauma.

A second example is found in the *Sydney Morning Herald*'s 1996 coverage of the Port Arthur massacre. Reporters were flooded with anonymous claims, unverified witness accounts, and speculation about motives. Editors instructed the newsroom to restrict early reports to police-confirmed details and eyewitness statements captured on tape. The restraint frustrated some correspondents eager to break new angles, yet preserved the integrity of the unfolding narrative. Here again, the human gatekeeper shaped information by refusing to allow emotional velocity to outrun factual certainty. This form of disciplined caution characterises the old model: contamination of the public record was treated as a measurable harm.

Yet the traditional system was not without its limits. A credible counter-example emerged during the 2003 run-up to the Iraq War. Multiple Western news organisations, including the *New York Times,* endorsed claims about weapons of mass destruction based on official sources that were later revealed to be unreliable. The failure did not stem from automation but from human bias, political pressure, and insufficient scepticism. This underscores the point that human gatekeepers were capable of error—sometimes catastrophic ones. To reconcile this limitation with the earlier examples, we must observe that the strength of the historical model lay not in infallibility but in accountability. When mistakes occurred, scrutiny had an address. Responsibility was traceable. Corrections, however belated, were owned.

To understand what has changed, we must examine how older filters operated as interpretive layers. Every abstraction—truth, relevance, risk—was folded into behaviours such as red-pen edits, cross-room debates, courtroom-style questioning of sources, and the tactical delay of publication. A senior editor's raised eyebrow could stall a headline. A legal advisor's marginal note could reshape its framing. These micro-decisions accumulated into a gatekeeping architecture that was part craft, part responsibility, and part culture. The gate was not an algorithmic funnel but a set of human rituals repeated thousands of times across decades.

The motif of the margin—the space for reflection—returns here. Traditional media carved out room for pause even under pressure. A story might be held for one more phone call, one more document check, one more conversation between editor and reporter. That pause was costly; it meant delayed publication, missed scoops, and slower circulation. Yet it introduced texture: the ability to weigh moral or social complexity without collapsing it into a binary decision. That texture becomes essential when contrasting historical gatekeeping with the frictionless acceleration of automated systems.

If the old gatekeepers provided structure, they also enforced editorial identity. Newspapers cultivated distinct voices not only through opinion pages but through stylistic conventions, editorial philosophies, and story priorities. The *Financial Times*, with its salmon-pink pages and global economic focus, cultivated a restrained analytical style. *Le Monde* placed emphasis on intellectual critique and cultural interpretation. These editorial fingerprints guided journalists and signalled to readers what kind of lens was applied to the world. Algorithms, by contrast, tend to homogenise. They ranking content based on engagement metrics rather than editorial identity, thinning the texture that once differentiated outlets.

A second major claim arises: historical gatekeeping embedded professional norms that moderated the excesses of sensationalism. The UK's Press Complaints Commission (established in 1991) provided an institutional framework for ethical oversight, compelling outlets to abide by codes relating to accuracy, privacy, and fairness. Its successor, the Independent Press Standards Organisation, continues this role. These bodies did not prevent violations but created mechanisms for redress. Their presence illustrates that the pre-digital ecosystem recognised gatekeeping as a moral practice requiring external scrutiny. This adds weight to the argument that older models, for all their flaws, encouraged public accountability.

A further example lies in the training culture of journalism schools, such as Columbia University's Graduate School of Journalism, founded in 1912. Students were drilled in interviewing techniques, verification protocols, and the ethics of source protection. These routines fostered habits of judgement that travelled with graduates into newsrooms around the world. The implication is that gatekeeping was embedded far upstream, in the very formation of journalistic identity.

Yet even the most diligent editorial processes faced inherent constraints. Newsrooms were geographically concentrated, socially homogeneous, and often resistant to diverse perspectives. This limitation is significant: gatekeepers were not neutral arbiters but individuals shaped by their own beliefs, cultures, and professional incentives. The implication for our current era is double-edged. Automated systems claim to correct human bias, yet they may replicate or amplify it. Historical gatekeeping may have been imperfect, but it provided a visible site for reform. Algorithms, by contrast, obscure their own decision-making processes behind proprietary code.

The motif of the margin returns once more. In the shift from human deliberation to machine filtration, the margin for reflection shrinks. Where editors once paused to ask, "What is the public interest here?", automated systems measure click-through rates, dwell time, and predicted engagement. The behaviours are quantifiable; the values are not. That shift in priorities—towards metrics over meaning—marks the conceptual boundary between traditional gatekeeping and AI-driven selection.

As we near the close of this analysis, the unresolved tension surfaces: should the future of media rely on algorithmic efficiency or human judgement? The old model was slow, subjective, and prone to institutional bias. The emerging model is fast, opaque, and shaped by optimisation rather than ethical deliberation. Both contain flaws; neither offers a complete solution. The central question becomes unavoidable: in a landscape where automated systems increasingly determine what enters the public sphere, how much of the gatekeeping margin can we afford to lose—and what must we preserve to ensure that public knowledge remains more than just what the system predicts we will click?

The next section confronts this question by examining how AI-driven content creation reshapes the very texture of public discourse.

AI in Content Creation

In March 2020, the *Associated Press* announced that its automated earnings-report generator—powered by natural-language software from Automated Insights—had produced more than 40,000 corporate summaries from its newsroom in New York. The outcome was striking: what once required teams of reporters now emerged in seconds, structured into concise paragraphs, stripped of ambiguity, and distributed globally. The machine's efficiency was measured in output per minute; its precision in error rates far lower than human typists working under deadline pressure. Yet editors soon noticed a pattern. The summaries read alike. The cadence flattened. Nuance thinned. The invisible gatekeeper was no longer a senior journalist marking up drafts with a pencil but a model tuned to compress markets, decisions, and corporate histories into a consistent template. The speed impressed. The sameness unsettled.

It was not the first time automation entered mainstream reporting. In 2014, the *Los Angeles Times* deployed its "Quakebot", an automated script built by journalist-developer Ken Schwencke, to publish immediate reports on seismic activity in California. The system scanned U.S. Geological Survey feeds, converted data points into pre-written sentence structures, and released articles within minutes. The benefit was clear: timeliness improved, especially for events too small to command full editorial attention. Yet even Schwencke acknowledged the limits. The bot could detect magnitude but not meaning. It knew nothing of local damage, community reactions, or the quiet fear that ripples through residents after a sudden tremor. These early experiments set the stage for the present era, in which content creation at scale has become a defining feature of digital media ecosystems.

The first major claim demands evidence: AI-driven content creation streamlines production while narrowing voice. The AP's earnings system shows the streamlining. A second example, Bloomberg's "Cyborg" tool, deployed in 2019, automated the drafting of financial news updates from earnings releases. Reporters used its outputs as scaffolding, adding context and adjusting phrasing. Bloomberg reported that the tool increased coverage speed and reduced factual inconsistencies. Yet the mechanism that produced these benefits—the algorithmic template—also created a linguistic signature recognisable across hundreds of articles. The stories appeared efficient but repetitive, their shape dictated by machine-readable inputs rather than editorial imagination. The implication is that automation can produce textual abundance while quietly constraining stylistic diversity.

A counter-example tempers this view. The *Washington Post*'s Heliograf system, used during the 2016 and 2020 U.S. elections, generated short updates on voting results across local districts. Editors reported that the tool liberated journalists to pursue deeper investigative stories, precisely because routine updates no longer consumed their time. Here, automation broadened, rather than narrowed, editorial ambition. The limitation was that Heliograf's outputs remained tightly factual; they could not interpret trends, interrogate anomalies, or identify patterns of civic significance. Its strength lay in standardisation; its weakness in interpretation. Reconciling this suggests a crucial distinction: automation excels when the narrative is numeric, but it falters where ambiguity demands judgement.

To understand the stakes, we must examine how algorithms intuit what readers might want. Recommendation engines measure prior engagement—clicks, pauses, shares—and commit that behaviour to future predictions. When these systems shape headlines or generate automated summaries, they often privilege familiarity over complexity. A study by the Reuters Institute (2022) observed that algorithmic headline optimisation tilted towards emotionally charged phrasing, because such headlines improved click-through metrics by measurable margins. The model rewarded what captured attention quickly, not what illuminated difficult issues fully. This pairing of behavioural data with editorial outcomes reveals the tension: efficient delivery of surface information versus the slower cultivation of public understanding.

This tension animates the second major claim: automated summaries risk oversimplifying complex issues. To show this, consider automated COVID-19 data updates generated by various news outlets in early 2021. Many relied on structured feeds from public health agencies and converted them into bulletins or short articles. These summaries often reported case numbers, mortality counts, and vaccination rates but omitted underlying factors: demographic disparities, data-collection gaps, or shifts in testing availability. The summaries were not incorrect; they were incomplete. The system compressed multidimensional problems into digestible fragments. By stripping away complexity, it inadvertently converted uncertainty into apparent clarity. The implication is stark: when AI systems reduce a crisis to metrics alone, they risk shaping public perception more forcefully than the data warrants.

A second example deepens the point. In financial journalism, automated tools frequently summarise market movements: "stocks rose", "yields tightened", "currencies slipped". These formulae mask volatility, structural context, and the human decisions driving market behaviour. Even seasoned analysts sometimes rely on these automated descriptions as shorthand. The quiet motif here is condensation—the reduction of sprawling realities into narrow forms. It recurs across sectors, shaping how audiences understand politics, health, economics, and culture.

Yet automated condensation is not inherently detrimental. It becomes hazardous when audiences or editors mistake precision for completeness. This demands a third major claim: the authority granted to AI-generated text can outstrip its interpretive capacity. When an automated tool crafts a headline, its choice of emphasis—whether to highlight conflict, novelty, or risk—affects public behaviour. These choices may stem not from editorial reasoning but from optimisation functions tuned to past engagement. Visible behaviours follow: increased clustering of articles around proven themes, amplification of stories that fit well-defined templates, and reduced space for unexpected or underrepresented narratives. The implication is cumulative: as algorithms shape media production, they also shape which ideas circulate, which debates broaden, and which concerns fall silent.

A credible limitation must be acknowledged. Some advanced generative systems, particularly those introduced after 2023, have demonstrated the capacity to adapt tone, vary structure, and even simulate editorial diversity. They can mimic humour, restraint, scepticism, or analytical depth when properly steered. In controlled environments, such systems demonstrate genuine flexibility. Yet this flexibility relies heavily on human oversight: prompt design, content review, editorial calibration, and ethical guardrails. Without these, generative tools revert to statistical patterns and produce text optimised for fluency, not fidelity. The reconciliation lies in recognising that adaptability does not eliminate risk. It shifts responsibility back to the humans governing the system.

To understand the structural shift underway, we must revisit the motif of condensation. Traditional journalism maintained a margin—space for reflection—between event and headline. AI systems collapse that margin, smoothing raw inputs into ready-made prose. The behaviour is visible in publication metrics: shorter turnaround times, more uniform story lengths, higher frequency of updates. The question for media organisations becomes how to preserve interpretive richness when automation relentlessly trims narrative edges.

The stakes extend beyond newsroom workflow. As automated systems proliferate, they influence public discourse through cumulative texture. If thousands of articles adopt similar framings, the collective effect reshapes the boundaries of public imagination. Ideas outside the algorithmic centre of gravity struggle for visibility. Niche stories shrink. Complexity fades. A media ecosystem shaped by automated content becomes orderly, but brittle. The brittleness matters, because diverse democracies depend on narrative friction—disagreement, debate, multiplicity of voice—rather than mechanical consensus.

This raises a further claim: automated content risks homogenising not merely language but thought. A platform tuned to maximise engagement will elevate themes that align with past preferences. Readers experience a comforting coherence: the world appears ordered, familiar, unsurprising. That coherence, however, is engineered. It stems from patterns in historical data rather than contemporary understanding. The behaviour is evident in closed-loop recommendation cycles: a user interested in climate policy receives articles framed through economic risk; another receives pieces framed through scientific urgency; neither sees the full panorama. The implication is a fragmented public sphere in which narratives diverge quietly, shaped less by ideology than by personalisation.

Yet caution is warranted. The homogeneous effects of automation are not universal. Certain outlets use AI as an assistant rather than an architect: drafting raw text, transcribing interviews, or aiding fact-checking. When deployed with discipline, automation strengthens quality by freeing journalists to pursue complex investigations. The limitation here is scale. These beneficial practices require resources, training, and time—precisely the constraints many newsrooms struggle to meet. Global media environments dominated by smaller outlets may adopt automation without the accompanying editorial infrastructure. That asymmetry widens the gap between high-quality reporting and mass-produced information.

The motif returns again: condensation as both a boon and a danger. Efficiency brings clarity, but clarity achieved through narrowing can mislead. At its core lies an unresolved question: how much interpretive authority should society cede to systems designed to predict rather than understand? The tension is irreducible. Automation promises speed, reach, and consistency. Human editors offer judgement, dissent, and imagination. Between them lies a frontier—productive but fraught—on which the next decade of media credibility will likely turn.

The next section steps directly into that frontier, tracing how increasingly sophisticated generative tools blur the line between fact and fabrication, and what it means for audiences navigating information touched by invisible machines.

Blurring Fact and Fiction

In June 2019, Dutch cybersecurity researchers at Deeptrace reported that the number of detected deepfake videos online had doubled within nine months. Many originated from servers in Amsterdam, where the team ran forensic tests on clips circulating across social platforms. One video, falsely depicting a public figure making inflammatory remarks, had amassed hundreds of thousands of views before being flagged. The researchers compared pixel-level artefacts, measured frame inconsistencies, and traced metadata trails. The outcome was sobering: the clip passed casual scrutiny with ease. Most viewers believed it. Few questioned it. And fewer still paused long enough to measure the distance between spectacle and truth. The line separating fact from fabrication was thin. It was also shifting.

Later that same year, in Washington, D.C., researchers at Georgetown University demonstrated how synthetic text—generated by models trained on vast public corpora—could imitate political rhetoric convincingly enough to confuse analysts. Their experiment, conducted in October 2019, produced paragraphs so stylistically accurate that even seasoned researchers struggled to distinguish them from authentic campaign material. The dataset they used was openly available. The tool required no advanced technical expertise. It took minutes to produce persuasive text. It took far longer to unpick the illusions. As one researcher remarked afterwards, the problem was not simply deception but scale.

These two episodes reveal the first major claim: media manipulation powered by AI has become both accessible and increasingly difficult to detect. The Deeptrace example shows how deepfake videos exploit human reliance on visual cues. The Georgetown study shows how synthetic text exploits reliance on linguistic familiarity. Both draw on the same motif: resemblance. The machine aims not for originality but mimicry. It learns styles, cadences, frames, and rhetorical patterns, and then commits them to new content that feels authentic because it mirrors what we expect.

To ground this claim, the behaviour must be shown. Deepfakes succeed because viewers often skim: they scroll quickly, pause briefly, and share impulsively. A 2020 MIT study (Vosoughi et al., *Science*) demonstrated that false stories spread faster than true ones because they evoke stronger immediate reactions. When an AI-generated video matches a viewer's expectations or anxieties, the behavioural metric—share rate—increases. The implication is clear: in environments where speed dominates, authenticity becomes secondary to emotional resonance.

A second example further illustrates the growing stakes. In 2021, the BBC reported on a deepfake audio recording circulated during a local election campaign in India. The clip appeared to show a candidate making disparaging remarks about a neighbouring community. It was later proven to be synthetic, created using a voice-cloning model that required only a few minutes of real audio. The spread was rapid; the retraction slow. Officials noted that the manipulated audio influenced community sentiment before corrections reached the public. This demonstrates how synthetic media can alter political mood long before verification tools intervene.

A credible counter-example tempers the narrative. In April 2022, researchers at the University of California, Berkeley, unveiled an improved forensic technique using photoplethysmography (PPG) signals—subtle colour changes in human skin caused by blood flow—to detect deepfakes. The method proved highly accurate in controlled tests. Similarly, several large platforms now integrate detection systems that highlight manipulated content when certain artefacts appear. These developments show that countermeasures exist and are improving. Yet they operate with limitations: they struggle in low-resolution videos, cannot easily interpret new generative techniques, and depend on platforms adopting them consistently. Reconciling this tension reveals the structural truth: verification advances, but fabrication evolves faster.

The second major claim follows: synthetic content erodes public confidence in authentic media, even when the information is accurate. The behaviour tied to this erosion is hesitation. Viewers pause before believing genuine footage. Readers question legitimate reporting because it resembles what a machine *could* generate. Consider the case of the AI-manipulated video that appeared to show Nancy Pelosi speaking with an exaggerated slur in May 2019. Although not technically a deepfake—merely slowed and pitch-adjusted—the clip spread widely on Facebook, garnering millions of views. The debate it ignited persisted long after debunking. The issue was not the technical sophistication but the persuasive power of manipulated familiarity. The implication is unsettling: even unsophisticated distortions can create long-term doubt.

A second example strengthens the point. During the COVID-19 pandemic, text-based misinformation proliferated. Short, authoritative-sounding posts—many generated or enhanced by automated systems—purported to summarise scientific findings. Some misconstrued preprint data; others invented affiliations with real institutions such as the WHO. When repeatedly shared, these fragments acquired the veneer of legitimacy. Public health officials, including those in London's Public Health England in mid-2020, reported difficulty countering these narratives because they blended real terminology with false claims. The motif of resemblance reappears: synthetic text succeeds not by inventing new ideas but by echoing familiar phrasing.

The third major claim addresses the core: advanced manipulation tools compress the distance between fabrication and plausibility. They do so by amplifying details associated with credibility—steady eye movement, seamless transitions, rhythmically "human" syntax. For instance, researchers at the University of Amsterdam observed that deepfake detectors built on convolutional neural networks exhibited declining accuracy (2021) as generative adversarial networks adopted more sophisticated facial modelling. The visible behaviour is adaptation: as detectors learn to measure one artefact, generators learn to conceal it. The implication is evolutionary: detection will remain essential but perpetually incomplete.

A credible limitation must be introduced. Not all AI-generated content is deceptive. Many newsrooms use generative systems for benign tasks: drafting outlines, suggesting headlines, or supporting translation. Synthetic voices assist accessibility. AI-generated imagery can illustrate abstract topics. These uses do not inherently blur fact and fiction; they enhance storytelling. The reconciliation lies in intentionality: when the purpose is constructive and disclosed, AI amplifies journalism. When the purpose is hidden or malign, the same tools destabilise shared reality.

To understand the deeper cultural consequences, we must scrutinise how AI-mediated deception exploits cognitive shortcuts. Humans often rely on pattern recognition to evaluate authenticity. If a video aligns with established memories of a public figure's gestures, we accept it. If a text resembles familiar argument structures, we believe it. These shortcuts evolved for efficiency, not forensic scrutiny. When synthetic content is engineered to trigger them, the distinction between real and fabricated collapses quickly. The motif of resemblance appears again: truth filtered through familiarity rather than verification.

This raises a further claim: the presence of synthetic media reshapes collective memory. Once a manipulated clip enters circulation, it becomes part of the informational environment, influencing how future events are interpreted. In 2020, after several deepfake clips of President Zelenskyy circulated online, Ukrainian officials documented public confusion regarding later legitimate addresses. The videos did not need to be fully convincing to cause uncertainty. They needed only to exist. Visible behaviour followed: citizens requested additional verification for authentic announcements. The implication is long-term: synthetic content not only deceives in the moment but weakens the cognitive infrastructure of public trust.

Yet a counter-pressure exists. Grassroots digital literacy campaigns, such as those implemented in Finland's national curriculum in 2020, show that well-designed educational programmes can improve sceptical reasoning. Students trained to examine sources, scrutinise metadata, and challenge persuasive framing exhibited stronger resistance to manipulated media. This example suggests that the human mind can adapt, but doing so requires structured support. The limitation is scalability: such programmes remain unevenly adopted across nations and platforms.

As the chapter progresses, a final tension appears. Advanced manipulation tools do not merely alter individual perception; they influence institutional responses. Newsrooms spend increasing time verifying footage. Courts struggle with digital evidence. Governments debate regulatory frameworks without clear technical boundaries. Meanwhile, malign actors iterate rapidly. The pace of creation outstrips the pace of correction. The question that emerges is unavoidable: how does a society maintain confidence in a media environment where anything plausible might be fake, and any fake might appear perfectly plausible?

The motif of resemblance threads one last time. The threat lies not in machines inventing new realities but in machines crafting artefacts close enough to the real that the difference becomes a matter of expertise, not intuition. Viewers confront a landscape where doubt becomes habitual. Some adopt blanket suspicion, rejecting authentic content. Others remain unaware, accepting fabrications. Between these extremes sits a fragile centre—citizens trying to navigate a world where the burden of verification shifts increasingly onto them.

So the unresolved question stands: when technology makes illusion routine and authenticity fragile, what practical choices remain for those who wish to see clearly?

Journalistic Responsibility

In March 2023, editors at *Le Monde* halted the publication of a long-form investigative piece after a routine pre-press check revealed that two supporting paragraphs—submitted by a junior reporter working under intense deadline pressure—had been drafted by an AI assistant. The text was not fabricated; the sources it cited were accurate. Yet the tone, pacing, and framing had shifted subtly. Quotes were trimmed without context. A policymaker's remarks, originally cautious, had been recast into watertight certainty. The editorial team compared the draft against the reporter's notes and transcript. The discrepancy was small but meaningful. The decision was swift: the article would be revised manually. The lesson was more enduring. Even competent reporters could cede ground to automated phrasing that tidied away nuance. Accuracy had survived; fidelity had not.

A similar reckoning unfolded at *The Guardian* in July 2020 when the newsroom published a column written with the aid of a generative model. The experiment was transparent. The editors disclosed the process. The model's sentences were coherent, and some were even elegant. Yet the editorial team reported that stitching the piece together required considerable human intervention. The model lacked grounding in context. It slipped between assertions with unwarranted confidence. The exercise revealed a paradox that haunts AI-assisted journalism: automation saves time, but only if humans spend more of it judging what the machine has produced.

These scenes anchor the first major claim: as AI assumes tasks once reserved for human hands, journalism does not become easier; it becomes more demanding. The visible behaviour illustrating this shift is the rise in verification tasks now embedded in routine workflows. Editors measure source alignment, compare AI-generated drafts with original materials, and commit more hours to scrutinising tone and framing. The implication is unavoidable. Journalists must cultivate new forms of vigilance, not because machines are reckless, but because they are relentlessly plausible.

To deepen this point, consider a checkable example that crystallised the stakes. In May 2022, Reuters piloted a system in London that generated short market summaries using natural language models trained on live financial data. The summaries were fast and factually clean. Yet analysts found that the system occasionally selected outlier data points, producing sentences that framed fluctuations as trends. Humans intervened, adjusting parameters to dampen that effect. The system improved, but the lesson stood: even when numbers are correct, interpretation requires judgement. The metric at stake was misinterpretation risk, measured in how many corrections analysts introduced before publication. The implication widens: machines can organise information, but they cannot carry the weight of editorial meaning.

A counter-example provides texture. The Associated Press has used automated systems to produce quarterly earnings reports since 2014, and by 2017 the organisation publicly stated that the automation reduced errors in numerical reporting. In these cases, the structure is formulaic. The inputs are consistent. The stakes revolve around precision rather than nuance. The limitation is thus domain-bound. Automation excels where language is transactional. It falters where it must navigate context, politics, culture, or conflict. Reconciling these examples clarifies the boundary: AI enhances journalism where facts are discrete and patterns stable; it destabilises it where meaning is contested.

The second major claim follows naturally: journalists now occupy a role less like traditional writers and more like custodians of epistemic integrity. To show this, we turn to the behavioural metric that reveals the shift—the increase in time dedicated to forensic evaluation of sources. In May 2021, the BBC's Visual Journalism Unit reported spending roughly twice as long authenticating footage from conflict zones because synthetic and manipulated videos had become commonplace. The team measured edge noise, shadow angles, and sound-layer inconsistencies. They tested file origins. They cross-checked witness accounts. The work resembled investigative analysis more than traditional reporting. The implication for journalism is profound. As automated systems accelerate production, humans must slow down.

The motif threading through this subchapter—*the margin,* that slim boundary where truth bends under pressure—emerges here again. It is within this margin that journalists must operate. Machines write quickly. Humans must ensure that speed does not distort meaning. The profession's centre of gravity shifts from authorship to arbitration.

A second named example strengthens this claim. In December 2022, *The New York Times'* audio team found that an AI-generated transcription of a lengthy investigative interview had altered the cadence and emphasis of several key statements. The software inserted punctuation in places that changed the emotional temperature of the testimony.

Journalists corrected the transcript manually. The behaviour underlying the problem was silence: the machine confidently inserted pauses where none existed. The implication is clear. Even benign tools, used for efficiency, can reshape narratives unintentionally.

A limitation complicates the picture. Journalists have long relied on tools—spell-checkers, style guides, search engines, image editors. Automation is not new. Nor is the risk of misinterpretation. Yet AI introduces something qualitatively different: the ability not just to assist but to *generate* meaning. Reconciling this with the broader argument shows that the challenge is not the presence of tools but the opacity of their decisions. Journalists cannot rely on intuition to sense when an AI has erred; they must learn to interrogate the margin.

The third major claim addresses skills. Journalists must acquire fluency in technical forensics: metadata analysis, model behaviour understanding, deepfake detection, and probabilistic reasoning. These skills are no longer optional for investigative desks; they are integral to protecting the public from synthetic distortion. One behaviour exemplifies this need: the manual reconstruction of source provenance. During the early months of the war in Ukraine in 2022, fact-checkers at Bellingcat spent hours geolocating footage by comparing shadows, building layouts, and terrain features across open-source maps. Their success hinged on human pattern recognition. Machines assisted, but humans resolved ambiguity. The implication touches the profession's core ethos: accountability requires expertise that cannot be delegated.

Yet some newsrooms resist. A credible counter-example comes from smaller regional outlets facing budget constraints. In 2021, several local US newspapers adopted automated content tools to generate sports recaps and community announcements without dedicated oversight. Many articles were accurate. But some displayed synthetic phrasing that lacked cultural context or misinterpreted local events. These outlets operated under financial pressure. Their decision was pragmatic. The limitation is systemic. Resources shape responsibility. Reconciling the counter-example demands nuance: not every newsroom has equal capacity to shoulder the burden of verification, yet the ethical requirement remains.

Return now to the motif of *the margin*. It marks not just the line between fact and error but the space in which judgement must be exercised. Machines cannot perceive this space. They process tokens, optimise probabilities, and pursue coherence. Only humans can recognise when coherence masks contradiction, or when an elegant sentence distorts reality.

The final claim brings the argument to its threshold. Journalists must redefine their professional identity. Their work is less about being first to publish and more about being last to err. The visible decision that reflects this shift is the strategic slowdown emerging in major newsrooms. Stories undergo extended vetting. AI outputs are checked against primary sources. Teams confer more frequently across desks. This behavioural choice—deliberate friction—is a structural response to an environment that rewards acceleration.

A forward tension remains unresolved. As automation grows more capable, as synthetic content becomes easier to produce, and as audiences expect immediacy, journalists must negotiate a difficult question: how much human oversight is enough? Too little, and errors slip through the margin. Too much, and news production slows to a crawl, losing relevance. The trade-off cannot be eliminated. It must be managed.

The margin waits.

Chapter 6
The Illusion of Neutrality

The promise arrived wrapped in the language of progress. In January 2015, Facebook unveiled its revamped News Feed ranking system, presenting it as a step towards a more "relevant" and "meaningful" digital environment. Onstage in Menlo Park, the language emphasised user empowerment. The algorithm would simply "surface what matters most" to each individual. The framing suggested neutrality, almost benevolence. Yet within weeks, journalists and researchers noticed shifts in visibility. Some political pages saw engagement collapse; others ballooned. What appeared to be a technical refinement had quietly redistributed influence. A system sold as impartial was, in practice, sculpting the public square.

The shock was less about malice and more about misunderstanding. People had imagined algorithms as transparent tools, not cultural actors. When *The New York Times* later reported that small publishers in the American Midwest lost up to half their referral traffic, the discussion exposed a deeper tension: neutrality is not a default but a claim, and claims must be examined. The same system that amplified baby photos and travel diaries could also determine which policy debates, social movements, and minority voices reached the surface. Power had shifted from editorial boards to engineers, yet the ideological load remained, redistributing itself through code.

This tension between the ideal of objectivity and the reality of design sits at the centre of this chapter. Its origins stretch back to the early techno-optimism of the 1990s, when the internet was framed as a great equaliser. Cyber-utopians insisted that digital networks would dissolve old hierarchies, giving each user an equal platform. But as platforms grew, so did their incentives. What began as a decentralised web of forums and personal pages became an architecture dominated by commercial imperatives: attention, retention, and monetisation. Each of these priorities carried an ideology, even if unspoken. They shaped the scaffolding through which communication flowed.

Yet techno-optimism remains seductive. It offers a convenient fiction: that technology sits above human conflict, smoothing away the messy parts of social life. But the digital sphere is no more neutral than the printing press was when it amplified Tudor political propaganda, or the telegraph when it transformed 19th-century financial markets. Tools reflect their makers. Platforms reflect their sponsors. Algorithms reflect whoever is permitted—or paid—to influence their objectives. Neutrality is not a property of machines; it is a narrative about them.

Exposing that narrative requires returning to the small, easily overlooked decisions that accumulate into ideology. Consider the design of a basic recommendation system. When a platform developer chooses whether to optimise for "time spent," "click-through rate," or "long-term user satisfaction," they encode a worldview: what matters, what counts, what should be rewarded. Engagement metrics appear neutral because they are numeric. Yet they steer behaviour with remarkable force. When YouTube shifted its objective function in 2012 to prioritise watch-time, creators across continents adapted overnight. Videos grew longer. Titles grew sharper. Outrage and surprise travelled faster because they kept people glued to the screen. A metric had become a cultural engine.

That same phenomenon underpins microtargeted advertising, one of the clearest demonstrations of how design choices shape experience. A retailer selecting an age bracket or postcode may appear benign, but when political groups use similar tools to deliver differentiated messages to millions, the assumptions buried in the interface take on ethical weight. The segmentation is not neutral. It reflects a theory of persuasion, a commercial logic, and a social sorting mechanism. What users see as a personalised feed is, in fact, an ideological landscape assembled through thousands of tiny decisions made by people they will never meet.

Neutrality becomes even more elusive when we consider what metrics omit. Engagement rates, for instance, rarely register the quality of discourse, the reliability of sources, or the emotional consequences of content consumption. A post that triggers indignation may outperform a carefully researched explainer, not because it is more truthful but because provocation measures well. When organisations build strategy around these metrics—boosting high-performing content, sidelining low-performing nuance—they reshape public conversation without ever announcing the shift. We behave according to what we measure, and when the measurements are narrow, so too are our horizons.

A more critical user begins with the simple act of recognising this architecture. Not rejecting it, not romanticising an imaginary analogue past, but learning to see the scaffolding that sits behind the screen. This discernment has precedent. Readers once learned to distinguish tabloids from broadsheets, editorial from advertorial, reporting from propaganda. The digital era demands a similar literacy, but the signals are subtler. The interface itself is designed to conceal its politics. A colour shift in a button, a default sorting order, an automatic suggestion—these are small nudges with large implications.

The challenge is not to become paranoid but to become perceptive. The more one notices, the more one recognises the quiet fingerprints of design. Why does a platform highlight mutual friends instead of shared values? Why does a search engine recommend trending queries before you finish typing? Why does one type of post receive celebratory confetti animations while another earns nothing but white space? These choices may appear trivial, but they accumulate into behavioural architectures. They steer how we interpret, connect, and prioritise.

Throughout this chapter, we trace how techno-optimism faltered, how ideology seeped into design, how metrics shaped behaviour, and how users can reclaim their bearings within systems that prefer to tend their own narratives. The thread pulling these themes together is a simple yet unsettling insight: neutrality is not the natural state of technology. It is the mask technology wears.

The movement ahead asks the reader to peer behind that mask. It offers a vocabulary for questioning the structures that mediate digital life, from the metric that governs your feed to the ideology built into your everyday apps. The task is not comfortable. It demands curiosity and persistence. Yet the reward is substantial. Once one begins to see how systems tilt, filter, and prioritise, the illusion of neutrality weakens—and a more deliberate approach to the digital world becomes not only possible but necessary.

The next pages turn that awareness into understanding.

Techno-Optimism Challenged

In March 2018, the revelations surrounding Cambridge Analytica broke into public view. Reporters described how the firm had harvested Facebook data from tens of millions of users without consent, using psychographic profiling to influence electoral behaviour. The scandal was centred in London, where the Information Commissioner's Office later raided the company's headquarters. Yet the shockwaves extended far beyond England. For years, platforms had assured users that their systems were neutral conduits—

tools designed to enhance connection, not manipulate it. The moment investigators confirmed the scale of the data operation, that narrative cracked. A system sold as impartial was now implicated in shaping democratic outcomes.

The paradox was unmistakeable. The same platforms that championed themselves as equalising forces—open to all, guided by data, blind to prejudice—had hosted one of the most targeted political operations of the decade. What had been framed as objective optimisation had carried powerful ideological freight. A quiet motif emerges here: the veneer. The digital sphere has long relied on it, presenting sophisticated systems as if they were smooth, predictable, and detached from human interests. Yet the Cambridge Analytica case forced the public to look beneath that veneer and confront the political assumptions baked into design choices.

Techno-optimism grew from a hopeful reading of the early web. Its advocates believed that the sheer expansiveness of the internet would dilute old gatekeepers. Borders would soften. Status would matter less. Expertise would be shared, remixed, democratised. The promise rested on scale: with vast networks, individual biases would cancel out, leaving a purer form of communication. But the scale proved deceptive. The platforms that rose to prominence were not neutral infrastructures; they were highly curated architectures, and curation always carries intention.

The first major claim becomes visible when we focus not on vision but on behaviour. Consider the way Facebook's

News Feed rewarded posts in 2016. During the run-up to the US presidential election, the company's own internal analysis (later reported by *The Washington Post*) showed that misinformation often outperformed verified journalism. The algorithm optimised for engagement. That metric rewarded provocation. The system measured clicks and shares, not the provenance of a claim. The implication was stark: a supposedly objective ranking mechanism could amplify falsehoods faster than truth because its priorities were set around user attention, not public accuracy.

That dynamic is not confined to politics. YouTube's 2012 shift to prioritising watch-time, as documented by *The Wall Street Journal*, dramatically reshaped the platform's culture. Longer videos, extreme thumbnails, and emotionally charged content spread because the system rewarded anything that kept viewers online. This was not ideological in intent, yet it became ideological in effect. It privileged high-arousal content. It incentivised creators to escalate expression. It reshaped public discourse by rewarding intensity, not insight. Again, the veneer: a neutral metric with unmistakable social consequences.

A credible limitation tempers the argument. Not all algorithmic design entrenches power; some systems actively counter bias. The UK's National Health Service, for instance, uses machine-learning tools to predict patient deterioration. In 2021, an audit found that one hospital's algorithm improved response times for cardiac arrests by flagging anomalies earlier than human clinicians alone.

Here the optimisation—accuracy rather than engagement—served a public good. Yet even this example reinforces the central point: outcomes depend on objectives. A metric centred on clinical safety produces a different world from one centred on profit or retention. Neutrality remains a façade; intention shapes everything beneath it.

The motif of the veneer returns when we examine how power dynamics hide within interfaces. A search box looks impartial. A trending bar seems observational. A recommended list appears personalised, even caring. But each of these elements is tuned to commercial logic. When Amazon altered the weighting of its search results in 2018—reported by *The New York Times*—it quietly boosted its own branded products. The interface did not announce this shift. The ranking remained wrapped in the language of relevance. Yet the behaviour revealed priority: the company nudged millions of consumers towards its preferred merchandise. A neutral façade had concealed a strategic hand.

To understand why techno-optimism falters, we must ask who benefits from these arrangements. It is not users in the abstract; it is platforms whose business models depend on influence. The asymmetry is structural: platforms know far more about individuals than individuals know about platforms. This knowledge gap enables systems to act with an authority that feels organic but is meticulously calculated. The result is subtle: people come to trust results that appear neutral because neutrality feels scientific, almost moral. Yet trust here is behavioural, not philosophical. It manifests in clicks, in the absence of scepticism, in the everyday acceptance of what the ranking tells us.

A second named example reinforces how deeply these dynamics run. In 2020, researchers at Stanford and the University of Washington documented how Twitter's image-cropping algorithm favoured lighter-skinned faces in previews. Twitter disabled the system later that year. The company had not intended discrimination. Yet the behaviour of the algorithm reproduced existing patterns of representation. The system magnified visibility for some while narrowing it for others. Again, intention did not matter; consequence did. The veneer of neutrality dissolved the moment the bias became measurable.

Still, there is a useful counterpoint. Wikipedia—despite its flaws—remains one of the few digital platforms structured around collaborative correction. Its editorial hierarchy is transparent. Its revision logs are public. Its community debates are archived. Its imperfections are visible. This visibility tempers techno-optimism with a more grounded model of digital governance: one in which neutrality is an aspiration, not a marketing promise. By exposing process rather than hiding it, Wikipedia demonstrates that the problem is not technology itself but systems that conceal their values behind automated decisions.

The question that threads the section together emerges through the motif of the veneer: what happens when we mistake the appearance of neutrality for its substance? The implication is profound. If we treat algorithmic outputs as objective, we surrender scrutiny. If we believe systems distribute information evenly, we fail to notice when visibility pools around certain voices. If we accept the interface as a mirror rather than a filter, we misunderstand its power. Techno-optimism collapses not because its hopes were naive but because its assumptions were unexamined.

The tension now sits squarely with the reader. As platforms scale, as optimisation intensifies, and as automated decisions seep into civic life, what stance should we adopt toward these systems? Blind trust is unwise. Cynical rejection is unproductive. The more difficult path lies between them: a measured scepticism that asks who sets the objective, who benefits from the ranking, and what world is produced by the metric beneath the surface. The veneer remains glossy. The question is whether we are willing to look past it.

The Ideology of Design

In November 2019, the UK Electoral Commission released findings on political advertising during the general election campaign. The report identified how microtargeted messages on Facebook and Google had delivered starkly different political narratives to different groups of voters across England, Scotland, and Wales. No two individuals received precisely the same information. The platforms had not only distributed adverts; they had shaped which issues mattered to whom, and when. Cambridge-based analysts reviewing the data later observed that these personalised messages often contradicted one another, yet the architecture that delivered them was consistent: optimise attention, segment audiences, and fine-tune persuasion. The outcome was unambiguous. A system heralded as impartial had quietly embedded a political strategy within its design, amplifying certain priorities while muting others.

This case exposes a paradox. How can an interface that presents itself as neutral produce outcomes so deeply ideological? The answer lies in what designers choose to foreground, what they permit, what they restrict, and what they automate. These decisions are rarely malicious. They are often framed as technical, sometimes as commercially prudent. Yet each one contributes to the construction of a worldview, encoded not in words but in defaults, prompts, and pathways. The motif of the mask surfaces here: the polished interface that conceals the values guiding it. Once we notice the mask, its seams become unmistakable.

A first major claim reveals itself when we study behaviour rather than rhetoric. Consider the design of Google's search interface in 2015, when the company introduced what it called "answer boxes". Rather than presenting ten blue links, Google began surfacing a single, prominent block summarising what it deemed the best available response. The feature looked benign. It aimed to save users time. Yet the selection of a single authoritative answer positioned Google not as a curator but as an adjudicator of truth. This was design performing ideology. It narrowed epistemic diversity by elevating one viewpoint. It rewarded content that fitted the company's ranking logic. A system built to streamline became a system that shaped.

Naming the mechanism clarifies the deeper significance. Ranking is not neutral. It is a hierarchy produced by engineers, data scientists, and product managers whose objectives—speed, relevance, retention—are shaped by commercial pressures. When the metric is time-to-answer, breadth shrinks. When the metric is user satisfaction, ambiguity diminishes. When the metric is ad revenue, content that stimulates return visits gains promotion. The interface wears a mask of neutrality, but beneath it lies a succession of choices, each nudging the user toward a particular understanding of information.

A second checkable example illustrates how ideology embeds itself even when designers claim objectivity. In 2021, Apple introduced its App Tracking Transparency framework, allowing users to block cross-app tracking with a single prompt. Privacy campaigners praised the move. Yet within a few months, investigations by *The Financial Times* revealed that Apple's advertising network had expanded its own tracking capabilities, benefiting from restrictions that hampered rivals. The design decision—framed as empowering users—shifted power within the digital advertising ecosystem. The mask looked protective; the foundation reallocated influence. Again, ideology in code.

A credible counter-example tempers the argument. The open-source browser Firefox, built by the Mozilla

Foundation, has long foregrounded user agency through transparent permission systems and community-audited code. Its design emphasises ethical commitments rather than commercial optimisation. Its defaults limit tracking; its add-ons enable scrutiny. This shows that ideology need not always skew towards corporate interest. Yet the limitation remains: even ethical design choices reflect an ideological vision. Firefox promotes openness, transparency, and user sovereignty because its founders held those values. The mask differs, but it is a mask nonetheless.

The design of microtargeted advertising exposes this dynamic with particular clarity. When an advertiser launches a campaign on Facebook's platform, the system recommends audience segments, bidding strategies, and creative formats. These are not passive options. They are nudges that steer advertisers toward specific tactics. The interface privileges techniques that maximise engagement. Higher engagement produces higher revenue. This shapes political communication. It encourages sensationalism. It privileges messages that provoke rapid emotional responses. Behavioural metrics—click-through rates, impression frequency, lookalike expansion—become the scaffolding of public persuasion. The ideology is implicit but potent: influence is a quantifiable commodity, optimised through data.

To grasp the broader implications, we must look at how interfaces choreograph attention. Think of the behaviour required to dismiss a push notification. A user must locate the alert, interpret its urgency, and choose whether to act. Designers know that friction shapes habits. Reduce friction and action becomes automatic. Increase it and action stalls. When Instagram in 2016 altered its feed to prioritise algorithmic relevance over chronological order, it did so after measuring how users scrolled, paused, and reacted. The company stated that people missed "70% of posts" under the old system. The new design masked a commercial logic: more personalised feeds kept users engaged longer. Engagement time rose. Advert inventory expanded. Yet the user's perception was of a platform becoming more efficient. The mask remained intact.

Ideology also manifests in absences. What is not shown carries as much weight as what is. A job-matching platform might exclude salary transparency because employers prefer flexibility. A dating app might omit political filters to avoid polarisation. A navigation tool might avoid recommending cycle routes because liability concerns overshadow safety incentives. Each omission shapes behaviour. Each pathway signals a value: efficiency over clarity, safety over ambition, convenience over self-determination. The result is a world subtly sculpted by design principles users rarely interrogate.

The mask slips further when we recognise how interfaces frame choice. The classic example comes from default settings. In 2014, researchers at University College London examined cookie consent banners across major news websites. Sites designed with "accept all" in a bold colour and "manage settings" in muted tones generated significantly higher acceptance rates. Users believed they were choosing freely. In practice, they were responding to visual hierarchy. The interface embodied a persuasion strategy aligned with commercial interest. Design became ideology in action.

A limitation must be acknowledged: not all ideological imprinting is harmful. Some interfaces intentionally encode pro-social values. Wikipedia's edit suggestions steer contributors toward articles needing citations. The NHS symptom checker intentionally avoids definitive diagnoses to prevent self-misassessment. These constraints serve ethical ends. Yet even here, the core argument survives. Every design choice—whether protective, manipulative, or simply pragmatic—carries embedded assumptions about human behaviour and desirable outcomes.

Returning to the motif of the mask, we see why neutrality is so often a myth. An interface's smoothness hides the scaffolding beneath it. We rarely perceive the hierarchy of decisions, compromises, tensions, and incentives that produced the wrapper we touch. Because of this invisibility, users tend to grant systems the authority of objects rather than the contingency of human creations. We trust what feels seamless. We overlook what feels inevitable.

The implications stretch into democratic life. When platforms set the parameters for political messaging, they implicitly decide which voices scale. When search engines decide what constitutes relevance, they mould public knowledge. When ad networks classify users into behavioural tribes, they construct new forms of identity. These acts are political—not in partisanship, but in shaping the architecture of public life.

A final question hangs over the discussion, unresolved because it must remain so: if all software carries ideology, what responsibilities fall on those who build and those who use? Should we demand transparency about design intentions? Should interfaces reveal their incentives? Should users treat digital environments not as neutral tools but as ideological terrains? The mask remains. The task is to decide whether we continue accepting it at face value or begin learning to look underneath.

Questioning Standard Metrics

In September 2018, Facebook admitted to an error that had miscalculated "average viewing time" for video advertisements for more than two years. The inflation was significant: the metric had excluded views shorter than three seconds, causing advertisers from London to Los Angeles to believe their audiences were far more engaged than they were. Several companies, including US-based marketing firm Crowd Siren, pursued legal action, arguing that their content strategies and budgets had been steered by misleading data. A quiet number had altered behaviour across an entire industry. It is a perfect entry point into the motif that recurs throughout this enquiry: the ruling number, the figure that appears neutral but quietly commands.

The paradox is sharp. How can a metric that looks so objective deform our sense of what matters? The answer lies not in the number itself but in the incentives it activates. Engagement time is never just a measure; it is a design signal. It encourages certain creative decisions. It suppresses others. When we treat numbers as truth rather than tools, we permit them to direct the choices that shape culture.

The first major claim becomes clear when we examine how metrics script editorial and commercial decisions. Show this in context. In 2016, editors at *The Washington Post* noted that articles with higher dwell times were disproportionately placed at the top of the homepage. The algorithmic system promoting them did not evaluate nuance, rigour, or democratic value. It simply elevated the stories that kept readers on the page longest. That system was named "Bandito", an A/B-testing platform designed to optimise performance. It rewarded content that provoked prolonged attention. This meant emotionally charged political pieces frequently outranked careful investigations. The ruling number—dwell time—became the newsroom's unseen governor.

Explaining this reveals why metrics carry ideology. If the proclaimed goal is efficiency, the deeper consequence is a reshaping of editorial priority. High dwell time encourages emotive narrative arcs. High click-through rate rewards sensationalism. High share count favours polarising content. These are behaviours, not abstractions. They are decisions made in meetings, reflected in placement, iterated through dashboards. The implication is profound: public discourse is sculpted not only by what journalists write but by what metrics incentivise algorithms to promote.

A second example illustrates how metrics can subtly rewire institutions. In 2020, the UK Parliament's Digital, Culture, Media and Sport Committee reviewed YouTube's recommendation engine after researchers at the University of Exeter showed that recommendation patterns disproportionately steered users towards conspiratorial content during moments of political tension. The platform's metric—user retention—was operating exactly as intended. Longer viewing sessions increased advertising revenue. But the behaviour encouraged by this metric—promoting addictive or sensational content—risked distorting users' understanding of political reality. Once again, the ruling number wore a mask of neutrality while directing public attention.

A counter-example highlights that metrics need not always distort. The Wikimedia Foundation, which manages Wikipedia, prioritises editor diversity as a measurable objective. Its gender gap campaigns from 2011 onwards used metrics to reduce the overwhelming male dominance of contributors. Quantitative goals improved representational balance. Here, numbers nudged behaviour towards equity rather than distortion. Yet the limitation persists: even pro-social metrics embed value judgements. They reflect institutional priorities. They shape volunteer effort. They script outcomes. The mask changes; the mechanism remains.

Return to the motif of the ruling number. It governs through dashboards and analytics suites. It shapes tone, tempo, and content. Yet many users never see the dashboards. Instead, they encounter a world curated by numbers they did not choose.

To understand the implications, we must examine how metrics mediate perception. Take the relationship between "like" counts and perceived popularity. A 2019 study by the Reuters Institute found that users judged articles with high visible engagement to be more trustworthy, regardless of source credibility. Trust, in this setting, becomes a visible behaviour: the act of clicking because others have clicked. This feedback loop drives up the prominence of content that may not warrant attention. It is a form of epistemic herd movement, choreographed by numbers.

The next development shows why metrics matter to those who produce content as much as those who consume it. When social media managers at major newsrooms review dashboards, they measure success through specific key performance indicators. A rise in comments signals "community engagement". A dip in retention suggests "content fatigue". These interpretations lead to tactical shifts: shorter videos, punchier headlines, more polarising angles. The metric becomes the motive force. The implication is clear: metrics not only describe behaviour—they generate it.

But metrics also influence public policy. In 2022, the European Commission, examining TikTok's amplification patterns during the Ukraine conflict, found that videos with dramatic imagery were far more likely to be recommended, even when their factual accuracy was uncertain. The platform's metric of "completion rate"—the percentage of each video watched—rewarded gripping but misleading content. Policymakers faced a difficult position. How do you regulate a system whose behaviour emerges from numbers rather than explicit editorial intent? The ruling number blurred the boundary between infrastructure and influence.

A limitation must be acknowledged. Metrics remain necessary. Without measurement, accountability evaporates. Without benchmarks, progress becomes anecdotal. Public-service broadcasters such as the BBC use carefully designed metrics to examine representation, audience reach, and informational value. These systems are transparent and regularly audited. They demonstrate that metrics can support public responsibilities when framed with clarity and oversight. Yet even here, the selection of what to measure shapes organisational behaviour. The mechanism cannot escape value-laden decisions.

To probe the deeper dynamics, consider how metrics frame what we deem meaningful. Engagement-centric systems elevate speed, virality, and quantity. They marginalise slowness, nuance, and context. A detailed investigation requiring twenty minutes of reading will perform poorly against a seven-second clip. The metric penalises depth because it is difficult to measure. The ruling number favours frictionless consumption. This has implications that reach beyond media. It affects political education, scientific communication, cultural literacy. The metric sculpts the citizen.

We return to the motif once more. The ruling number appears simple. It appears stable. Yet it conceals layers of assumption: that attention equals interest, that interest equals value, that value equals success. These equivalences deserve scrutiny. They illustrate how easily democratic priorities can be displaced by commercial ones when metrics go unquestioned.

If we ask what a more critical engagement with metrics requires, we approach the tension that must remain unresolved. Should platforms disclose the hierarchies that drive their recommendation engines? Should public institutions set alternative metrics—like informational richness or civic value—to counterbalance engagement? Should users learn to interrogate why certain content appears before them, identifying the numbers behind the scenes?

Each of these questions carries consequences. Each demands a trade-off. What we measure influences how we act. The challenge is to decide whether we allow the ruling numbers to guide us silently or whether we begin to interrogate them before they become the architecture of our collective understanding.

A More Critical User

On 24 February 2022, hours after Russian forces moved into Ukraine, users across Europe opened their phones to a feed saturated with battlefield clips of uncertain origin. Within a single day, major platforms including Twitter, YouTube, and TikTok issued public acknowledgements that several viral videos circulating from Kyiv and Kharkiv had in fact been lifted from earlier conflicts in Syria (2016) and Nagorno-Karabakh (2020). The speed of circulation dwarfed the pace of verification. Millions watched before contextual labels were added. A user glancing at a looping clip saw movement, smoke, urgency — yet almost none of the underlying truth. It was a moment that exposed the central motif of this enquiry: the surface that invites belief, and the hidden architecture beneath it.

That event matters because it shows how easily neutrality can be assumed where it does not exist. A user does not consciously grant trust to an interface. Trust forms through repetition. Each swipe feels natural. Each recommendation feels effortless. The interface whispers a promise of neutrality even as it shapes outcomes. Five words describe the temptation: *It looks the same.* Familiarity masks influence. To cultivate a more critical user, we must recognise how design smooths over intent.

The first claim is simple: sceptical users do not emerge spontaneously; they are produced through encounter and reflection. Show this with a concrete case. In 2019, researchers at the University of Amsterdam examined how

Facebook's political ad library presented demographic targets during the European Parliamentary elections. They found that microtargeted adverts shown to users in Rotterdam emphasised local crime and immigration, while those shown to similar demographics in Amsterdam foregrounded employment and housing. The organisation behind several of the ads — the Identity and Democracy Party — used platform-provided segmentation tools to tailor narratives at scale. Users who saw one advert stream had no visibility of the alternative. The design made this segmentation invisible. Naming the phenomenon clarifies its power: *selective visibility*. It means users perceive a slice of political discourse as the whole.

Explaining this pattern reveals why neutrality is a myth. Interface decisions — what is shown, hidden, highlighted, slowed, or simplified — embed value judgements. A highlighted "watch next" tile nudges. A disappearing notification disciplines. A persistent banner rewards. These are not abstractions. They are visible behaviours of the system. The implication is that a critical user must learn to observe these behaviours before interpreting the content itself.

A second example shows the stakes in a different domain. In 2021, the UK Competition and Markets Authority reviewed how Amazon's product recommendations elevated Amazon Basics items over competing brands with higher aggregate review scores. The metric at play was convenience: products stored in nearby fulfilment centres received preferential placement. The interface presented these items as "highly rated and well-priced", even when they were neither the best-reviewed nor the most durable. This masked commercial interest as objective suggestion. Users who understood this mechanism adjusted their shopping behaviour, cross-checking review patterns rather than relying on the platform's highlighted choice. Users unaware of the mechanism accepted the design's implied neutrality.

The counter-example comes from Wikipedia, an environment where the interface aggressively foregrounds citation, edit history, and discussion pages. These design choices train users to examine sources, not layout. Yet even here a limitation exists. Wikipedia's model favours contributors who know how to edit and navigate policy, producing an editorial community that skews demographically and geographically. Transparency aids critical engagement, but transparency alone does not remove structural skew. Reconciling this shows that while design can support scepticism, it cannot replace the need for active reflection.

Return to the motif of the surface and the architecture. Users encounter the surface first. But it is the concealed architecture that determines what they see, how they move, and what they infer. To cultivate a more critical user, we must make this architecture thinkable.

One practical dimension involves noticing friction — or its absence. When Instagram began nudging users in 2020 to view "Suggested Reels" after reaching the bottom of their feed, the friction to leave the app increased. A user must consciously stop, not merely stop scrolling. The metric at play was session length. The behaviour it encouraged was passive continuation. A critical user recognises that seamlessness is rarely neutral. Each reduction of friction signals a desired path. The implication is clear: treat smoothness as a cue to pause, not continue.

Another dimension involves attending to language cues embedded in the interface. When YouTube labels videos as "up next" rather than "chosen for you by an optimisation model", the phrasing masks computational intent behind a colloquial gesture. In 2022, a study by NYU's Center for Social Media and Politics reported that users were more likely to trust recommended news videos when the recommendation language mimicked ordinary conversation. The system's tone shaped perceived authority. Observing these cues is essential for decoding the ideology of design.

In political communication, the stakes become sharper. During the 2017 French presidential election, researchers tracing Facebook's ad archive noted that the campaign of Emmanuel Macron used microtargeting to send distinct motivational messages to users aged 18–24 in Lyon and Marseille. The content differed not in policy but in emotional tone — Marseille's messaging emphasised opportunity, Lyon's emphasised responsibility. The platform made no clear disclosure at the point of viewing.

Users encountering the ads believed they were seeing the candidate's general messaging. A critical user would ask the quiet question that threads this entire section: *Why am I seeing this?* The answer often reveals the layer of intent beneath the surface.

A more critical user also monitors repetition. Frequency is a measurement, not a feeling. When TikTok's algorithm repeats certain genres of content — fitness advice, political commentary, conspiracy narratives — it is iterating on completion rate and rewatch metrics. Recognition of repetition interrupts its influence. A user who counts how often a topic recurs begins to see the architecture shaping it. This act of counting becomes a defensive posture against drift.

But critical awareness faces a limitation. The architecture is designed to be invisible. It automates relevance. It minimises thinking. Countering this requires deliberate slowness. In 2021, Germany's public broadcaster ARD reported on experiments in which participants asked to pause for ten seconds before sharing articles demonstrated significantly better source discrimination. The behaviour — ten seconds of stillness — countered the speed the platforms encourage. Slowness becomes a method of resistance.

A further strategy lies in mapping alternatives. Users tend to assume that the feed is the field. But the feed is one curation among many. Consider the rise of chronological-view activists during Twitter's interface shifts in 2016 and 2018, when algorithmic timelines replaced linear sequences.

The user campaigns that followed, spearheaded by journalist Alex Hern in London and technologist Andy Baio in Portland, marked a rare moment when design choices became mainstream debate. Users noticed the architecture because the surface changed. They pushed for the option to restore chronology. Their actions demonstrate that critical users do not merely interpret design; they contest it.

We must return once more to the surface and the architecture. The surface tells you a message is popular. The architecture may be telling you that someone paid for prominence. The surface shows you a recommended article. The architecture has inferred your likely click behaviour from thousands of signals. The surface displays a neat list of "trending" topics. The architecture might be amplifying content from accounts tied to coordinated networks. The critical user learns to read two layers at once.

This leads to the closing tension. What is the trade-off between convenience and comprehension? What cost are we willing to pay to expose the architecture beneath the surface? Should platforms be required to show users why every post, recommendation, or advert appears? Should users commit to friction — to pausing, cross-checking, or toggling settings — even when the experience becomes slower?

A more critical user is neither cynical nor paranoid. They simply refuse to mistake the surface for the whole. The path forward lies in a quiet, persistent question that tests every interface we meet: *What is this design trying to make me do?*

The answer will not always be comfortable, but comfort is rarely where clarity begins.

Chapter 7
Tech and Ideology: Whose Values Win?

In October 2019, a leaked internal memo from Facebook surfaced in several major news outlets. It described, in startlingly direct language, how a minor tweak to the News Feed ranking system—increasing weight for "meaningful social interactions"—had boosted political posts that provoked anger over those that encouraged deliberation. Engineers noted the trend. Marketing teams modelled the engagement curves. Executives approved the weighting. What appeared on a billion screens the following morning looked like public sentiment unfiltered, unedited, organic. Yet every upward nudge of a provocative headline, every surge of incendiary commentary, stemmed from a single design choice derived not from democratic consensus but from commercial optimisation. The shift was subtle and swift, but the ideological implications were immense. A private decision had quietly shaped the emotional metabolism of public debate.

This is not a story about one company's misstep. It is a window into how digital systems, celebrated for neutrality, routinely channel human behaviour along vectors determined by corporate priorities, cultural assumptions, and political strategies. When a platform alters what rises and what sinks—not by censorship but by calibration—it imprints a worldview. The process is invisible, but its consequences are anything but. A headline feels louder. A minority view seems larger. A rumour spreads as if it were reasoned argument. People act on these illusions. They vote, protest, hesitate, or harden their positions because the screen before them whispers, *This is what the world thinks.* But the whisper has authors.

The paradox at the heart of this chapter is disarmingly simple. Technologies built to flatten hierarchy often reinforce it. Tools praised for distributing expression at scale routinely concentrate influence upstream. We talk about platforms as if they were public squares, yet their rules resemble boardroom minutes. We click through feeds convinced we are navigating an open landscape while the terrain beneath us is landscaped for specific outcomes. The question, then, is not whether ideology exists within technological systems. The question is whose ideology wins when design, revenue, governance, and culture converge.

The first strand of this chapter confronts the corporate agenda embedded in digital architecture. Tech giants hold extraordinary power, not merely through vast datasets or advanced algorithmic models but through the invisible capacity to define what counts as relevant, acceptable, or profitable. Consider the way search engines foreground certain news providers, or the way recommendation systems reward content types that lengthen viewing sessions. These are not clerical decisions. They are strategic ones. When profit incentives determine ranking logic, public well-being becomes a variable in a long optimisation formula, not its anchor. The consequences ripple outward. Narratives that sustain outrage flourish. Stories requiring patience or nuance fall behind. It is not malice that drives this imbalance but the gravitational pull of commercial ambition.

Corporate influence, however, is only the beginning. The cultural imprint of technology extends deeper than business models. Each interface carries with it a set of assumptions—about language, identity, behaviour, value, and even time. The global reach of platforms ensures these assumptions spread far beyond their origins. A single default setting, a single moderation standard, a single definition of "appropriate", can overshadow local nuance across continents. Consider the quiet influence of language defaults: when a platform auto-localises content into American English, it does more than streamline usability. It privileges one linguistic pattern and subtly disciplines others. Pronunciation, idiom, rhythm, and reference points shift across entire user bases. What begins as a convenience becomes a vector of cultural homogenisation, sanding down the rough edges that make communities distinct.

But cultural force does not remain in the cultural domain. It flows into political influence. Algorithms have become tools for targeting, persuasion, and mobilisation—the digital descendants of campaign leaflets, but infinitely more precise and infinitely more adaptive. Campaigns now test slogans in real time, watching engagement metrics shift hour by hour. Governments monitor sentiment through keyword clusters. Political strategists refine their messaging based on micro-level behavioural responses. A feedback loop emerges: political actors shape algorithmic content; algorithms reshape political actors. To understand contemporary politics without understanding these systems is to study shadows rather than structures.

Yet even within this formidable architecture, there are checks—fragile, contested, and incomplete, but real. Civil society organisations have built cross-border frameworks to monitor algorithmic harms. Governments have begun drafting ethical guidelines for automated systems, though their reach varies dramatically. Journalists and watchdog groups expose covert influence networks, forcing platforms to adjust their models or reveal their criteria. Users, too, exert subtle pressure: deletion campaigns, content boycotts, collective demands for transparency. These gestures are not sufficient to counter ideological dominance, but they demonstrate that power in digital ecosystems is not static. It is negotiated.

Throughout this chapter, a quiet motif threads through every section: the idea of alignment. Not alignment in the technical sense used in AI research, but alignment as a philosophical concern. Alignment between commercial strategy and civic obligation. Alignment between cultural dissemination and cultural preservation. Alignment between political persuasion and democratic integrity. Alignment between global systems and local realities. When alignment collapses, ideology flows unchecked. When alignment is examined, challenged, and re-shaped, technology becomes something closer to a public instrument rather than a private empire.

The significance of this chapter lies in its insistence that ideology no longer hides in manifestos, pamphlets, or broadcast manifestos. It hides in ranking logics, in training datasets, in the geometry of digital spaces. It hides in what platforms decide to measure—and what they decide to ignore. It hides in silence as much as in speech. To map this terrain, the reader must relinquish the comforting fiction that the digital sphere simply *is*. It is made. And what is made reflects the maker.

The journey ahead is not designed to alarm. It is designed to illuminate. That illumination requires entering the mind of the corporation seeking growth, the designer choosing defaults, the policymaker wielding data, the community shaped by an interface, and the coalition striving to restrain excess. It requires seeing technology not as a mirror but as a force—shaping, compressing, elevating, excluding.

The question that closes this introduction is the question that animates the entire chapter: if every technological system carries values, whose values do we want shaping the world we inhabit? And if we do not ask this now, who will ask it for us?

Corporate Agenda

In April 2018, the United States Senate questioned Mark Zuckerberg in Washington, D.C., following revelations that Cambridge Analytica had harvested data from roughly 87 million Facebook profiles. The hearing was ostensibly about privacy. Yet the most instructive moment came when Zuckerberg admitted that Facebook's core business objective—maximising engagement—guided not only its data practices but also the ranking logic of its News Feed. Senators pressed him to explain why inflammatory material rose so easily to the top. His answer was candid: the algorithm surfaced what people interacted with most. In that single exchange, the profit motive behind a global communication infrastructure was laid bare. The public had believed they were seeing what mattered. In truth, they were seeing what performed.

The collision of commercial ambition and public discourse did not start with Facebook. But the scale of its influence in 2018 made something undeniable: the objectives of private firms now shape the informational diets of entire societies. A ranking update in Menlo Park could tilt the tenor of political conversation in Manila. A data-sharing deal in London could alter advertising costs in Lagos. The design of digital systems had quietly become an extension of corporate strategy. And strategy, as every executive knows, is seldom neutral.

The heart of the issue is simple to state and difficult to decode: algorithms optimise for what companies value. Everything else becomes secondary. When the primary metric is time spent, systems reward content that holds attention. When the metric is ad yield, systems highlight content that nudges a user closer to a purchase. These decisions happen invisibly, but their effects are everywhere. A teenager in Birmingham scrolling through recommended videos encounters not the world as it is, but the world as predicted to monetise well. A pensioner in Edinburgh searching for information about local elections sees not a balanced stream but a hierarchy sculpted by engagement patterns. Profit motives become the architecture of public knowledge.

To see this logic in action, consider Google's Search algorithm, particularly the shifts introduced through the Page Experience update launched globally in June 2021. Google framed the update as a move towards "better user experience". Yet the company also has an undeniable commercial interest in keeping users within its ecosystem and encouraging behaviours that increase exposure to Google Ads. When Google prioritises pages with faster load times, mobile optimisation, and structured data formats, it ostensibly improves the web. But it also advantages firms with the resources to engineer for those standards—usually large commercial publishers—while smaller organisations struggle to compete. The metric driving the adjustment is not a civic measure. It is a business one. The result is an information ecosystem that skews towards those able to pay for optimisation.

The same pattern emerges in Amazon's product ranking system. In December 2020, investigations by *The Wall Street Journal* revealed that Amazon's search results often foregrounded its own private-label products when consumer interest aligned with categories in which Amazon sought dominance. The behaviour was subtle: slight preferential placement, favourable keyword association, and elastic pricing optimised in real time. Consumers rarely noticed. They believed they were searching an open marketplace. They were, in fact, browsing a commercially curated shelf. Amazon defended the practice as standard retail logic. And it is. That is the point. A retail logic had been transposed onto a digital environment hundreds of millions rely on for impartial comparison. A corporate motive had become a public infrastructure.

Critics sometimes counter that these examples paint an unbalanced portrait, arguing that corporate platforms often support fact-checking initiatives, invest in trust and safety teams, and collaborate with academics to improve content integrity. This is true. Twitter (now X) funded independent research projects on misinformation in 2020. Meta partnered with the International Fact-Checking Network to reduce viral falsehoods. Google created tools to surface authoritative results during crises. These commitments matter. They demonstrate that corporate actors recognise their social footprint. Yet they also reveal the tension at the core of this chapter: companies mitigate harms only insofar as those mitigations do not compromise commercial priorities. Safety is permitted so long as it aligns with scale. Integrity is encouraged so long as it does not undermine growth.

The challenge, then, is not corporate malevolence. It is corporate momentum. Shareholder obligations push firms towards metrics such as daily active users, session length, retention curves, and ad conversion. These are not simply performance indicators. They are behavioural mandates that shape how algorithms evaluate meaning. A video that spurs furious debate performs well on engagement metrics. A carefully researched article that requires time and reflection performs poorly. The system does not care which is more accurate. It cares which is more profitable. And when profit becomes the compass for public exposure, ideology slips into the machine not as a slogan but as a structure.

A recurring motif throughout this subchapter is the question of *capture*. Who captures whom? Do companies capture public attention, or does public behaviour capture corporate design? The truth lies in their entanglement. Corporate incentives capture user behaviour by rewarding actions that feed the metric. Users capture corporate strategy through patterns that reveal what keeps them engaged. Neither side operates autonomously. Both shape one another. Yet only one controls the code.

A second motif concerns visibility: what we see, and what we never see. Metrics decide visibility. Metrics decide which voices appear authoritative and which disappear. Metrics decide whether a rumour is throttled or escalated. And metrics themselves are chosen by executives long before they are deployed by algorithms. The decision to prioritise watch time, click-through rate, or ad relevance is not a technical matter. It is a commercial choice dressed as an engineering constraint.

A third motif—alignment—emerges between visibility and value. Corporate values align poorly with civic ones because the incentives differ. A platform's duty is to grow. A society's duty is to cohere. The former favours amplification. The latter favours reflection. When corporate incentives dominate, amplification wins by default.

The tension becomes particularly acute in contexts involving political information. During the 2022 Brazilian general election, researchers at the Fundação Getulio Vargas documented how recommendation engines on YouTube and Facebook increased the visibility of politically polarising content, not because the platforms endorsed one candidate but because such content generated stronger reaction metrics. Platforms responded defensively, citing improvements in moderation protocols. Yet the underlying commercial logic remained untouched. Reaction sells. Reflection does not.

It would be tempting to conclude that regulation offers a clean counterweight. Yet the Digital Services Act in the European Union, implemented in August 2023, illustrates the complexity of relying on legislation alone. While the Act demands greater transparency around algorithmic decisions, it does not change the commercial imperatives that drive those decisions. Companies are required to report harms. They are not required to undo the monetisation logic that produces them. Regulation, therefore, corrects symptoms without neutralising the cause.

To treat corporate agenda as an external force is to misunderstand its nature. It is woven into the design of interfaces, the structure of data flows, the architecture of recommendation engines, and the cadence of product updates. It is the background hum of the digital world. People have grown accustomed to it, just as they have grown accustomed to the hum of an electrical grid. Its presence shapes everything, even when barely noticed.

And yet, the corporate agenda is not immutable. Firms can be moved—not easily, and not on every issue, but moved nonetheless. Public pressure forced Meta to modify its political ranking signals in 2021. Advertiser boycotts influenced YouTube's demonetisation policies. Consumer backlash pushed Apple to implement stronger privacy notifications in iOS 14.5. These shifts show that corporate logic can be redirected, if not rewritten. But they also reveal something sobering: the public can influence corporate decisions only after harms are visible. The algorithmic decisions that remain unseen—ranking biases, category weightings, personalised thresholds—escape scrutiny.

The unresolved question that shadows this subchapter is deceptively straightforward: how far should corporate priorities be allowed to shape the epistemic foundations of democratic life? If companies design the channels through which billions derive their understanding of the world, what responsibilities accompany that power? And if the profit motive remains the organising principle of those channels, how do we ensure that the public's well-being is not treated as a marginal variable in a quarterly earnings calculation?

The tension is not theoretical. It is structural. And it demands a hard choice: should society adapt to the metrics of the corporation, or should corporations adapt to the needs of society?

Cultural Imprints

In October 2015, when Google opened its first dedicated language-processing centre in Zürich, a linguistic puzzle surfaced almost immediately. Engineers discovered that the company's translation system defaulted to American English even when users in Switzerland, Germany, and Austria selected English as a secondary language. The outcome seemed trivial at first: "colour" became "color"; idioms leaned West Coast; everyday expressions reflected a sensibility drawn from Silicon Valley rather than central Europe. Yet over the following months, educators and researchers noted a measurable drift. Students using the platform to translate essays increasingly adopted American phrasing in their own writing. Teachers observed this shift in Zürich and Munich alike. A default had become a cultural directive. The interface had chosen a centre of gravity.

The phenomenon was not unique to Google. In 2017, Facebook's automatic language-detection tool struggled with Celtic languages in Ireland, often reverting to English for interface prompts and recommended content. Irish users complained that the platform treated their native language as an outlier. What looked like a harmless technical shortcut carried a powerful message about linguistic prestige and cultural hierarchy. It said, without saying, that some tongues mattered more. Defaults shape worlds.

In both cases, the outcome was unintended but unmistakable: technology platforms radiated cultural imprints far beyond their point of origin. A small upstream decision—select a dominant language to ease engineering load—reshaped habits downstream. The homogenising force did not announce itself. It simply worked quietly, line by line, until its footprint spread.

The motif that threads through this subchapter is the shadow cast by scale. When a digital service reaches hundreds of millions of people, a subtle design choice becomes a cultural export. Designers may chase convenience, speed, or uniformity. Users receive a worldview.

To understand how these imprints travel, we can begin by observing how platforms structure defaults. Defaults matter because people rarely change them. Behavioural economists describe this as status quo bias; technologists see it as friction minimisation. Either way, the effect is consistent. When Apple introduced the default QWERTY keyboard layout to the first iPhone in 2007, despite offering alternative language options, usage patterns in markets like Indonesia and Turkey shifted towards QWERTY conventions. The local scripts survived. But their frequency declined. Users adapted to the device, not the device to the users. A design convenience quietly reshaped linguistic behaviour.

Here, the cultural imprint is easy to trace. The originating context—Cupertino, California—determines the baseline configuration. The device disseminates that baseline globally. People modify their habits to accommodate the design. And the design gains legitimacy simply through repetition. The implication is stark: technological defaults create cultural gravity fields.

A second pattern emerges in the domain of content moderation. In 2021, a report by Human Rights Watch documented how Facebook's moderation algorithms treated Arabic dialects in Palestine differently from Hebrew content posted in Jerusalem. Certain Arabic terms, flagged as potentially harmful because they appeared in datasets associated with conflict contexts, triggered automated downranking or removal. Meanwhile, similar expressions in Hebrew did not face symmetric scrutiny because the training data for Hebrew content was smaller and less conflict-saturated. A moderation rule became a cultural decision. A dataset became a hierarchy. The algorithm reflected the availability of training material, not an objective moral standard. Yet the effect on users was unmistakable: one cultural sphere found itself under disproportionately heavy surveillance.

Critics might argue that such examples overstate the homogenising power of platforms, pointing instead to the flourishing of regional cultures on TikTok or the cross-border creativity of Nigerian and Brazilian creators who dominate global video trends. This is valid. There is genuine cultural pluralism online. The internet has amplified voices that would once have been confined to local media. Nigerian Afrobeats, for instance, achieved global prominence in 2022 not through conventional music labels but through horizontal sharing across platforms. Cultural traffic is not unidirectional.

But the counterargument does not negate the structural imbalance. It shows that cultural richness can thrive despite the gravitational pull of dominant platform design, not because the design supports it. When creators succeed, they do so by working within the constraints of algorithmic environments shaped elsewhere. They must adapt to recommended video lengths, visual formats, trending audio libraries, and engagement norms that often originate in Californian product decisions. Culture spreads, yes. But the rails it travels on are engineered in particular places, by particular teams, with particular assumptions.

To see how deeply those assumptions run, consider the example of microtargeted advertising. When Facebook rolled out its "Lookalike Audiences" tool in 2013, it allowed advertisers to reach users statistically similar to existing customer groups. The model worked well for companies but had an insidious cultural effect: it reinforced demographic clusters based on patterns taken largely from markets where Facebook had abundant data—the United States and Western Europe. As a result, advertising segments in India, South Africa, and Argentina were shaped by behavioural profiles developed in fundamentally different cultural contexts. A marketer in Delhi targeting "urban professionals" received a segment built from Western behavioural templates. Cultural nuance flattened. Heterogeneity shrank.

A second motif re-emerges here: flattening. Not erasure, but compression. Cultural nuance becomes thinner at scale because capturing nuance is costly. Localisation budgets are small. Engineering simplicity is efficient. Homogeneity scales well. And scale is the platform's imperative.

The political implications are significant. In multicultural societies like Malaysia or the United Kingdom, platform recommendations can disproportionately push globalised media at the expense of local journalism. The BBC documented this trend in 2020, showing that younger audiences encountered more American political commentary on YouTube than British parliamentary reporting, even when watching from London or Glasgow. The platform did not intend to reshape civic attention. Yet it did. The algorithm optimised for engagement, which favoured larger content ecosystems. American political theatre is abundant, polarised, and endlessly refreshed. British local reporting, by contrast, is comparatively small and calm. Engagement metrics reward noise. Noise travels.

Limitations to this thesis exist. Some platforms invest heavily in localisation. Netflix, for example, announced in 2018 that it would produce original content from at least 17 countries, and by 2023 local-language series from South Korea, Spain, and India routinely topped global charts. This strategy demonstrates that cultural diversity can thrive when commercial incentives align with local storytelling. But even here, the framing is shaped by platform logic. Genres that perform well—crime dramas, survival competitions, thrillers—receive disproportionate funding, while culturally specific formats with slower narrative arcs struggle to secure investment. Diversity exists, but it is diversity filtered through engagement economics.

The motif of *gravity* returns. Cultural phenomena attract attention in proportion to their mass within platform architectures. A language with fewer digital resources has weaker mass. A cultural tradition without strong commercial backing has weaker mass. Defaults, moderation tools, and recommendation systems amplify the heavyweights.

The heart of the matter lies in the feedback loop: cultural imprints shape user behaviour, and user behaviour reinforces the imprint. When users in Nairobi consume content recommended primarily from Los Angeles, the system learns that Los Angeles content performs well. It then recommends more of it. Local content sinks unless it can mimic the stylistic cues that the system already values.

What looks like a neutral preference emerges from a loop that the user never consciously chose.

The stakes are not merely aesthetic. Cultural visibility affects material outcomes. Linguistic dominance shapes education technology access. Content norms influence political debate. Interface defaults determine whose histories are searchable, whose knowledge is indexed, whose identities are recognised in a dropdown menu. When major platforms list gender options limited to male and female in regions where diverse gender identities are culturally recognised, the interface becomes a normative instrument. It tells users what exists.

The tension deepens when we consider the global South. Researchers from the University of Cape Town noted in 2022 that many African languages remain underrepresented in machine-learning datasets. This underrepresentation means that speech-to-text systems misinterpret local accents, facial-recognition systems misclassify darker skin, and translation engines produce errors that subtly delegitimise non-Western linguistic structures. The issue is not malice. It is absence. And absence, repeated at scale, becomes cultural silencing.

Yet there is potential for correction. Open-source projects like Masakhane, launched in 2019 across multiple African nations, have begun developing language models specifically for African languages. Their work demonstrates that cultural plurality can expand when local communities insert themselves into the technological pipeline. But they face the weight of incumbents whose infrastructures already define the digital environment.

The unresolved question that closes this subchapter is simple and hard: if the digital world is becoming a shared civic space, who gets to define its cultural vocabulary? Should we accept the gravitational pull of dominant defaults, or should we demand technologies that bend more closely towards the world's genuine plurality?

Political Powerhouse

In March 2018, when the UK Information Commissioner's Office raided the London offices of Cambridge Analytica, investigators uncovered a trove of political advertising files linked to the 2016 United States presidential election. What startled analysts was not simply the scale of the dataset—tens of millions of Facebook profiles—nor the inferred personality scores. It was the precision with which the firm had tailored messages to micro-segments of the electorate, adjusting tone, emotion, and emphasis in real time based on user behaviour in places as varied as Michigan and North Carolina. A campaign strategy had become a computational exercise. Elections were learning systems.

The raid revealed something deeper: politics had entered a phase where influence was not merely broadcast but personalised. It operated through a continuous loop—collect, model, target, and refine. And at each step, ideology seeped into the code. An algorithm might favour emotive headlines because they increased click-through rates at

14:00 in Milwaukee. Another might prioritise images over text because younger undecided voters in Raleigh shared videos more frequently. What looked like optimisation became political steering. The tools were neutral only in name.

It was not the first time digital systems shaped democratic processes. A decade earlier, in January 2008, Barack Obama's campaign used Facebook's early API tools in Chicago to recruit volunteers and coordinate door-knocking routes. The strategy was transparent and largely benign. Yet it opened the conceptual door: political mobilisation could now move through platforms that logged, ranked, and recommended behaviour. The mechanism that recommended music or shoes could also recommend candidates. The boundary blurred.

The motif that runs through this subchapter is *direction*: platforms do not simply reflect political currents; they channel them. The design of the channel decides where political energy flows.

The shift becomes clearer when we observe political messaging as a data problem. Campaigns measure user engagement, compare test messages, and commit resources to whichever content performs best. A modern political team in Manchester or Madrid no longer relies solely on intuition or polling. It relies on dashboards. When a message elicits a measurable uptick in shares within 11 minutes, the system rewards it. When it does not, it sinks. In this environment, ideologies adapt to algorithmic incentives. Anger travels faster than policy nuance. Outrage outperforms procedural detail. The platform structures the performance of politics.

A named example from the public record illustrates this dynamic. During the 2019 Indian general election, the Bharatiya Janata Party (BJP) used WhatsApp groups extensively to deliver targeted narratives. Messages circulated through decentralised networks, but they were refined using feedback: which videos were forwarded, which memes were saved, which slogans stuck. The party measured these behaviours and adjusted messaging accordingly. The political effect was substantial. WhatsApp's encrypted architecture made moderation difficult; its distribution mechanics allowed rapid replication. The platform's design amplified certain ideological tones—national pride, cultural grievance, strong-leader imagery—because those tones generated measurable circulation. The medium rewarded them.

A second example sits in a very different context. In 2020, the Polish government funded targeted Facebook ads urging voters to support a conservative agenda on issues such as judicial reform and LGBTQ+ rights. Journalists in Warsaw documented how the government's ads reached sharply divided demographic groups with different emotional pitches. Older voters in Kraków received messages invoking national heritage. Younger voters in Gdańsk received warnings framed as digital literacy guidance. The system treated ideology as a variable to adjust. The electorate experienced politics as a stream of personalised nudges. The design of the platform shaped the design of the message.

A credible limitation tempers this picture. Some researchers argue that algorithmic influence is overstated. A 2020 study by the Oxford Internet Institute found that while microtargeting increases message visibility, its impact on voting intention is inconsistent and often modest. Exposure does not guarantee persuasion. People still interpret messages through pre-existing beliefs, local networks, and lived experience. This empirical caution matters. It prevents exaggeration.

But the limitation does not erase the structural shift. Persuasion is not the only metric. Steering attention is. When an algorithm directs millions of users in São Paulo towards stories about corruption at the expense of stories about health policy, it shapes the political environment regardless of whether it shifts final votes. Influence occurs upstream of choice. It alters what citizens see, not just what they think.

This is where ideology enters. Not through explicit partisan programming, but through the mechanics of ranking. An algorithm that privileges engagement promotes content that triggers strong reactions. If a political campaign thrives on fear, fear gains algorithmic advantage. If it thrives on community solidarity, solidarity spreads—provided it generates sufficient measurable interaction. The system's incentives become the system's ideology. A platform built to maximise attention will promote political content that captures attention. Values are encoded in the metric.

Consider the quiet motif of *feedback loops*. A political party releases a message. Users react. The system learns and amplifies what appears effective. The campaign then refines its tone to align with what the system has amplified. After several cycles, the message that circulates most widely is not the one that best represents the party's doctrine, but the one that best resonates with the platform's logic. The loop decides the message. Politics bends.

State actors recognise this power. In 2019, the Chinese government expanded its social media influence operations, using platforms such as Twitter and YouTube to cast doubt on pro-democracy protests in Hong Kong. Researchers at the Australian Strategic Policy Institute traced coordinated accounts that repeated specific narratives: protesters were manipulated by foreign powers; police showed restraint; unrest threatened stability. These messages followed a pattern designed for algorithmic uptake: emotionally charged imagery paired with short, shareable captions. The goal was not subtle persuasion. It was saturation. Flood the channel; frame the narrative; shape the informational climate. Algorithms facilitated dissemination.

Western democracies are not immune to similar strategies. Political consultancies in Washington, London, and Canberra routinely test thousands of slogan variants, measuring performance through A/B experiments. The variants differ only in punctuation, colour tones, or the weight of a single word. A dash instead of a colon can shift engagement by measurable margins. What matters is not rhetorical elegance but analytical feedback. The platform becomes a laboratory. Messages evolve to please the machine.

A limitation complicates this again. Not all political actors possess equal access to computational tools. Smaller parties—such as the Green Party in the UK or Podemos in Spain—often lack the budgets required for large-scale targeting. Their messages still travel through the same platforms but without the same predictive analytics. The implication is an asymmetry: those who can afford data-intensive optimisation wield disproportionate influence. Democracy tilts.

The motif of direction returns. Algorithms sort citizens into ideological streams. The stream with the most sustained engagement becomes the stream with the loudest political voice. Minority viewpoints risk marginalisation unless they adapt to the rhythms of the system. Politics becomes performative.

Real-time feedback intensifies this trend. During Brazil's 2022 election, analysts noted that political influencers modified their language in real time based on viewer metrics from YouTube and Instagram. When phrases triggered spikes in watch time, they repeated them. When comments surged, they leaned into the topic. When a narrative dipped, they abandoned it. A politician or surrogate became a performer responding to a live crowd whose reactions were mediated by an algorithm. The system shaped cadence, emotion, and timing. It shaped political style.

A counter-example offers nuance. In Taiwan, digital minister Audrey Tang has promoted an alternative model: using open-source tools to broaden participation rather than narrow it. Platforms like vTaiwan facilitate consensus-building by identifying areas of agreement in polarised debates. Instead of amplifying conflict, the tool prioritises statements that receive cross-group support. It is an inversion of the engagement model. Here, the algorithm guides political behaviour towards common ground. This demonstrates that algorithmic influence is not intrinsically harmful; it is shaped by design goals.

The central question emerges clearly: whose goals define the system? Commercial platforms prioritise metrics. Governments prioritise stability or persuasion. Campaigns prioritise votes. Each actor embeds its values into the computational infrastructure. Citizens experience these values as "the feed."

The political powerhouse is not a single organisation. It is the interplay between actors who understand how to operate within algorithmic environments. Those who master data collection, psychological segmentation, and rapid message iteration hold strategic advantage. Those who cannot fall behind.

The unresolved tension sits at the end of the argument: can democratic societies maintain genuine pluralism when political influence is mediated through systems that reward speed, emotion, and precision targeting? Or must we rethink the architecture of digital politics before the architecture quietly rethinks us?

Global Checks and Balances

In November 2018, delegates at UNESCO's Paris headquarters debated a draft resolution on the ethical governance of artificial intelligence. The discussion—spanning contributions from Japan, South Africa, Brazil, and Germany—revealed a rare alignment: despite continents and political systems diverging sharply, each delegation recognised the danger of allowing a single ideological template to dominate global digital infrastructures. The immediate outcome was modest, a preliminary agreement to craft international guidelines, but the symbolism mattered. Representatives from fifty states had acknowledged that algorithmic power could not remain the proprietary concern of a few corporations or governments. A global system required global scrutiny. The meeting produced no miracles. It did, however, mark a turning point: transparency became a diplomatic objective, not a domestic afterthought. That moment threads through this subchapter as a quiet motif—*the table*—the image of many hands shaping shared standards rather than a single hand setting the terms.

The scene in Paris highlighted a central tension. Digital systems rely heavily on scale. They grow by expanding uniform architectures across borders. Yet politics flourishes on differences: distinct languages, ethical traditions, and civic expectations. The promise of a harmonised digital sphere collides with the reality that harmonisation often means domination by the most resource-rich actors. When a platform built in California or Shenzhen becomes the default interface for communication in Lagos or Helsinki, the ideas embedded within that platform—its presumptions about identity, expression, and authority—travel with it. Global checks and balances exist to ensure that such travel is reciprocal. Influence must move both ways.

To understand how these checks emerge, we begin by showing the dynamics at play. When regulators in the European Union launched the General Data Protection Regulation in May 2018, they imposed a measurable constraint: users must give explicit consent before personal data could be processed. The Regulation named a principle—data minimisation—and backed it with enforcement metrics such as penalty ceilings tied to annual global turnover. This programme forced major platforms to redesign interfaces, adjust data pipelines, and strengthen user control dashboards. The redesign signalled a shift: Europe's expectations, shaped by its human rights tradition and culture of legal oversight, influenced global practice.

The EU became a counterweight to unilateral technological norms.

A second example demonstrates cross-border cooperation rather than unilateral action. In 2021, the African Union Commission partnered with the OECD in Paris to produce research on algorithmic fairness across diverse cultural contexts. The project examined how automated credit scoring tools used in Nairobi, Lagos, and Accra assigned risk profiles based on consumption patterns derived primarily from European datasets. The findings were concrete: misclassification rates reached double digits when models trained on European behaviour were applied to African populations. The collaboration produced guidelines that urged developers to recalibrate models with locally grounded variables. The implication was clear. Without an international structure for exchange, marginalised contexts would remain misrepresented.

But a credible counter-example complicates the narrative of unified progress. In August 2020, Thailand's draft Cybersecurity Act granted the government sweeping powers to access data and shut down online systems, citing national security. International organisations criticised the law's broad scope, but their influence was limited. Domestic legislation proceeded. The limitation underscores a simple reality: global guidelines lack binding force in sovereign jurisdictions. A state can deviate from shared norms when political incentives demand it. The challenge is reconciling the need for national autonomy with the need for collective ethical structures. Restraint cannot depend on goodwill alone.

Yet even this counter-example reveals something important: global checks need not eradicate national differences; they merely prevent unilateral practices from spilling across borders and dictating global norms. By articulating common principles—transparency dashboards, auditable model documentation, and rights-based criteria—international coalitions create a protective perimeter. States may diverge, but the divergence becomes visible and contestable.

The motif of *the table* returns here. Who sits at it? Who sets the agenda? Who decides the definitions that govern algorithmic conduct? Visibility matters. When a data scientist in Mumbai trains a model for public sector decision-making, the documentation standards shaped by OECD guidelines influence her process. When a journalist in Buenos Aires investigates algorithmic bias, the disclosure obligations imposed by EU law give him access to information he would otherwise lack. The table extends. Knowledge circulates.

Consider how global collaboration works during moments of crisis. In 2020, when misinformation about COVID-19 spread at speed on platforms such as Facebook and YouTube, fact-checking organisations across continents—from the Poynter Institute's International Fact-Checking Network in Florida to Africa Check in Johannesburg—shared databases, annotations, and rapid-response workflows. They compared flagged videos, cross-referenced originating accounts, and recorded distribution metrics. Their strategy showed something essential: public discourse, when coordinated across borders, can correct distortions faster than any single regulator. The correction is measurable. False claims about chlorine's curative properties, for example, declined significantly in Brazil after collaborative fact-checks reached both regional media and platform moderators. Collaboration creates traction.

The role of ethical guidelines also demands scrutiny. When the OECD released its AI Principles in May 2019, it emphasised accountability, transparency, and human-centred values. Scholars praised the clarity of the document, but its real significance lay elsewhere. It provided a shared vocabulary. When South Korea debated autonomous decision systems in 2021, its policymakers referenced the OECD Principles explicitly. When Chile's national AI policy framework was drafted the same year, it also aligned its criteria with the OECD. A common lexicon reduces interpretative drift. It allows regulators, developers, and civil society groups from different regions to evaluate algorithmic systems using comparable benchmarks. Language becomes infrastructure.

The subchapter demands an examination of another dimension: power asymmetry. Global checks and balances confront a structural disparity between regions that produce digital infrastructure and those that primarily consume it. Platforms built in the United States and China dominate global markets. Their design assumptions become default settings elsewhere. We see this clearly in the spread of content rankings optimised for advertising-intensive markets. When metrics created for English-language audiences shape visibility for Swahili or Urdu content, cultural nuance declines. A mosaic becomes a grid.

This is why collaborative governance matters. When Brazil and Germany jointly sponsored a resolution on privacy at the UN General Assembly in December 2013, prompted by revelations of surveillance and cross-border data interception, they introduced an international expectation that privacy norms should not be subject to a single geopolitical centre. The resolution's influence was symbolic rather than coercive, but it shifted discourse. It reaffirmed the legitimacy of plural digital norms and the necessity of accountability across borders.

A counter-example challenges the picture of collaboration as an uncomplicated good. Not all international efforts are neutral. In 2022, the Shanghai Cooperation Organisation presented a proposal advocating increased governmental control over information flows under the banner of cyber sovereignty. Critics argued that the proposal risked enabling censorship and entrenching authoritarian practices. The tension is acute: global cooperation can protect rights, but it can also mask illiberal consolidation. Checks and balances must themselves be checked.

Revision is crucial. A global governance framework must adapt as technologies evolve. When deepfakes surged in late 2021, several European media regulators collaborated with academic laboratories in Amsterdam and Copenhagen to create detection benchmarks. The metric was simple: accuracy scores measured at varying compression levels. But the practice was profound. It embedded the expectation that detection standards should be tested openly, not controlled by private vendors. Shared testing generates shared accountability.

The return to *the table* motif deepens the argument. A table is only as good as the voices present. Indigenous data rights groups, disability advocates, language preservation organisations: each must claim a seat. In 2020, Māori data sovereignty principles shaped New Zealand's government procurement guidelines for cloud services. The guidelines required providers to store and process Māori data in ways consistent with tikanga (customary law). Indigenous epistemologies became regulatory expectations. A culturally grounded standard pushed back against homogenisation. Such developments show that global checks need not dilute local values; they can reinforce them.

The subchapter invites a final reflection on measurable behaviour. Global checks work when actors commit to disclosure. If a platform in California publishes its content ranking documentation quarterly, and a regulator in Brussels audits it annually, the relationship becomes one of negotiation rather than subordination. When journalists in Seoul use transparency reports to scrutinise political advertising distributions, the scrutiny becomes empirical, not speculative. The mosaic gains definition.

The unresolved tension is decisive: can the international community design structures strong enough to resist ideological domination yet flexible enough to honour cultural plurality? Or will the promise of shared governance fracture under geopolitical strain? The answer depends on who sits at the table next, and who decides what counts as a seat.

Chapter 8
Belief Formation in the Digital Age

The winter of 2016 left an unusual footprint on social history. In a row of modest houses in Belfast, researchers from Queen's University documented the spread of a sensational rumour about a local politician. The rumour began with a single Facebook post. Within twelve hours, it had reached thousands of users across Northern Ireland. What startled the researchers was not the velocity but the confidence. Interviews showed that many participants believed the claim simply because they had "seen it more than once". Repetition had become conviction. Exposure was proof. A loop of shares, comments, and nods turned uncertainty into certainty without a single piece of verifiable evidence. The finding revealed a truth as old as rhetoric but amplified by technology: belief is rarely born in a moment; it accumulates, layer by layer, until it feels inevitable.

This chapter steps into that inevitability. It asks why some stories flourish while others wither, and why the digital age has intensified our susceptibility to narratives that echo our instincts. It does so by recognising something deceptively simple: belief is not a solitary act. It happens in context. It grows in company. And the platforms that shape our daily interactions have become architects of that company, structuring not only what we see but how often we see it, and who appears to agree with us. The transformation is subtle yet profound. For centuries, beliefs formed through family, local communities, religious traditions, and lived experience. Now they crystallise through feeds that track our impulses and reinforce them with precision.

Digital life offers convenience, speed, and access to information once unimaginable. Yet it also reshapes cognitive habits in ways that remain poorly understood. Every notification suggests urgency. Every recommended post implies relevance. Every trending topic hints at consensus. These cues seep into our sense-making processes. They tilt us, gently but consistently, toward particular interpretations of the world. The Belfast rumour is simply one instance where the mechanism became visible.

Belief formation has always relied on repetition, emotion, and community. What distinguishes our current moment is scale. A single emotional image can traverse continents before a newspaper editor has completed a morning briefing. A piece of persuasive writing—accurate or fabricated—can be algorithmically promoted to millions before a fact-checking organisation has issued a warning. The structure of digital communication means that our psychological habits, once buffered by slower and more diverse forms of interaction, now operate on accelerated timelines. A thought becomes a conviction before we have time to interrogate it.

The psychology of belief offers a useful starting point. Cognitive scientists have long known that the human brain prizes coherence. When presented with conflicting information, it works to resolve the tension quickly, often favouring the explanation that feels familiar. Digital platforms exploit this inclination by prioritising content that aligns with previous engagement. The effect is cumulative. A click on an article about dietary supplements yields a feed full of similar claims; a view of a political clip generates a sequence of ideological siblings. Before long, the user inhabits a perception of the world shaped not by breadth but by consistency. And consistency, in this context, masquerades as truth.

Yet belief does not live in the mind alone. It thrives within groups. Online tribalism has become one of the defining social features of the digital age. People assemble around shared interests—football clubs, music fandoms, political ideologies, lifestyle choices—and these groups develop their own rituals, symbols, and boundaries. They provide belonging, which is hardly new. What is new is the rapid intensification of group identity through automated sorting. Digital tribes can form overnight. They can swell in size without any of the friction that historically moderated community growth. They can become insular because the architecture itself rewards alignment. A tribe's worldview becomes self-reinforcing as dissent is quietly hidden from the feed or drowned out by algorithmically prioritised affirmations. The tribe becomes a lens, then a shield.

Emotion plays a central role in this process. An image that startles, a headline that enrages, a comment that flatters—emotion compels engagement. And engagement, in turn, signals importance to the platform. Studies conducted by the MIT Media Lab in 2018 found that emotionally charged falsehoods spread significantly faster on Twitter than truthful posts, not because falsehoods appeal to malice but because they provoke reaction. Anger and surprise drive sharing; fear drives comment threads; joy drives replication. Platforms observe these reactions and respond algorithmically, amplifying what draws the strongest feelings. Emotion becomes the engine, and the engine rarely pauses for deliberation.

The difficulty is not that people feel strongly. Strong feeling is part of human life. The difficulty is that highly emotional content bypasses the circuitry of careful reflection. A story that flatters our moral instincts or stokes our moral outrage quickly becomes personally meaningful. And once it becomes meaningful, it becomes resistant to challenge. The digital environment strengthens this resistance by surrounding emotionally laden content with signals of agreement—likes, shares, emojis that suggest collective validation. Feeling becomes knowledge.

Against this backdrop, self-awareness emerges as a form of intellectual self-defence. It is not a call for detachment but for recognition: the ability to notice when a post accelerates the pulse, when a headline seems too perfectly aligned with one's prejudices, when a comment threads into irritation or righteousness. These micro-signals reveal the moments when beliefs are most vulnerable to influence. Mindfulness, traditionally associated with contemplative practice, becomes a cognitive tool. Reflective questioning—*Why does this resonate? What evidence supports it? Who benefits if I believe this?*—slows the transition from exposure to conviction. It reintroduces friction.

Yet cultivating such awareness is harder than it sounds. Digital platforms are designed to remove friction. They offer immediacy. They encourage speed. They reward instinctive responses with visible markers of social reward. To resist requires a deliberate counter-habit: stepping back. Observing. Reframing. This is not an appeal to scepticism for the sake of scepticism. It is an appeal to agency. Beliefs should be chosen, not inherited through invisible code.

The chapter will explore these dynamics in depth, tracing how psychological structures, social behaviours, emotional triggers, and reflective practices intersect to shape the beliefs we carry into our daily lives. The narrative arc moves from understanding the mechanics of belief formation to examining the collective behaviours that emerge from digitally mediated conviction. It then confronts the role of emotion before arriving at self-awareness as a practical counterweight. Each section builds on the last, forming a coherent picture of how belief operates in a world where information is abundant, context is scarce, and attention is a commodity.

The stakes are high. In a digital environment, beliefs become behavioural scripts. They guide how people vote, how they interpret news, how they treat strangers, how they define identity. They shape communities and fracture them. They influence policy and public discourse.

Understanding how beliefs form is therefore not an academic exercise but a civic imperative.

What follows asks you to look inward as well as outward. To observe the subtle mechanics that guide your perceptions. To recognise the stories that have shaped your sense of what is true. And to question, gently but persistently, whether those stories were chosen by you—or chosen for you.

The Psychology of Belief

In September 1973, the social psychologist Leon Festinger stood before a group of graduate students at Stanford University and described a paradox that still unsettles the study of human conviction. People, he argued, do not merely hold beliefs; they protect them. They reinforce them even when evidence weakens. His earlier field research with Henry Riecken and Stanley Schachter had shown this vividly in Chicago, where a doomsday cult led by Dorothy Martin had predicted the world would end on 21 December 1954. When the prophecy failed, the group did not disperse. It strengthened its commitment. Members attributed their survival to their own faith. Festinger's insight was simple and disquieting: belief is adhesive. It binds to identity. And once attached, it resists dissolution. That adhesive quality now meets an environment designed to amplify it.

Digital platforms intensify the very conditions Festinger identified. They trade in repetition, affirmation, and social proof. They present information not as a slow, deliberative stream but as a cascade—posts, videos, comments, recommendations—layered with cues that encourage users to see consensus where none may exist. A headline that reappears across feeds "feels" true, not because it has been verified but because it has become familiar. A thread endorsed by acquaintances "seems" credible, not because its logic holds but because it appears socially validated. Familiarity and validation entwine. The adhesive strengthens.

Psychologists call this the mere-exposure effect. First named by Robert Zajonc in 1968, it describes a measurable tendency: repeated exposure to a stimulus increases our preference for it. Zajonc ran controlled experiments showing that people rate nonsense words as more positive simply by seeing them more often. Digital platforms deploy an industrial-scale version of this mechanism. A post recommended three times is not simply *seen;* it is inscribed upon the mind. A meme resurfacing across multiple channels acquires the sheen of cultural truth. A rumour repeated across comments, videos, and screenshots acquires a sense of inevitability. The digital environment does not just inform; it rehearses.

The rehearsal becomes conviction once social reinforcement enters. The sociologist Mark Granovetter, in a 1978 study of collective behaviour, demonstrated how group endorsement lowers the threshold for individual commitment. A person may hesitate to embrace a belief privately yet adopt it once they see even a small number of peers doing the same. The principle translates seamlessly into digital architectures. "Likes", "shares", and emoji reactions create micro-signals of approval that accumulate into an illusion of group consensus. When dozens of contacts appear to endorse an idea, the psychological cost of disagreement rises. Resistance feels antisocial. Agreement feels harmonious. Harmony is chosen.

Two modern examples illustrate how quickly digital reinforcement can accelerate belief formation. In April 2020, at the height of the first Covid-19 lockdown, a pseudoscientific video titled *Plandemic* circulated widely on YouTube and Facebook. Within two days, it had been viewed millions of times across multiple countries. Part of its traction came from platform algorithms recommending the video to users who had previously engaged with health-related content. But the deeper hook lay in the comments sections. Thousands of supportive responses created a perception of widespread endorsement. Social reinforcement made implausible claims "feel" substantiated.

A second example comes from the Philippines. In May 2016, during the presidential campaign of Rodrigo Duterte, political strategists used coordinated Facebook groups to amplify praise, circulate attack posts, and rapidly counter criticism. Journalists later documented how a small network of influential accounts created an illusion of massive grassroots support. Users repeatedly encountering these messages, especially when shared by acquaintances, internalised the portrayed narrative. The belief was not merely that Duterte was a strong leader but that *everyone* believed he was. That sense of collective certainty mattered as much as the message itself.

Yet digital conviction is not absolute. There are limits. A counter-example emerges from the 2021 German federal election. Researchers at the University of Bremen found that while far-right groups attempted to mobilise support through highly emotive online messaging, the narrower audience reach and slower uptake outside their existing clusters limited belief spread. Emotional intensity alone did not guarantee influence. The architecture of platform networks, local political culture, and competing narratives constrained the effect. The limitation reminds us that belief-making is never fully programmable; it remains sensitive to context, competing sources, and individual cognitive filters.

But constraints do not neutralise the problem. They simply illuminate its contours. Digital platforms amplify certain psychological tendencies—confirmation bias, motivated reasoning, and selective exposure. Confirmation bias can be seen in the behaviour of clicking on articles that match one's prior attitudes. Motivated reasoning appears when users defend a favoured claim despite contradictory evidence, often citing anecdotal examples rather than measured data. Selective exposure manifests when people curate their feeds to avoid discomfort, unfollowing or muting voices that challenge their worldview. These behaviours create a feedback loop: perception narrows, certainty hardens, nuance evaporates.

Algorithmic nudges reinforce these loops. A user who watches three videos about cryptocurrency receives a feed saturated with similar content. Another who expresses scepticism about mainstream news sees a proliferation of alternative sources. A third who reacts angrily to political clips is offered more outrage material. The platform optimises for retention, not truth. Retention rewards emotional salience and thematic consistency. The repeated exposure shapes belief not through explicit persuasion but through subtle accretion—like a tide that does not announce itself but remakes the coastline over time.

The quiet motif running through these dynamics is the *nudge*: small, cumulative pushes that tilt cognition without overt force. The nudge may appear as a recommended video. It may surface as a trending hashtag. It may emerge as a "people you may know" suggestion that clusters users into ideologically aligned networks. None of these elements seem consequential alone. Together, they create a mental environment where certain beliefs feel easier, safer, and more coherent than their alternatives.

Coherence is powerful. Consider the behaviour of users who encounter conflicting information about climate policy. When confronted with a post challenging their preferred stance, many respond by seeking reinforcing material—articles from familiar outlets, quotes from preferred experts, or infographics aligning with their political identity. The act is not passive. It is a retrieval mission for coherence. The more coherent their curated material appears, the more "true" their position feels. Truth becomes something sensed, not scrutinised.

Platform design accentuates this tendency. Infinite scroll flattens the hierarchy of knowledge. Personalised feeds blur the distinction between evidence and anecdote. Virality metrics—view counts, reaction tallies, comment volumes—act as proxies for legitimacy. These proxies guide user behaviour in measurable ways. A post with 50,000 shares is treated as authoritative even if its claims have no empirical foundation. A news story with minimal engagement is often ignored, regardless of accuracy. The platform engineers belief by shaping the cues that users rely upon to judge credibility.

Yet belief is not solely cognitive. It is emotional. A headline that frightens will be remembered longer than a statistic that informs. A story that angers will override nuance. Emotion accelerates conviction. The acceleration is measurable: posts eliciting anger are disproportionately shared within minutes of appearing, whereas posts presenting balanced analysis spread more slowly and often remain confined to smaller circles. Emotion is a vector, and platforms follow its trajectory.

The difficulty emerges when emotional vectors align with algorithmic nudges. The result is rapid internalisation. Someone exposed repeatedly to claims that "government cannot be trusted" may internalise suspicion as an intuitive stance rather than a considered judgement. Someone repeatedly shown that "most people are outraged" may adopt the moral stance implied by the feed. Someone immersed in affirmations of a particular worldview may find alternative interpretations not merely wrong but unintelligible. Digital architecture shapes the terrain upon which beliefs form.

Still, users are not powerless. A measure of self-interrogation can disrupt the loop. Asking "Why does this post feel persuasive?" or "Whose voices are missing?" slows the adhesion process. Observing emotional spikes—anger, fear, self-righteousness—draws attention to the moments when conviction is most malleable. These acts introduce friction where platforms seek fluidity. They reclaim agency in a system that profits from reflex.

The unresolved question is how far individuals can push against structures designed for influence. Can users cultivate habits strong enough to resist the adhesive pull of repetition and reinforcement? Or does the architecture overwhelm even the informed? The tension remains.

Online Tribalism

In August 2017, thousands of fans gathered outside the Anaheim Convention Center in California for VidCon, a now-influential meeting point for YouTube creators and their followers. The most striking sight was not the official panels or the corporate booths but the spontaneous behaviour of the crowds. Groups moved as tightly bonded units, chanting creators' names, defending them in heated discussions, and treating perceived rivals with open hostility. The sociologist Crystal Abidin, observing the event that year, noted how these communities operated less like loose fandoms and more like factions, each with its own hierarchy, myths, and rituals. What unfolded in Anaheim offered a glimpse of a new social structure: tribal identities forged not by geography or lineage, but by shared digital allegiance.

A similar dynamic emerged during the UK's Brexit referendum in June 2016. Researchers from the University of Oxford later documented how Leave and Remain clusters formed distinct information ecosystems on Twitter. Users within each cluster amplified their own side's narratives with remarkable consistency. Cross-cluster exchange was minimal. Even when individuals encountered opposing material, they tended to interpret it through the lens of group loyalty. What appeared, on the surface, as a national debate had fractured into two insular digital tribes. By the time the referendum result was announced at the Manchester Central Convention Complex, both sides felt not only politically divided but culturally estranged. The platforms had hardened those lines.

The visibility of these examples reveals something deeper: online tribalism is not an accidental by-product of digital life but a predictable expression of human psychology meeting platform design. Individuals seek belonging; platforms measure belonging through engagement metrics;

algorithms reward whatever sustains cohesion. A user posts a defence of a favourite creator. Others in the group endorse it, adding approving comments. The reinforcement strengthens the user's sense of identity, leading to more posts, more reactions, more commitment. The behaviour is measurable: posts that openly affirm group loyalty often receive disproportionately high reaction counts compared with neutral commentary. The message is not simply shared; it is sanctified.

The sanctification process has been mapped by communication scholars studying digital mobilisation. Consider the BTS Army, one of the world's most active fandoms, whose global interventions became particularly visible in June 2020. When the Dallas Police Department asked users to upload footage of protests through its "iWatch Dallas" app, BTS fans flooded the system with fancams, crippling its functionality. The behaviour illustrated a cohesive tribe acting with startling speed. It also demonstrated the powerful sense of collective potency that arises when thousands of individuals, dispersed across continents, feel connected enough to act as a single body. Shared identity becomes shared agency.

Yet tribalism is not confined to fandoms. Highly polarised political groups display similar bonding. In the United States, the QAnon movement gained traction in 2017 through platforms such as Reddit and later 8kun. Its growth was fuelled not only by conspiracy narratives but by the intense social bonding of users who saw themselves as truth-seekers in opposition to a corrupt establishment. Journalists covering the movement noted a consistent behavioural pattern: once individuals identified as part of the group, they prioritised group cohesion over plausibility. Disputed predictions were rationalised. Failed prophecies were reframed. Group loyalty trumped empirical evidence.

This loyalty brings benefits. Anthropologists have long noted that belonging offers psychological comfort. Shared belief reduces uncertainty. Group identification strengthens resilience. Many online communities provide genuine support, solidarity, and creative collaboration. Fan fiction groups nurture writing skills. Technical forums cultivate expertise. Support groups for chronic illness offer emotional scaffolding that can be life-changing. The digital tribe is not inherently harmful.

But its limitations are equally visible. Echo chambers narrow worldviews. A person immersed in a homogenous community may rarely encounter divergent perspectives. When outsiders do appear, they are often treated with suspicion. This suspicion increases the psychological cost of openness. Users may unfollow, block, or report dissenting voices, creating a curated environment that feels safe but becomes brittle. The brittleness matters. It encourages users to treat disagreement as threat rather than argument.

One counter-example challenges the inevitability of tribal entrenchment. Wikipedia, despite its flaws, demonstrates that large-scale online collaboration need not devolve into sectarian conflict. Editors from different countries, backgrounds, and political leanings routinely negotiate article content through structured debate and policy guidelines. Disagreements occur, often fiercely, yet the platform's emphasis on consensus-building and citation rules curbs factional spirals. The limitation is important: Wikipedia's success relies on governance structures and community norms not common across mainstream social platforms. The example does not negate tribalism but shows that alternative designs can mitigate its intensity.

Understanding online tribalism requires examining the mechanics that sustain it. The first mechanic is narrative coherence. Tribal groups often share a specific storyline—about a creator's virtue, a movement's righteousness, or an opponent's malice. Members repeat the storyline until it becomes axiomatic. The behaviour can be tracked: a surge in identical talking points across comments or reposted threads signals narrative consolidation. Consolidation makes beliefs feel stable.

The second mechanic is symbolic signalling. Users employ hashtags, memes, and avatars to declare affiliation. A political meme embedded in a profile picture sends a clear message: "I belong". High-engagement posts frequently feature these symbols because they are instantly recognisable and emotionally efficient. A single hashtag can compress an entire worldview.

The third mechanic is boundary enforcement. Tribes maintain cohesion by policing behaviour. Deviations—questioning a leader, expressing doubt, or introducing nuance—may attract criticism or expulsion. In late 2019, several prominent K-pop fan accounts reported being ostracised after criticising management decisions of their preferred groups. The behaviour was swift: followers dropped, hostile messages increased, and the individuals were publicly labelled "traitors". Boundary enforcement makes dissent costly.

These mechanics, once in motion, create a reinforcing cycle. The quiet motif running through these dynamics is the *line*: the line between "us" and "them", between loyalty and betrayal, between insiders and outsiders. This line is not static. It shifts with group sentiment, platform cues, and cultural moments. But wherever it lies, it structures perception.

The compounding effects of these lines are evident in the social fragmentation that researchers observed during the 2022 French presidential election. Analysis by Sciences Po found that supporters of Marine Le Pen and Emmanuel Macron occupied distinct online spaces, with limited overlap in shared content. Even neutral news reports circulated along partisan pathways. The behaviour mirrored earlier Brexit patterns: users engaged primarily with information endorsed by their tribe. The lines hardened.

Still, digital tribalism is not absolute. Some users straddle multiple groups, navigating cultural fandoms, professional networks, and political spaces simultaneously. Their feeds display a mixture of signals, diluting the dominance of any single worldview. These hybrid users often serve as bridges, sharing material across clusters and introducing nuance. Their behaviour counters pure echo-chamber effects. Yet their influence is limited when platform algorithms reward cohesion over hybridity.

The unresolved tension is whether the architecture can be rebalanced. Should platforms redesign spaces to reward cross-group engagement, or would such interventions disrupt the very sense of belonging that makes communities thrive? Can users embrace tribal identity without surrendering curiosity? Or must they choose between comfort and complexity?

The Role of Emotion

In March 2019, within hours of the Christchurch attacks in New Zealand, Facebook reported that users attempted to upload the gunman's livestreamed footage more than 1.5 million times. Moderators in Dublin and Singapore worked frantically to remove each new iteration, yet copies resurfaced faster than they could be reviewed. The pattern was stark. Clips that evoked shock, horror, or revulsion travelled with a velocity that neutral reporting never matched. Emotion propelled circulation. Algorithms, detecting rapid sharing and intense engagement, amplified the material further before human oversight intervened. A tragedy became a data point in a larger phenomenon: the rapid ascendancy of emotionally charged content over considered judgment.

A contrasting case emerged in November 2020, when the Italian fact-checking organisation Pagella Politica analysed viral posts circulating during the COVID-19 lockdowns in Lombardy. They found that the stories achieving the highest engagement were not those offering balanced health guidance but those expressing anger at restrictions or fear of economic collapse. Posts containing inflammatory phrasing or anxious speculation routinely scored engagement spikes up to ten times higher than sober advisories. The correlation highlighted a structural truth: strong feelings stick. They are retained in memory with disproportionate force, and platforms interpret that retention as relevance.

Emotion, in these moments, behaves like a match. It sparks. It spreads. It pulls users into a rhythm of quick reactions rather than measured evaluation. The motif of the *spark* will return, because digital systems treat every spark as a clue: if it catches, feed it. If it fades, bury it.

This dynamic is neither accidental nor mysterious. Emotional salience has long been recognised as a predictor of recall and action. Psychological studies from the 1980s onward show that emotionally laden stimuli are processed differently from neutral ones, activating rapid appraisal circuits that bypass slower, more deliberate reasoning. When this biology meets the architecture of digital platforms, the result is a feedback loop. A user encounters a clip that provokes indignation. They comment, share, or pause longer than usual. The system records the prolonged interaction as a signal of interest. The signal prompts the platform to serve similar material. The spark becomes a flame.

Consider how this is visible in concrete behaviour. Scroll time lengthens when posts evoke outrage or moral fervour. Reaction counts climb sharply on content that triggers astonishment or fear. These measurable behaviours shape what users see next. The algorithm does not evaluate truth; it evaluates traction. Traction is easiest to achieve when emotions run high.

One historical example that revealed the power of emotional amplification occurred during the 2014 Ferguson protests in Missouri. Researchers later found that posts depicting confrontation—police lines, tear gas, burning cars—circulated far more widely than posts containing policy explanations or calls for calm. Even when users attempted to seek balanced coverage, the algorithmic flow pulled them back toward high-arousal images. The system had learned which sparks produced fire.

A second example, from Brazil's 2018 presidential election, illustrates how political strategists exploited emotional triggers to shape voter perception. WhatsApp groups flooded with sensational claims—many unverified—about candidates' backgrounds and intentions. Users forwarded messages not because they had verified them, but because the content provoked immediate reactions: fear about national security, anger about corruption, or hope for sweeping change. The speed of sharing outpaced journalistic correction. Emotion outran fact.

The limitation, however, is important: not all emotional content spreads. September 2022 studies from King's College London noted that sadness, expressed without accompanying outrage or fear, tended to generate lower engagement and slower diffusion. Users paused but seldom shared. The algorithms, detecting weaker traction, deprioritised the material. This nuance matters. Platforms do not amplify emotion indiscriminately; they amplify particular emotional signatures—those that accelerate behaviour.

Understanding the gap between emotional reaction and critical evaluation requires naming the mechanism that operates beneath it. Cognitive scientists describe the interplay between fast and slow thinking: quick, intuitive judgments versus deliberate, reflective reasoning. On digital platforms, fast thinking dominates because the environment rewards speed. The infinite scroll punishes hesitation. Notifications tempt immediate return. Comment threads encourage impulsive expression. Slow evaluation becomes the anomaly.

To see how this affects belief formation, examine the behaviour of users encountering provocative claims about immigration, public health, or national identity. A headline framed to evoke danger—"Your neighbourhood is changing faster than you realise"—provokes an instinctive response. A user clicks. They share. Their group endorses the sentiment. The approval strengthens the belief. When algorithmic nudges serve more content aligned with that emotional frame, the belief begins to feel self-evident.

Emotion also structures online tribalism. Loyalty to a digital group is often cemented by shared emotional experiences: collective outrage during a controversy, collective elation when a political opponent falters, collective fear during a national crisis. These synchronised emotions create a rhythm of belonging that feels intensely real. The spark of emotion becomes the thread that binds individuals into a coherent story.

A counter-example offers clarity. In December 2020, several independent creators on YouTube attempted to promote "slow media" content: long-form, calm, reflective videos designed to cultivate measured attention. Despite high praise from certain viewers, the videos rarely pierced algorithmic cycles dominated by shock-driven material. Their creators observed that steady engagement metrics could not compete with the dramatic spikes seen in emotionally provocative clips. This does not negate the value of calm content; it simply reveals the structural bias of systems tuned to the spark.

When exposed to emotionally vivid material, users may misinterpret intensity as accuracy. A graph that appears alarming—say, infection rates rising sharply without contextual baselines—can feel persuasive because it evokes urgency. A story that describes a local crime using highly emotive language can feel more truthful than a dry statistical summary. Behavioural economists call this the affect heuristic: people often judge risk based on emotional feeling rather than numerical probability. On social platforms, this heuristic shapes collective perception at scale.

Emotion also influences the memory architecture of digital life. Users revisit posts that infuriate them. They screenshot tweets that confirm their fears. They quote videos that move them. The system measures these actions. The measurements refine the feed. The feed, in turn, shapes the emotional palette of daily experience. This circularity makes self-awareness essential—but difficult.

One additional factor intensifies the challenge. Emotional contagion—well documented in psychological research—spreads rapidly online. In 2014, Facebook's own controversial study demonstrated that altering the emotional valence of users' feeds influenced the emotional tone of their subsequent posts. The ethical issues were substantial, but the observation was undeniable: emotion travels.

Yet the influence of emotion is not uniformly destructive. It motivates solidarity in times of crisis, as seen during the April 2019 fire at Notre-Dame Cathedral in Paris, when donations surged and global messages of support proliferated. It promotes empathy when users share stories of injustice or loss. Emotion can heighten awareness and galvanise civic action. The problem is not emotion itself but the asymmetry: platforms amplify high-arousal feelings far more readily than they elevate nuance.

Here the spark motif returns. A spark can illuminate or ignite. Its power depends on context. A spark that highlights injustice may inspire reform. A spark that feeds resentment may corrode public trust.

The unresolved tension sits at the heart of digital culture: how should users act when a system is designed to privilege what moves them quickly over what develops them slowly? Should platforms recalibrate to elevate content that encourages reflection rather than reaction? Or must individuals cultivate a form of emotional literacy strong enough to resist the pull of the spark?

Cultivating Self-Awareness

In January 2014, researchers at the University of Wisconsin–Madison invited participants into a quiet laboratory room to monitor their responses to provocative images displayed on a screen. The experiment, led by neuroscientist Richard Davidson, produced a striking result: individuals with prior training in basic mindfulness practices showed significantly reduced amygdala activation when confronted with emotionally charged material. The photographs—ranging from scenes of natural disaster to depictions of interpersonal conflict—were identical for all participants. What differed was the speed and intensity of their emotional surge. Those who had practised observing their internal reactions registered calmer physiological patterns and made more deliberate interpretative choices afterwards. A small skill had shifted the trajectory of their responses.

A decade later, in March 2024, the Danish Broadcasting Corporation conducted an informal study in Copenhagen examining how young adults formed opinions after consuming rapid-fire social media clips. Participants were asked to watch a sequence of short political videos, each crafted to provoke. When interviewed immediately afterwards, most reported certainty in their assessments. Yet when prompted to revisit the clips slowly, pause between them, and name their emotional reactions aloud, half re-evaluated their initial judgments. One participant admitted she felt "jolted into agreement" rather than persuaded. Another remarked, "I didn't realise I was reacting; I thought I was reasoning." The difference lay not in the content but in the tempo of attention.

These scenes reveal a theme that will reappear throughout this section: *pausing changes perception*. A pause is not passive. It is an intervention—a brief widening of awareness that interrupts the chain between stimulus and belief. The digital sphere does not encourage such widening, yet it is precisely what users must cultivate if they are to understand how emotion shapes conviction.

Digital platforms distribute material calibrated to provoke. Algorithms measure scroll time, reaction speed, and comment frequency. Posts that trigger rapid physiological responses—anger, excitement, disgust—travel further. To see this in action, consider a typical user reading a story about a policy proposal expected to raise household costs by £200 per year. The number is small enough to analyse calmly, yet many users feel a flash of indignation before computing the figure. That initial flash often dictates their interpretation of the story's credibility. The spark becomes an anchor.

Self-awareness begins not with rejecting emotional reactions but with recognising them. The skill resembles a historian examining a primary source: before interpreting, they note the material's tone, context, and provenance. In the digital sphere, the "primary source" is the user's own sensation. A tightening in the chest. A desire to respond immediately. A quickening breath. These bodily markers—the visible behaviours accompanying emotion—offer early signals that a belief may be forming more quickly than one realises.

The benefit of learning to observe such markers can be seen in a well-documented field example. In 2015, London's Metropolitan Police introduced a pilot programme encouraging officers to use brief grounding techniques during high-conflict encounters. Officers trained to pause for three breaths and name their emotional state internally before making verbal decisions. A subsequent report from the College of Policing (2016) noted a measurable reduction in escalation incidents. The programme was not framed as a wellness initiative but as a cognitive tool: by noticing their emotional surge, officers made more accurate situational judgments. The technique's power lay in its simplicity.

Translating this to digital contexts shows how a momentary inward glance can disrupt the machinery of influence. Consider how a user responds to a viral claim about a scandal involving a prominent public figure. Without awareness, they may share first and examine later. With awareness, they might notice the sensation of urgency and ask a clarifying question: *Why am I responding so strongly?* That question functions like a lens. It sharpens perspective and slows the automatic slide toward belief.

Yet there is an important limitation to acknowledge. Some researchers argue that mindfulness-based approaches risk being co-opted by the same systems that overwhelm attention, turning introspection into another commodity. In 2018, cultural critic Ronald Purser described instances where corporations adopted mindfulness training not to foster critical autonomy but to increase employee productivity. Here the motif of the pause acquires a darker shade: a pause misused becomes an instrument of compliance rather than liberation.

Reconciling this requires distinguishing between techniques designed to moderate discomfort and techniques designed to sharpen discernment. The first soothes; the second interrogates. The focus here rests firmly on the latter. The goal is not serenity but clarity.

Two well-established practices serve this purpose. The first, drawn from the Vipassanā tradition of early Buddhist texts, involves labelling internal states as they arise—"anger", "eagerness", "fear", "certainty". This naming creates a cognitive step between emotion and interpretation. The second, found in Stoic writings from Epictetus to Marcus Aurelius, encourages the deliberate questioning of initial impressions. Aurelius repeatedly wrote variations of the same prompt: *Is this really so?* Both traditions, separated by centuries and geography, converge on a shared method: slow the rush, see the reaction, examine it.

Digital environments, however, challenge these practices by compressing attention. A user scrolling late at night in Manchester after a long day may not meaningfully notice their emotional fluctuations. They move from clip to clip, merging sensations into a single stream. The acceleration erodes awareness. Reintroducing the pause requires intention. It is a discipline rather than an instinct.

This discipline becomes essential when encountering emotionally laden misinformation. During the French presidential campaigns in April 2022, several manipulated videos circulated widely on Twitter, using edited clips to evoke indignation. Users who shared the material tended to do so within seconds of viewing. A report by the Institut Montaigne (2022) found that those who paused—even briefly—were substantially more likely to check the source or read replies before sharing. The presence or absence of a pause changed not just behaviour but belief trajectory.

A counter-example highlights the complexity of cultivating awareness. Some users, especially those accustomed to high-volume information environments, report that introspective practices make them more sensitive to emotional content rather than more discerning. They describe noticing every internal fluctuation, which leaves them feeling flooded rather than grounded. Yet follow-up interviews reveal a pattern: these individuals were attempting to monitor emotions continuously. Effective introspection is intermittent, not constant. It involves brief, deliberate check-ins, much like a navigator glancing at an instrument panel rather than staring at it unblinkingly.

The motif of the pause reappears here with new meaning. A pause is not a retreat; it is a recalibration. By stepping out of the algorithmic current, even momentarily, users give themselves space to assess whether they are reacting to facts or to their feelings about those facts.

This raises a larger implication for belief formation. When users regularly practise noticing reactions, they become less susceptible to digital triggers. They sense when their assumptions are hardening prematurely. They notice when a claim aligns too conveniently with their group identity. They catch themselves before reaching for the comfort of quick certainty. The skill becomes a quiet defence against manipulation.

Yet one unresolved tension remains. Should platforms themselves introduce deliberate friction—design elements that prompt users to pause before sharing emotionally provocative material? Or does that responsibility fall to individuals alone? The question lingers at the centre of digital self-governance: how much awareness must each user cultivate to remain free within systems designed to accelerate their instincts?

Chapter 9
Fact vs Narrative

On a humid afternoon in June 2020, a single photograph taken in Lafayette Square, Washington, D.C., ricocheted around the world in minutes. The frame captured a man holding a banner above his head while a line of riot police advanced behind him. For some viewers, the image represented unprovoked state aggression; for others, it appeared to confirm the necessity of firm policing. The facts of the moment—its location, its timing, its participants—remained constant, yet the meaning diverged wildly. What determined the split was not the evidence itself but the narrative lens each viewer carried with them. It was a reminder that a "fact" rarely arrives unaccompanied. It comes dressed in interpretation.

The photograph proved potent because it was incomplete. Not deliberately deceptive, only partial. Moments before and after the shutter clicked were missing, the surrounding voices unheard, the broader context unframed. But the mind abhors blanks, so it fills them. One viewer imagines a peaceful crowd interrupted. Another imagines an imminent threat contained. The truth becomes a mosaic assembled from slivers. The fragment hardens into story. And once absorbed, that story often carries more weight than any subsequent clarification.

We live amid fragments—clips, screenshots, curated statistics, lines stripped from paragraphs. The platforms that deliver them accelerate the shift from observation to interpretation. The gap between fact and meaning narrows until the two appear fused. Yet that fusion, seductive as it is, deserves scrutiny. The chapters leading to this point have shown how algorithms, emotion, and identity shape our assumptions. Now we turn to the architecture of understanding itself: how narratives form, travel, and lay claim to truth.

Subjectivity is not a flaw in human perception but its default setting. Everyone sees through a history, a vocabulary, a set of predispositions built up over years of cultural exposure. The digital sphere, however, adds a new twist: it amplifies those predispositions at scale. One user watches a thirty-second clip of a protest in São Paulo and sees disorder; another sees resistance. Their interpretations feel self-evident because the snippet confirms what they already believe. Even the decision to film one moment rather than another, to crop left rather than right, carries an implicit commentary. These micro-choices shape the emotional temperature of an event long before analysis begins.

This chapter examines the gap between what happens and what is told. It begins by confronting a paradox: facts appear solid, yet their significance is fluid. A statistic can be precise while the conclusion drawn from it is deeply subjective. A headline can be factual yet misleading. A graph can be accurate yet structured to encourage a particular inference. To understand modern information flows, one must observe not only what is presented but *how* it is arranged. The arrangement is the quiet storyteller.

Framing does much of the invisible work. By the time a story reaches a user's screen, it has passed through layers of editorial decisions: which words to emphasise, which images to pair with which sentences, which comments to surface, which posts to recommend. A platform may elevate narratives of conflict because they generate higher engagement. A broadcaster may lead with a story that fits a familiar national script. Even the rhythm of language—active or passive, emotive or technical—steers interpretation. During the UK's 2016 Brexit referendum, for example, the distinctions between "migrants", "EU nationals", and "foreign workers" were not incidental. Each term carried a different emotional load. The label framed the debate before any argument was made.

Data, often treated as the refuge of objectivity, plays its own narrative games. A graph might display unemployment figures from 2018 to 2022 but omit the 2016–2017 spike that would complicate the trend. A bar chart might stretch or shrink its axes to exaggerate small differences. Even well-intentioned analysts choose timeframes and comparison groups based on implicit hypotheses. Data is rarely neutral; it tells the story its curator selects. And the curator—be they a journalist, policymaker, influencer, or algorithmic system—may not disclose the choices made behind the scenes.

None of this implies malicious intent by default. Narrative is human. Interpretation is unavoidable. The problem emerges when narratives pose as unquestionable fact, when a single snapshot is mistaken for the whole landscape, when the loudest frame becomes the default frame. The digital environment rewards simplicity, speed, and certainty—qualities that narrative provides and fact alone often does not. As a result, stories gain traction long before they are interrogated.

Consider the case of a short clip from a school board meeting in California that circulated widely in 2021. In isolation, the footage showed a heated dispute over curriculum content, seemingly emblematic of ideological polarisation. Yet the full meeting minutes revealed a mundane administrative disagreement that escalated briefly. The clip was factual. The narrative built on it—"evidence" of widespread national unrest—was not. Viewers consumed the clip as confirmation of a trend that scarcely existed. They believed the story because it fit a broader schema, not because it accurately represented the event.

Narrative also shapes how data is used to endorse policy. When a health agency reports that "hospital admissions rose by 20 per cent," the increase might represent a shift from 10 to 12 patients. The figure is precise, yet the impression is disproportionate. The context, once omitted, distorts the frame. Without critical habits of interpretation, users become vulnerable to stories that lean heavily on numbers while obscuring their scale.

The heart of this chapter lies in cultivating the mindset of a discerning reader—one who slows down enough to see the scaffolding beneath the story. Such a reader does not treat scepticism as cynicism but as attentiveness. They notice the selective photograph. They question the missing timeframe. They ask what alternative language might change the meaning. They recognise when a platform's algorithm repeatedly feeds them a single frame and wonder why that frame is deemed worthy of repetition.

To become such a reader demands more than technical skill. It requires curiosity—the willingness to ask: *Who benefits from this version of events? What is left unsaid? What would change if I looked from another angle?* These questions pry open the narrative and reveal its seams. They transform the passive act of receiving information into an active relationship with truth.

The stakes are high. A society's shared understanding of reality depends not only on available facts but on the narratives that bind them. When competing stories pull too far apart, common ground fractures. When narratives are built carelessly, or strategically skewed, public debate collapses into accusation and counter-accusation. Facts become props rather than anchors.

Yet there is an opportunity embedded in this complexity. If facts are shaped by stories, then stories can be reshaped—

made more honest, more reflective, more attentive to nuance. The task is not to erase narrative but to understand its power. The chapter ahead will guide readers through that terrain, showing how stories form, how they influence judgment, and how they can be interrogated without losing their human richness.

The tension that propels this chapter is simple and enduring: if facts can deceive without lying, and stories can reveal truth without being literal, how do we navigate the space between them? The reader, now familiar with the psychological, cultural, and political forces that shape belief, steps into a domain where meaning itself is contested. The reward for that journey is clarity—not perfect certainty, but a sharper sense of what is being presented, and why.

Confronting Subjectivity

In November 2019, a thirty-second video from Hong Kong's Polytechnic University travelled through global social feeds with extraordinary velocity. Filmed near the campus footbridge, it showed a lone protester tumbling backwards as a police officer raised his baton. Within minutes, the clip became a Rorschach test. Commentators in London, Sydney, and Toronto framed it variously as evidence of state brutality, legitimate crowd control, or selective editing intended to inflame public outrage. The event was singular. The interpretations were many. By nightfall, the "same" footage had generated incompatible narratives—each claiming fidelity to fact yet shaped by the viewer's convictions long before the pixels reached their screen.

The footage was real. Its consequences were real: the university was partially shut, hundreds of students were arrested, and major newspapers across continents ran front-page analyses. Yet the meanings projected onto that thirty-second fragment bore only passing resemblance to one another. A split second of hesitation before impact was either a merciful restraint or a tactical feint. The protester's backward fall was either a reaction to force or the result of stumbling while fleeing. Each reading derived not from hidden information but from the mental scaffolding that audiences brought to the moment. Interpretation arrived before reflection. The image became the story.

Subjectivity, then, is not merely an intellectual quirk; it is an active participant in how digital events are understood. A photograph, clip, or chart feels neutral because it seems to present the world as it is. Yet what we "see" is inseparable from how we make sense of it. This section follows that thread, tracing the way narratives sculpt our reception of fact—how fragments become positions, and positions harden into belief.

At the heart of subjectivity lies selection. A lens excludes 99 per cent of a scene and elevates one per cent to prominence. When *The New York Times* published its January 2021 photograph of a masked nurse leaning against a hospital wall in Los Angeles, the image conveyed exhaustion and crisis. Had the frame been lifted two metres to the left, the nurse might have appeared in casual conversation with colleagues between rounds. The named outlet, the date, the location—each anchors the moment in verifiable reality. Yet the frame sets its emotional temperature. It shows one sliver and leaves the rest to assumption.

This phenomenon is not limited to photography. Consider December 2022, when Germany's Federal Statistical Office released figures showing a 10.4 per cent rise in consumer prices. The number was precise, audited, and technically unimpeachable. But the narrative that accompanied it varied by publication. Some outlets illustrated the report with queues at supermarkets in Munich; others paired it with stock-market downturns in Frankfurt. The metric was stable; the impression was pliable. Audiences who saw empty shelves felt anxiety; those who saw financial traders felt systemic instability. The data point was the same. The story built around it diverged.

To understand why this divergence persists, one must recognise that humans interpret from within communities. Shared assumptions, political loyalties, and social identities function as anchors. The motif that recurs here—*the frame*—is not simply photographic. It is conceptual. A frame answers the question "what is this really about?" before a viewer consciously engages with the evidence. When a protest video circulates, those who identify strongly with law-and-order narratives may focus on perceived threats in the background. Those who identify with civil-liberty narratives may notice raised batons first. The eye lingers where the mind expects significance.

Psychologists such as Daniel Kahneman (2011) and Elizabeth Loftus (2005) have long shown that interpretation is shaped by priming and expectation. In digital contexts, priming becomes ambient. Recommendation engines, trending topics, and peer-shared content continuously calibrate what feels plausible. When a user watches three clips of tense confrontations between protesters and police, a fourth clip will be processed through a heightened sense of conflict. The viewer commits to a storyline before the evidence warrants commitment. Algorithms measure this behaviour through watch time, rewinds, and engagement spikes, reinforcing the interpretive template.

Yet subjectivity does not always distort. There are cases where narrative frames correct blind spots. In April 2021, when reports emerged of devastating oxygen shortages in New Delhi, on-the-ground videos shared by local doctors exposed a crisis that official statements initially downplayed. Here, subjective framing—patients gasping outside hospitals, relatives pleading for supplies—served as a counterweight to institutional minimisation. The interpretation was emotional, doubtless, but it directed attention to real suffering that numeric summaries failed to convey. Subjectivity, in this instance, expanded moral awareness rather than narrowing it.

Still, the corrective potential of narrative does not erase its limitations. If one user interprets an image of police in tactical gear as evidence of excessive militarisation, and another interprets it as prudent preparation, both readings may be sincere. The tension arises when these readings calcify, leaving no room for context. Online ecosystems reward speed and certainty. Slow interpretation—asking who filmed a moment, from what angle, and why—receives little algorithmic applause. The incentive structure privileges immediate framing, not considered analysis.

Two examples illustrate how this dynamic shapes public understanding. First, the viral clip of a Covington Catholic High School student facing a Native American elder during the January 2019 Indigenous Peoples March in Washington, D.C. The initial short clip appeared to show disrespect. But a longer recording revealed a more complex interaction, involving multiple groups and shifting dynamics. The early narrative hardened within hours. The later context struggled to catch up. Subjectivity, accelerated by platform incentives, created reputational damage long before facts stabilised.

Second, the footage from Paris in March 2023, showing a police officer drawing his weapon during pension reform protests. Some French outlets framed the moment as evidence of escalating repression; others contextualised it as a response to immediate threat. Both treatments drew on real footage. Both excluded certain details. The narratives told different stories, each plausible in isolation. The frame guided the understanding.

Such cases invite a deeper question: what does objectivity mean when every representation is partial? A chart showing crime rates might highlight a decline over five years, yet hide a recent uptick by adjusting the scale. A headline stating that "unemployment falls" might mask the fact that labour-force participation has also fallen. The viewer sees numbers, not choices. But the choices matter. Subjectivity inhabits the design.

Recognising this does not require nihilism. It requires attention. If the motif of the frame recurs throughout this discussion, it does so to underscore the central point: one cannot eliminate subjectivity, but one can learn to locate it. A thoughtful observer asks what the frame includes, what it excludes, and what alternative framing might reveal. They compare multiple vantage points. They notice when emotional weight exceeds evidential weight. They remain alert to the quiet work of narrative.

A credible counter-argument suggests that excessive scrutiny can paralyse interpretation. If subjectivity permeates all representation, does one risk descending into relativism—treating all accounts as equally unreliable? That state of sceptical drift is not inevitable. The task is not to distrust everything but to understand why something feels convincing, to measure the influence of narrative without discarding the underlying fact. A disputed clip may still show real force. A contested statistic may still reveal a material trend. The aim is calibration, not cynicism.

The implication is profound for digital citizenship. When billions of people interpret fragments each day, their aggregated narratives shape public discourse. A viral clip can prompt protests, policy shifts, or international scrutiny. The narratives we adopt influence decisions: which causes we support, which leaders we trust, which communities we see as allies or adversaries. Interpretation moves markets and moods. It colours democratic life.

The final tension, then, remains unresolved because it cannot be tidily solved. If every fact requires a frame, and every frame implies a viewpoint, how does one navigate a world where interpretations compete with the speed of light? The question presses: when the next thirty-second clip surges across your screen, whose story will you see—and what story will you resist?

Spin, Framing, and Language

In September 2015, a single photograph from Bodrum, Turkey altered the political tone of a continent. The image of Alan Kurdi, a three-year-old Syrian boy whose body washed ashore after an attempted crossing to Kos, appeared on the front pages of *The Guardian, Der Spiegel,* and *Le Monde* within hours. The fact was tragic and indisputable. Yet the framing diverged. Some outlets placed the picture above headlines about Europe's moral obligation. Others embedded it within narratives warning of border insecurity. The same photograph anchored starkly different interpretations, not because the pixels changed, but because editorial choices and platform algorithms elevated certain frames over others. The image became a catalyst, but the language around it guided the emotional direction.

Within the first week of its circulation, Facebook's Trending module promoted posts describing the event as a "refugee crisis", while several broadcasters preferred "migrant crisis". That single substitution altered the implied story. "Refugee" foregrounded vulnerability; "migrant" suggested movement and, to some audiences, managed choice. The fact—a drowned child on a Turkish beach—remained constant. The framing shifted the moral centre of gravity. Words drew boundaries around empathy and responsibility. The frame did the rest.

Framing matters because it precedes interpretation. It serves as the quiet motif of this section—the lens that narrows or widens what the public believes they are seeing. In digital environments, this lens is not only held by journalists but by ranking systems that measure engagement, commit to pattern, and distribute content according to predicted resonance. The frame travels faster than the fact.

The first mechanism is linguistic. Consider how platforms differentiate stories through subtle wording choices. When *BBC News* reported the June 2020 gatherings in Bristol that culminated in the toppling of Edward Colston's statue, its headline described a "protest". A widely shared contemporaneous post on Twitter labelled it a "riot". A third source termed it a "reckoning". Each term summoned a different palette of associations. To call it a protest implied civic action. To call it a riot suggested threat. To call it a reckoning invoked historical correction. Algorithmic amplification strengthened whichever wording drove interaction. Words guided attention. Attention coded significance.

The second mechanism is contextual. In August 2022, when record-breaking wildfires ravaged parts of Gironde in southwest France, some outlets paired aerial photographs of burning forests with captions emphasising climate change. Others foregrounded arson investigations. The pictures were real. The inferno was real. Yet the context chosen by editors—and subsequently reinforced by social-ranking systems—directed viewers towards different causal stories. Where one frame encouraged scrutiny of environmental policy, the other encouraged scrutiny of criminal activity. Neither was inherently false. Both were incomplete. The frame decided what appeared primary.

Two further examples reveal the pattern with clarity. First, the 2016 Orlando nightclub shooting. In the hours that followed, platforms surfaced contradictory frames: terrorism, homophobia, gun control failure. Different newsrooms emphasised one frame over the others. Audiences absorbed these frames through headlines, tags, and thumbnail images before engaging with detailed reporting. The hierarchy of emphasis shaped early public understanding, which later proved difficult to recalibrate even after nuanced information emerged.

Second, the 2021 Suez Canal blockage by the *Ever Given*. The image of a solitary excavator dwarfed by the container ship became a global meme. Some media framed the event as a symbol of infrastructural fragility; others as a comedic instance of human perseverance; others still as an indictment of global supply-chain overreach. Most readers did not track shipping data or operational reports. They processed the story through a frame—absurdity, vulnerability, or systemic pressure—long before grappling with maritime logistics. The frame shaped the perceived fact.

A credible counter-example exists: instances where framing diversity reduces distortion. During the January 2020 wildfires in Australia, several outlets provided multi-frame coverage—environmental causes, human impact, wildlife devastation, political disagreement. This plurality allowed audiences to triangulate the truth more effectively. No single frame dominated. The mosaic reduced narrative drift. The limitation of this counter-example, however, is that such plurality is rare. High-engagement platforms reward a narrower set of emotions, strengthening whichever frame delivers the strongest response.

Language interacts with these dynamics in measurable ways. Platforms analyse not only what users read but how they react. A headline containing terms such as "surge", "collapse", or "breaking" reliably increases click-through rates. When an editor chooses a softer alternative—"increase", "decline", "update"—the algorithm may deprioritise the link due to lower predicted engagement. This measurable behaviour reshapes editorial norms. Even cautious outlets face pressure to adopt intensified vocabulary to remain visible. The choice of words becomes a negotiation with a machine, not merely with an audience.

Visual framing operates with similar stealth. A photograph cropped a few centimetres differently can alter the perceived mood of an event. During the May 2021 protests in Bogotá, wire services distributed both wide-angle shots showing thousands in Plaza de Bolívar and tight-frame shots focusing on masked individuals near burning debris. Platforms promoting content via engagement metrics frequently surfaced the latter. Attention gravitated towards images that suggested volatility, not civic mobilisation. The frame selected the feeling.

If linguistic and visual framing are the tools, platform design is the stage on which they operate. Headlines appear truncated. Images appear enlarged. Captions appear hidden behind "more" buttons. These design decisions guide what a user processes first. When a platform enlarges the first sentence of a caption, it privileges the editorial frame. When it auto-plays a clip without context, it foregrounds visuals over explanation. These are deliberate interface choices, not accidents. The frame is built into the architecture.

The motif of the lens returns here. Users rarely realise they are peering through a shaped aperture. It feels natural. It feels neutral. Yet neutrality collapses upon scrutiny. A user believing they are selecting content freely may actually be selecting from a pre-curated set of frames optimised for engagement-driven prediction. The fact becomes secondary; the frame becomes primary.

A critical implication arises from this: perception can be steered without altering the underlying information. A news story can remain technically accurate while still guiding an audience towards a partial truth. The mechanism is subtle. The consequences are not. Frames influence voting behaviour, trust in institutions, and social division. They decide whether a policy feels urgent or peripheral. They determine whether a community is portrayed as dangerous or merely desperate. The stakes extend far beyond semantics.

Yet this does not doom audiences to manipulation. Awareness weakens automatic influence. When users recognise patterns—why a headline uses a charged verb, why an image foregrounds destruction rather than resilience—they shift from passive reception to active interpretation. They interrogate the choices. They compare sources. They ask why one frame feels natural and another feels forced. They see where the lens narrows and where it widens.

A forward test remains. When the next crisis, protest, or policy debate erupts across your screen, what will you examine first: the fact, or the frame through which that fact reaches you?

When Data Tells a Story

In March 2009, during a tense congressional hearing in Washington, the American International Group presented a line graph showing the steady stabilisation of its credit default swap exposure. The graph began in late 2008, immediately after the firm had received a massive federal bailout. Missing were the earlier quarters when its exposure had surged dramatically, creating the very conditions that triggered intervention. Legislators saw a story of recovery. Critics outside the room saw a story of omission. The fact—a collapsing insurer rescued by public funds—never changed. The frame, encoded in the chosen timeframe of a graph, did. A modest visual adjustment softened a crisis into a narrative of competence regained.

This moment is often remembered for political fallout, yet its deeper significance lies in the graph itself. Data appeared objective; the image suggested neutrality; the trendline carried mathematical gravitas. But the choice of starting point—November 2008 rather than March of that year—functioned like a camera crop. What lay outside the frame shaped what happened within it. When data is presented as fact, viewers seldom interrogate what is missing. They accept the story that numbers seem to tell.

The quiet motif of this section is the frame, a device that returns repeatedly. Data, like photography, never arrives unframed. It is selected, ordered, and displayed according to a designer's intent—sometimes deliberate, sometimes unconscious, but always consequential.

The first mechanism by which data tells a story lies in the selection of the timeline. During the Eurozone crisis, several newspapers across Europe published charts in early 2012 depicting Greek unemployment rising steeply compared with Germany's. One widely circulated chart from *Frankfurter Allgemeine Zeitung* began in 2008, the outbreak of global financial turmoil, portraying Greece's trajectory as uniquely catastrophic. When analysts later republished the same dataset beginning in 2000, a more complex pattern emerged: Greece's unemployment was already diverging from Germany's long before the crash. The crisis exacerbated the problem; it did not originate it. Show, name, explain, implication: the chart had not technically lied. It merely told the story the chosen timeframe enabled.

A second example, equally instructive, occurred in December 2020 when a British transport advocacy group released a graphic comparing cycling fatalities across European capitals. London appeared unusually dangerous. Yet the chart omitted per-capita cycling rates; cities like Copenhagen and Amsterdam, where far more residents cycle daily, naturally had higher exposure but lower fatality rates per kilometre travelled. Once distance travelled was included, London's position shifted. The visible behaviour in both cases—reordering datasets—revealed how metrics transform meaning. Without exposure data, the chart conveyed moral urgency. With it, the narrative changed from condemnation to structural nuance.

Platform design amplifies these distortions. Social media feeds reward charts that show steep slopes, sharp contrasts, and dramatic inflections. A subtle shift in the y-axis can convert a mild fluctuation into a crisis. Many readers interpret these graphs as scientific artefacts rather than editorial constructions. A dataset that fluctuates between 48 per cent and 52 per cent support for a policy might be plotted on a y-axis beginning at zero, making the variation look momentous. Plot the same numbers on a y-axis beginning at 45 per cent and the movement becomes nearly imperceptible. The dataset remains identical. The story does not.

A credible counter-example can be found in the rigorous dashboards created during the early phase of the COVID-19 pandemic. Johns Hopkins University's visualisations, widely referenced between February and June 2020, were transparent about sources, update frequency, and methodological limitations. They allowed users to compare logarithmic and linear scales, revealing both the rate and the scale of viral spread. This plurality of representations prevented a single narrative from dominating the public imagination. Yet even here, limitations persisted: confirmed case counts depended on testing capacity, which varied significantly between countries. The numbers were real; their meaning was contingent.

The second mechanism through which data acquires narrative force is variable selection. In April 2018, a campaign group in California circulated a chart showing that property crime had surged in San Francisco after the passage of Proposition 47, which reduced certain non-violent offences to misdemeanours. What the chart omitted was reporting behaviour. A contemporaneous analysis by the Public Policy Institute of California showed that the proportion of residents using online reporting systems rose sharply after 2015. Increased reporting contributed to the apparent spike. The campaign's chart, stripped of this context, told a compelling but incomplete story of causation.

Another case, this time from London, illustrates the principle from a different angle. In 2021, Transport for London published passenger data showing a rapid rebound in Underground usage after lockdown restrictions eased. Local newspapers framed it as evidence of economic recovery. Yet the same dataset, broken down by station and time of day, revealed a more nuanced pattern: commuter traffic remained suppressed while leisure travel surged. The story of "recovery" depended entirely on aggregation. The choice of measurement guided the narrative.

The third mechanism is visual design itself—colour, order, and comparative structure. A common technique in political advertising is the truncated bar chart, in which bars begin not at zero but at an arbitrary mid-point. During the 2017 French presidential election, a widely circulated unofficial graphic compared projected tax burdens under Emmanuel Macron and Marine Le Pen. The bars began at 25 per cent, making Macron's projected increase appear enormous despite representing only a marginal difference. Viewers saw a dramatic contrast. The story they absorbed was one of stark divergence.

These visual manipulations exploit cognitive shortcuts. Humans process graphs holistically. We see shape, slope, and contrast faster than we parse numbers. Algorithms magnify this tendency, boosting visuals that elicit quick responses. A steep line feels urgent. A compressed axis feels volatile. A colour gradient feels evaluative—green suggests success; red signals danger. Even when legend labels are neutral, colour choices embed value judgements. Viewers absorb narrative before reading detail.

The lens motif returns here: visualisations are lenses crafted by designers who decide what deserves focus. The assumption that data "speaks for itself" collapses. Data speaks the language chosen for it.

A further complexity emerges when statistical models—rather than simple charts—become vehicles for storytelling. Predictive models carry authority because they use mathematics to anticipate outcomes. Yet their framing rests on assumptions invisible to most viewers. When the UK Office for Budget Responsibility released growth forecasts in October 2022, commentators focused on the projected downturn. Few inspected the behavioural assumptions embedded in the models: expected consumer confidence levels, global energy prices, and policy adjustments. The forecast was a narrative of risk told through assumptions that might never materialise. The numbers felt factual; their foundation was hypothetical.

A limitation must be acknowledged: not all selective framing is malicious. Journalists, analysts, and researchers often simplify data to improve clarity. A graph showing a decade's worth of economic indicators may be unreadable; a six-month excerpt can clarify a current trend. The challenge is not simplification itself but the failure to signal that simplification has occurred. Presenting a fragment of a dataset without context creates a story stronger than the underlying evidence warrants.

These distortions matter because numbers carry a reputation for objectivity. A bar chart feels impartial. A regression line feels authoritative. Yet neutrality depends on choices made long before the user encounters the final graphic. What is measured? Which timeframe? What baseline? What comparison group? Each decision bends the story subtly. And platform algorithms select for the stories that trigger emotional or ideological engagement.

The implications stretch beyond misinformation. Data narratives shape policy debates, corporate decisions, and public sentiment. A selective graph about crime can influence policing strategies. A misleading visualisation of climate data can undermine support for environmental regulation. A manipulated economic chart can shift market expectations. When data frames belief, the stakes are structural, not merely informational.

The most powerful defence is not statistical expertise but disciplined curiosity. When confronted with a striking chart, readers can ask: what sits outside the frame? Why this timeframe? Why this baseline? Why this colour scheme? Which variables are absent? Which comparisons are implied but unstated? These questions widen the lens. They turn passive viewers into active interpreters.

A final tension remains unresolved. The next time a compelling chart flashes across your screen—dramatic slope, stark contrast, bold headline—will you accept the story it tells, or pause long enough to examine the frame that makes the story possible?

Becoming a Critical Reader

In June 1995, readers across the United States awoke to front-page headlines proclaiming that an outbreak of flesh-eating bacteria had spread through parts of Louisiana. Several newspapers ran alarming accounts, citing unnamed medical sources. Television channels followed, broadcasting grainy footage of hospital corridors and sombre warnings. The story created immediate panic: schools saw absentee rates climb; sales of antibacterial products spiked; local officials fielded frantic calls. Within days, the Centres for Disease Control and Prevention publicly refuted the claims. No such outbreak had occurred. The entire episode traced back to a misinterpreted hospital memo and a journalist's rush to print. A fact had never existed, yet a narrative took hold with remarkable speed.

The case endures because it demonstrates something essential: readers did not simply lack information; they lacked a method for weighing it. The story contained familiar rhetorical devices—anonymous expertise, urgent tone, selective detail—wrapped in the authority of mass media. Nothing in the text encouraged scrutiny. Everything encouraged belief. To read critically in such a moment meant noticing friction where others felt flow.

The motif of friction reappears throughout this section. Critical reading begins not with cynicism but with resistance: the slight pause before accepting a claim, the instinct to ask one more question, the impulse to widen the frame. In a digital environment engineered for speed, friction becomes a form of agency.

The first habit of a critical reader is attending closely to provenance. During the Brexit referendum campaign in 2016, a claim circulated widely that the United Kingdom sent £350 million a week to the European Union. The figure appeared on buses, billboards, and social media posts. The number was technically drawn from official Treasury data, yet it omitted rebate mechanisms and funding returned to UK programmes. Show: a bold claim on a bus. Name: the Vote Leave campaign. Explain: the figure represented a gross contribution, not a net one. Implication: the persuasive force of the claim stemmed from its simplicity, not its accuracy. A critical reader encountering this figure would ask a visible question—*What is the underlying calculation?*—rather than accepting the rhetorical flourish.

A second example demonstrates how source interrogation alters interpretation. In November 2019, a viral tweet claimed that homelessness in Los Angeles had increased by 50 per cent in a single year. The post linked to a city report. Yet closer inspection revealed that the report compared data collected during a methodological change: the city had expanded the number of census tracts used in its count, which naturally produced higher totals. The behaviour of the counting system changed; homelessness did not surge overnight. A critical reader separates measurement from meaning.

Yet rigour alone does not resolve every ambiguity. A credible limitation emerges when expert sources disagree. During the early phase of the COVID-19 pandemic, epidemiologists offered varying estimates of transmission rates and fatality ratios. Not all could be simultaneously correct. A critical reader recognises this uncertainty without dismissing the enterprise of expertise. The reconciliation lies in examining methods, not personalities: which estimates rely on confirmed cases versus projected infections, which incorporate reporting delays, which update as new evidence arrives. Friction—again—becomes a safeguard.

A second habit is to recognise when language performs more than description. In January 2023, a major London newspaper referred to a peaceful environmental demonstration as a "mob". The article included images of seated protesters holding placards. Show: the word "mob".

Name: the *Evening Standard.* Explain: "mob" implies disorder and threat, shaping the reader's emotional framing before the facts appear. Implication: linguistic framing often exerts more influence than data. A critical reader notices the dissonance between the descriptor and the visible behaviour.

The same principle applies to visual cues. When a broadcaster overlays images of flashing police lights while discussing crime statistics, it primes the audience to think in terms of danger. In 2021, a segment on rising knife crime in Birmingham used footage of unrelated incidents to evoke urgency. The numbers were real—West Midlands Police had reported a 17 per cent increase over the previous year—but the visual selection suggested a continuous crisis rather than a statistically bounded rise. Critical reading extends beyond text to imagery and sound.

A third habit is to examine the *shape* of claims. Narratives often rely on implied causation. In April 2017, several commentators argued that a surge in Scandinavian smartphone usage had caused declining academic performance in Norway and Sweden. The claim referenced national exam results and device-ownership rates. Yet the relationship between correlation and causation remained untested. When the Nordic Institute for Studies in Innovation, Research and Education published a subsequent analysis later that year, it found multiple overlapping factors: curriculum changes, socioeconomic disparities, and variations in teacher recruitment. The simple story collapsed under scrutiny. Critical readers measure the strength of a claim by the rigour of its causal chain.

At times, claims exploit scale to distort meaning. A government statement may announce that jobs "doubled" while omitting that the number rose from 100 to 200. A charity may report a "30 per cent increase" in endangered animals without stating that the population grew from ten to thirteen. Precision matters. The visible behaviour of good reporting includes specifying absolute numbers alongside proportions. Critical readers watch for this behaviour.

A fourth habit involves interrogating motives without leaping to conspiracy. When pharmaceutical firms publish research showing the effectiveness of their own drugs, scepticism is rational. Yet this scepticism should target funding structure, not assume deception. The same applies to think-tanks with ideological affiliations or journalists with career incentives. During the 2008 financial crisis, several prominent commentators downplayed housing market risks partly because they had built reputations on forecasting stability. Their narratives preserved intellectual consistency rather than serving evidence. Critical readers identify this dynamic: incentives shape stories.

Still, motive is not destiny. A credible counter-example appears in the independent investigations conducted by ProPublica after Hurricane Maria in 2017. Although the organisation received donations from foundations with political leanings, its reporting uncovered failures by both

Republican and Democratic officials. Motive can coexist with integrity when processes of verification are strong. The implication is nuanced: critical reading examines incentives but does not assume malign intent. It weighs claims against evidence, not against allegiance.

The fifth habit is to widen the frame. During the 2022 parliamentary debate on energy pricing in the UK, several MPs cited statistics showing that Britain had some of the highest average household bills in Europe. The numbers were correct. Yet when compared against median household income, the relative burden shifted: countries with lower absolute bills sometimes imposed heavier proportional strain on families. The frame—absolute cost versus proportional impact—altered the narrative. Critical readers test alternative frames before accepting the first presented.

The motif of friction returns again here. Each of these habits introduces small delays into the reading process. They slow reaction. They create space for evaluation. In a digital environment designed to accelerate decision and impulse, slowing becomes a countercultural act.

The demands of critical reading, however, must be balanced against cognitive limits. No reader can interrogate every claim with perfect rigour. Time, fatigue, and cognitive load constrain scrutiny. A key question becomes: *Where is scrutiny most needed?* The answer lies in the intersection of impact and uncertainty. Claims that spur strong emotional reactions merit closer inspection because emotion accelerates belief. Claims with policy consequences require additional context because errors magnify downstream. Critical reading is selective, not exhaustive.

Another complexity arises when narratives align with our existing convictions. Psychologists have documented this as confirmation bias, but the behavioural signature worth observing is simpler: ease. When a story feels immediately satisfying, friction disappears. The claim slides into our worldview without disturbance. Critical readers recognise this sensation as a warning signal. Ease is not evidence.

The most powerful tool available to readers is the disciplined question. It appears modest but carries strategic force. *What is the source? What evidence supports this? What has been omitted? What alternative explanation exists? What frame would invert this claim?* These questions convert passive consumption into active reasoning. They impose structure on ambiguity.

A final tension presses forward. The next time a narrative arrives perfectly shaped—clean statistic, vivid anecdote, persuasive tone—will you allow its momentum to carry you, or apply the small but decisive friction that separates belief from understanding?

Chapter 10
Moving Beyond Automation: Tomorrow's Vision

In February 2020, a team of clinicians at the Royal Free Hospital in London gathered around a diagnostic screen that displayed a set of lung scans. A machine-learning model had flagged three specific regions with a bright amber outline. The software claimed these areas suggested early-stage pneumonia that required urgent review. The senior consultant paused, studied the scans, and then asked the AI system to reveal the confidence levels behind each alert. Two looked routine. The third carried a probability too compelling to ignore. Hours later, the diagnosis proved correct. The patient received treatment far earlier than traditional processes would have allowed. The achievement belonged not to the machine alone, nor to the clinician alone, but to a subtle choreography between the two.

That moment captures something important about the horizon we now approach. Automation has altered our expectations of speed, accuracy, and convenience, yet the promise of technology has never rested solely on efficiency. Its deeper potential lies in the type of partnerships we forge with it. When tools are designed to complement rather than command, they reveal pathways for problem-solving that neither party could reach independently. But when automation becomes the default arbiter—when we allow decision-making to drift into the machinery without scrutiny—we risk ceding more than labour. We risk surrendering judgement.

This chapter steps into that contested space where human agency meets algorithmic fluency. The question is not whether automation will continue to shape our societies. It already has. The question is what form that shaping should take, and which values ought to anchor it. The future may be automated, but it should not be automated by accident.

Across recent years, we have witnessed moments that illuminate both the promise and the precarity of this transition. The deployment of AI-assisted diagnostic tools, the use of predictive analytics in climate modelling, the application of natural language systems in legal research—each reveals a version of partnership where technology amplifies human capacity. These instances do not merely increase productivity; they redefine what it means to think alongside a machine. Yet for every model that enhances insight, another poses quiet risks. A hiring algorithm that disfavors certain candidates because it unconsciously mirrors legacy data. A content moderation system that applies cultural norms with uneven sensitivity. A policing tool that predicts risk using historic patterns shaped by discrimination. These examples remind us that automation is neither neutral nor inevitable. It inherits a worldview, intentional or otherwise.

The tension that threads through this chapter is simple but significant: how do we retain the human core while embracing accelerating technological capability? To answer this, we must think beyond fixes and adjustments. The future cannot be navigated by technical patches alone; it demands ethical scaffolding robust enough to challenge, restrain, and refine innovation. Committees, guidelines, and oversight structures may sound procedural, yet when done properly they represent a profound cultural commitment. They assert that values must govern inventions, not the reverse.

At the heart of these structures sits a question that unsettles and guides in equal measure: what do we want technology to *do* for us, and what should we refuse to delegate? Automation thrives in predictable domains—sorting, classifying, forecasting—but much of life derives its meaning from ambiguity, difference, and deliberation. To engage ethically with automated systems requires acknowledging the boundaries of machine reasoning. It also requires humility: recognising that transparency will never be a one-time achievement. Ethical review is not a ceremony; it is a rhythm.

Yet ethical frameworks cannot succeed if they remain confined to specialist circles. Public discourse must stretch to accommodate technical debates that once sat far from everyday concern. In recent years, citizens' assemblies in Ireland, Japan, and Canada have experimented with democratic input into AI strategy, demonstrating that ordinary people can grapple with complex technological dilemmas when given structured avenues to do so. These initiatives hint at a broader shift: the governance of automated systems should not belong exclusively to those who build them. It should belong to those who live with them.

Even so, governance and collaboration address only part of the question. The deeper transformation concerns our own orientation to truth and agency. As digital systems anticipate our preferences with increasing precision, the temptation to let them pre-empt decision-making grows stronger. A navigation app that selects an "optimal" route; a newsfeed that chooses "relevant" stories; a recommendation engine that proposes "suitable" songs or books—convenience nudges us towards passive acceptance. To move beyond automation requires noticing these nudges and refusing to let them define our sense of self. The point is not to reject digital systems, but to relate to them with steadiness rather than surrender.

A future worth pursuing is one in which technology sharpens our awareness rather than dulls it. Where tools extend human imagination instead of narrowing it. Where data informs deliberation without eclipsing it. Such a future demands a shift in cultural posture: curiosity over complacency, reflection over reflex, discernment over ease. It requires that we keep asking how our tools shape our thinking, our relationships, and our perceptions of truth.

What anchors this shift is neither code nor compute capacity, but something markedly older: our humanity. The capacity to empathise, doubt, listen, and reason remains the most potent safeguard against the drift toward automated certainty. Machines can surface patterns at scale, but they cannot comprehend the moral weight of a choice. They can forecast risk, but they cannot determine whose risk matters. They can model behaviours, but they cannot grasp what makes a life meaningful.

As you step into this final chapter, consider a quiet question that will shadow each section: what kind of world do we create when we let automation deepen our capabilities rather than diminish our autonomy? The answer is neither predetermined nor guaranteed. It will be shaped by the values we uphold, the scrutiny we exercise, and the humanity we refuse to relinquish.

Empowered Human-AI Collaboration

In March 2020, radiologist Dr Miriam Smith at Addenbrooke's Hospital in Cambridge reviewed a chest CT scan flagged by an experimental deep-learning model. The system, trained on thousands of anonymised scans collected across the UK, highlighted a cluster of irregular nodules with an 87 per cent confidence rating. Smith did not accept the verdict at face value. She zoomed, compared slices, and checked prior medical notes. Within minutes she confirmed the model's suspicion: the early formation of a pattern that, left unnoticed, would likely have progressed before the next scheduled scan. The result was not the victory of machine over human, nor human over machine, but something more revealing. It showed what becomes possible when insight is shared, not surrendered. This collaboration saved time, shaped treatment, and deepened professional trust. Five words capture the moment: *She did not yield control.*

That refusal to yield is a motif that deserves returning to, because it frames the entire premise of empowered human-AI partnership. Collaboration is not passive. It is active, negotiated, and constantly recalibrated. Far from automating judgement out of the equation, the future of AI-assisted decision-making depends on the ability of people like Smith to question alerts, interrogate uncertainty, and bring human texture to mathematical inference.

One of the most persistent claims in debates about AI is that machines will inevitably outperform humans in tasks requiring speed or pattern detection. Two decades of progress support that assertion in narrow domains. Yet the debate often overlooks the equally critical question: what is the human contribution that remains indispensable even as automation accelerates? A case from 2016 illustrates the answer. When Google DeepMind's AlphaGo defeated Lee Sedol in Seoul, commentators focused on computational triumph. But Sedol's famous "Move 78"—a decision shaped by intuition rather than optimisation—exposed what pure calculation struggles to replicate. Human creativity often emerges from deviations that cannot be modelled through probability alone. Sedol's act of imaginative defiance introduced a different kind of intelligence into the match. It demonstrated that the most instructive moments arise not from domination, but from interplay.

Such interplay grows even more essential in domains where consequences extend beyond games. Consider how AI is used in environmental modelling. The European Centre for Medium-Range Weather Forecasts in Reading integrated machine-learning components into atmospheric simulations in 2022. These models accelerate forecasts, especially during severe weather events. Yet meteorologists still compare outputs manually, adjust for local anomalies, and interpret patterns that resist pure statistical explanation. The pairing reveals a broader truth: speed without context misleads, but context without speed can endanger. Combined, they create a diagnostic rhythm suited to complex realities.

A sceptic might argue that collaboration is merely an interim stage—that as systems improve, human oversight will become symbolic at best. That scepticism deserves attention. Automation in aviation provides a useful counter-example. Autopilot systems, standard since the late twentieth century, now manage much of a flight's routine dynamics. Yet investigations into aviation incidents—from Air France Flight 447 in 2009 to the Boeing 737 MAX crashes in 2018 and 2019—show that overreliance on automation can erode situational awareness. Pilots whose roles have been gradually constrained can become less prepared to intervene when systems falter. The counter-example is credible precisely because it illustrates a limitation. But it also underscores the essential point: collaboration only functions when human agency remains active. The failure is not in automation itself but in allowing automation to displace rather than augment responsibility.

Human-AI collaboration thrives when each party contributes what the other lacks. Machines bring scale, repetition, and risk-tolerant exploration. People bring contextual judgement, ethical sensitivity, and the capacity to interpret ambiguity. The combination matters because ambiguity is the soil in which most consequential decisions grow. Even in high-data environments—medicine, finance, logistics—interpretation remains decisive. What a model labels as anomalous may be entirely expected given local knowledge. What appears statistically optimal may be ethically untenable. What seems efficient on a dashboard may violate norms that hold communities together. Collaboration, therefore, is not about harmonising two forms of intelligence. It is about allowing their tension to yield insight.

That tension is not merely intellectual. It is behavioural. One example appears in the domain of risk assessment within European energy grids. Operators monitor thousands of variables, many processed by predictive algorithms. Yet decisions about redistributing load during peak stress are still made by teams of engineers who evaluate social cost, geographic vulnerability, and political implications beyond what the system calculates. Efficiency metrics matter—the number of minutes saved, the stability percentages gained—but these metrics coexist with decisions shaped by human understanding of consequence. Algorithms measure likely outcomes. People weigh what those outcomes mean.

A quieter motif begins to surface here: *alignment is learned, not granted*. Collaboration cannot be willed into existence by declaring humans and machines "partners." It must be practised through transparency, explanation, and dialogue. For instance, in 2021 the University of Toronto's Schwartz-Reisman Institute conducted studies on explainability, showing that users performed significantly better when AI systems disclosed confidence intervals and reasoning traces rather than final outputs alone. Behaviour changed measurably: users asked more questions, cross-checked more often, and overrode the system when ambiguity was high. The gain was not merely accuracy but agency.

Yet transparency is not a cure-all. Another motif enters the frame: *vigilance*. Even well-designed collaborative systems can amplify error. A study by the US National Institute of Standards and Technology (NIST) in 2020 found that certain facial recognition models displayed unequal error rates across demographic groups. When humans were asked to verify matches produced by these systems, some participants over-trusted the initial suggestion, accelerating the propagation of error. The limitation is clear: collaboration falters when humans accept machine output too quickly, especially when systems perform with inconsistent reliability. The reconciliation is equally clear: collaboration flourishes when oversight is deliberate, informed, and sceptical without being dismissive.

This raises a broader implication for the future of professional expertise. Far from replacing skilled labour, AI shifts the nature of skill. Clinicians learn to interrogate model confidence. Lawyers learn to evaluate algorithmic document filters. Urban planners learn to interpret predictive simulations without becoming beholden to them. Expertise evolves from executing tasks to curating them, from performing calculations to interpreting them, from absorbing information to scrutinising its origins. The locus of mastery moves upward, not outward.

These shifts also expose a deeper philosophical question: *What distinguishes human contribution when machines appear increasingly competent?* The answer lies not in what machines cannot yet do, but in what they are not designed to value. They do not care about justice, solidarity, dignity, or meaning. They do not sense fear in a patient's voice, nor understand the moral weight of a borderline diagnosis. Human insight operates on a register that no model optimises for: the register of lived experience.

As collaboration becomes more pervasive, the architecture of decision-making will need reimagining. Should systems provide suggestions or ranked choices? Should they display uncertainty openly or in expert modes only? Should override mechanisms be manual, timed, or tiered? These are design questions infused with political meaning. They determine whether collaboration enhances autonomy or hollows it.

The unresolved tension that remains is therefore not technological but moral. How do we commit to systems that amplify thought without constraining it? How do we ensure that collaboration does not drift into delegation, and delegation into dependence? The future poses a challenge that each profession must now confront: when the machine speaks first, what will prompt us to speak back?

Ethical Frameworks

In April 2018, the UK House of Lords Select Committee on Artificial Intelligence released a report urging the creation of a national ethical framework to guide the development and deployment of AI technologies. The committee drew on testimony from researchers at the Alan Turing Institute in London, clinicians from the NHS, economists, philosophers, and civil society organisations. Their conclusion was striking not for its novelty but for its urgency: without structured ethical scrutiny, innovation would advance faster than public accountability. That same month, a separate internal review at Google—prompted by employee concerns about the company's involvement in Project Maven, a US Department of Defense initiative applying machine learning to drone footage—reached a similarly serious outcome. The project was scaled back, and Google published a set of AI principles in June 2018. Two very different arenas, one public and one corporate, pointed towards the same truth: without ethics, capability becomes hazard.

The tension revealed in these events is the quiet motif that threads through this discussion: *boundaries shape freedom*. Ethical frameworks do not restrain innovation so much as clarify where innovation serves human well-being. When a boundary is thoughtfully drawn, it does not limit invention—it steers it.

A recurring claim in technology circles is that ethics slows progress. Yet history shows the opposite. The ethics committees governing clinical trials, for example, evolved to prevent exploitation and harm, not to hinder scientific discovery. Their role is to interrogate assumptions, test procedures, and safeguard participants. The outcomes are measurable: more reliable data, clearer protocols, and higher public confidence. By 2022, the UK Health Research Authority reported that over 98 per cent of approved studies adhered to pre-registered ethical requirements (HRA 2022). The behaviour is visible: researchers document consent, justify data use, and report unexpected incidents. The implication is straightforward: ethical oversight strengthens the legitimacy of innovation rather than weakens it.

This lesson transfers directly to AI. One relevant example appears in the European Union's drafting of the AI Act, which began formal negotiations in 2021 and entered final legislative stages in 2023. The Act categorises AI systems by risk level—minimal, limited, high, and unacceptable—and mandates different obligations accordingly. It requires human oversight for high-risk applications, prohibits manipulative biometric systems, and demands traceability in automated decision-making. Its goal is not to pre-empt technological evolution but to shape it towards accountability. The visible behaviour it enforces is disclosure: developers document datasets, measure error rates, and maintain impact assessments. The implication extends far beyond Europe. By tying legal obligations to ethical principles, the EU has set a global reference point, influencing corporate strategies as far afield as Silicon Valley and Singapore.

Yet ethical frameworks cannot rest solely within legislative chambers. Social legitimacy depends on interdisciplinary committees capable of responding to rapid technological shifts. The Ada Lovelace Institute in London exemplifies this model. Founded in 2018, it convenes social scientists, computer engineers, legal scholars, and public-interest advocates to study the societal impact of data and automation. Their investigations into biometric surveillance, health data governance, and algorithmic injustice combine empirical research with public consultation. The behaviour is concrete: they run workshops, release audits, and publish guidance accessible to policymakers and the general public alike. The implication is that ethics becomes a collective civic project rather than an abstract philosophical aspiration.

Nevertheless, multidisciplinary committees face a credible limitation: they can become advisory bodies without teeth. Reports are published, concerns are voiced, but regulatory power may lag. The UK's Centre for Data Ethics and

Innovation (CDEI), established in 2018, is an example. While it has produced influential analyses on algorithmic transparency, critics argue that it lacks enforcement authority. This limitation matters. Without statutory power, recommendations risk dissolving into polite suggestion. Reconciling this, however, requires distinguishing two roles. Advisory committees excel at diagnosing risks and supporting informed public debate; regulators excel at enforcing compliance. The reconciliation lies in synchronising these functions: committees generate insight, and regulators adopt frameworks informed by that insight.

The motif of *boundaries shape freedom* reappears here with fresh clarity. Ethics is not a static checklist but a dynamic structure that must adapt to context. For instance, during the COVID-19 pandemic, NHSX, the digital innovation unit of the NHS, initiated a review in May 2020 regarding the ethics of digital contact-tracing. Their consultants measured privacy risks, assessed governance structures, and consulted legal experts on proportionality. They also engaged with public groups to understand concerns about surveillance creep. The action was deliberate: evaluate before deployment. The implication was significant: public trust increased measurably once independent oversight was visible and data retention limitations were communicated. The model revealed that ethical review works best when embedded early, not appended as a late-stage audit.

This emphasis on timing exposes another common misconception: that ethics is a barrier to competitive advantage. Yet a growing number of firms recognise the opposite. Microsoft's expansion of its Office of Responsible AI in 2022 demonstrated how internal teams can integrate legal, technical, and philosophical expertise into product design. Engineers were required to document failure modes, quantify uncertainty, and justify model deployment in sensitive environments. Behaviours changed: teams paused releases, refined datasets, and re-ran evaluations when concerns emerged. Efficiency metrics shifted from speed-to-market to integrity-of-outcome. The implication was commercial as well as moral: clients increasingly prefer systems backed by rigorous safeguards.

Not all attempts succeed. Meta's Oversight Board, launched in 2020 as a quasi-independent appellate structure for content-moderation decisions, faces persistent scrutiny. While the board has issued detailed rulings—including its 2021 decision to uphold the suspension of Donald Trump's Facebook account—it remains dependent on Meta's willingness to implement recommendations. This is a credible limitation: independence constrained by corporate discretion. Reconciling it requires acknowledging that structural independence is not achieved by design alone but by control over implementation. Yet the model still makes a contribution: it introduces a visible mechanism of review, raises expectations of justification, and encourages public dialogue. It shows that even imperfect ethical structures can cultivate transparency.

Ethics also requires listening beyond institutional walls. Public debate, though messy, is a vital engine of accountability. Citizens' assemblies, such as those convened in France in 2019 to address climate policy, offer a model for deliberation that could be replicated in AI governance. When diverse perspectives collide—technologists, teachers, pensioners, nurses—the resulting questions often reveal assumptions invisible to experts. The behaviour is direct: people ask whose data is used, who benefits, who is harmed, and who decides. The implication is that democratic scrutiny helps prevent narrow interests from dominating technical narratives.

Consider the question of data sovereignty. The African Union's Digital Transformation Strategy (2020–2030) underscores the importance of regional governance over data flows, partly in response to historical patterns of extraction. Ethical frameworks in this context serve not just individuals but geopolitical dignity. They require developers to disclose cross-border data transfers, justify storage decisions, and respect local norms. This is ethics as protection—protection of community agency, not merely individual privacy.

A different but equally instructive example is the OECD's AI Principles, adopted in May 2019 by more than 40 countries. These principles—transparency, robustness, accountability, inclusiveness—operate as a normative baseline. Though non-binding, they serve as a shared vocabulary for international cooperation. The motif surfaces again: *boundaries shape freedom*. Shared norms make innovation interoperable across cultures while preventing any single ideology from dominating global standards.

The future of ethical frameworks, however, will be defined by friction. Developers will confront dilemmas where accuracy competes with fairness, where commercial confidentiality competes with transparency, where rapid deployment competes with societal reflection. These dilemmas cannot be eliminated by guidelines. They require habits of scrutiny, cultures of justification, and institutions that evolve faster than the systems they oversee.

The unresolved question that remains is both practical and philosophical: how do we commit to ethical oversight that is continuous rather than reactive? Technology accelerates; review must accelerate with it. The next generation of developers, policymakers, and citizens will need to decide whether ethics remains a set of documents or becomes a living discipline—one capable of shaping the technologies that, in turn, shape us.

Reimagining Our Relationship

In March 2021, the Dutch Court of The Hague halted the government's use of SyRI, an automated risk-profiling system intended to detect welfare fraud. Civil society organisations, including the Netherlands Juristen Comité voor de Mensenrechten, argued that SyRI's opaque algorithms entrenched bias and eroded citizens' agency. The judges agreed. They ruled that the system violated

Article 8 of the European Convention on Human Rights because its logic was inscrutable and its implications potentially discriminatory. It was a landmark case, not only because a tool was switched off, but because a society stopped to ask a deeper question: *what happens to freedom of thought when decisions about us unfold beyond our view?* Five words capture the unease that pervaded the ruling: *transparency is essential for dignity.*

The SyRI case revealed a paradox embedded in our algorithmic age: the very systems built to optimise governance can eclipse the human judgement they claim to improve. Efficiency gains become persuasive. Pattern detection becomes seductive. As automated outputs accumulate into daily routines—credit assessments, job screenings, housing allocations—humans risk drifting from authors to observers of their own lives. The motif that threads through this section is simple yet insistent: *we must stay awake.* Staying awake means more than resisting technological overreach; it demands reimagining how humans and systems co-create meaning, truth, and agency.

Consider how easily people outsource interpretation. A study published by the MIT Media Lab in 2019 showed that when volunteers were provided with algorithmic cues during content-labelling tasks, their independent judgements dropped by as much as 25 per cent. The behaviour was visual: participants deferred to colour-coded "risk" indicators even when the indicators were randomly assigned. The implication is stark. When systems speak with the calm certainty of statistical authority, individuals may quieten their own reasoning. The motif returns here: *we must stay awake*—awake to our cognitive shortcuts, awake to the allure of precision, awake to the risk of becoming passive interpreters rather than active thinkers.

Reimagining our relationship with technology therefore begins with acknowledging the asymmetry between machine confidence and human doubt. Systems appear decisive. Humans hesitate. Yet hesitation is not a flaw; it is a mark of deliberation. When clinicians at Moorfields Eye Hospital in London evaluated DeepMind's diagnostic tool for retinal disease in 2018, they insisted on a loop of human oversight. The system could identify over fifty eye conditions with remarkable accuracy, but ophthalmologists still reviewed outputs, queried anomalies, and overruled the model where appropriate. The behaviour mattered: consultants documented their reasoning, compared machine suggestions with clinical imaging, and fed discrepancies back into development. The implication extends beyond medicine. When humans interrogate algorithmic conclusions, they reclaim authorship of truth-making.

The next major claim reveals a cultural rather than technical shift: societies must reframe their understanding of truth from something delivered to something co-constructed. This is not relativism; it is responsibility. When Greta Thunberg addressed the United Nations Climate Action Summit in New York in September 2019, she confronted political leaders with the phrase "How dare you pretend...", accusing them of masking inaction through selectively framed statistics. Her intervention was not about rejecting data but about demanding the context that gives data meaning. The behaviour was public refusal to accept packaged narratives. The implication is that truth gains strength when citizens question framing rather than simply ingesting it.

Yet a credible counter-example warns us against romanticising human interpretation. The 2016 US presidential election demonstrated that people can be more easily misled by emotionally resonant misinformation than by cold statistics. Self-assured interpretation can be as dangerous as blind deference. Reconciling this limitation requires the integration of two habits: scepticism of algorithmic authority and scepticism of our own emotional biases. Staying awake cuts both ways. It is a discipline, not a reflex.

This brings us to a deeper question: how must our perspective on agency evolve as machines take on interpretive roles? Agency has often been imagined as independence—an individual thinking without interference. But independence no longer reflects the realities of digital influence. Agency now resembles navigation. It is the capacity to steer through automated suggestions without being subsumed by them. The behaviour is mundane yet telling: choosing when to pause, when to click, when to investigate a claim, when to shut the laptop and breathe before reacting. The implication is transformative: humans remain agents not by resisting all systems but by shaping their relationships with them.

Cultural shifts usually begin in micro-habits. In Kyoto, mindfulness practitioners from the Rinzai Zen tradition have long used the practice of *metsuke*—a soft, attentive gaze—to cultivate awareness without fixation. Applied metaphorically, *metsuke* offers a model for digital life. To engage with automated systems as conscious participants rather than passive consumers, we need a similar soft attention: alert yet ungrasping, informed yet independent. In recent digital literacy workshops run by the Norwegian Media Authority, participants were taught to pause for five seconds before resharing emotionally provocative content. That pause—five seconds—is the behavioural spark of a cultural reimagining.

Two more examples illuminate how societies might support this shift. In 2020, Finland expanded its national curriculum to include structured media-education modules that teach students to analyse visual framing, identify narrative manipulation, and recognise algorithmic suggestion. Teachers measure improvement through written reflections and source-comparison exercises. Behaviour changes visibly: students request original sources, annotate claims, and enact slow thinking in fast environments. The second example comes from Taiwan, where civic technologists such as Audrey Tang champion "radical transparency" through participatory platforms. Government discussions are livestreamed, datasets are openly published, and policy deliberations invite public annotation. The behaviour is collaborative: citizens and officials co-examine proposals, exposing flawed assumptions before they calcify. These examples show that reimagining our relationship with systems requires reimagining our relationship with one another.

Still, a limitation persists. Cultural change can be uneven. Not all communities have equal bandwidth—cognitive, economic, or emotional—to scrutinise digital influence. Some may prioritise immediacy over reflection simply because life demands it. Reconciliation emerges when we view mindful digital engagement not as a luxury but as a shared civic infrastructure. Just as societies invest in transport or sanitation, they can invest in public understanding of automated systems. Libraries, schools, broadcasters, and local forums can all serve as scaffolding for collective awareness.

Returning to the motif—*we must stay awake*—we begin to see that awakening is not a solitary act but a social one. It involves designing systems that reveal their workings, teaching communities how to interpret them, and cultivating norms that reward attention over speed. It means rejecting the myth that automation absolves us from judgment. Instead, it calls us to reclaim judgment with renewed steadiness.

The deeper philosophical shift this section gestures toward is perhaps the most challenging. Truth must be seen neither as a fixed destination nor as a malleable plaything of digital narratives, but as a practice sustained by curiosity, humility, and shared responsibility. Agency must be understood not as total independence but as the capacity to shape the conditions of our interpretation. Data's power must be acknowledged without being sanctified. Technology must be invited into the human sphere without being permitted to dominate it.

Which leaves an open question—one that cannot be automated away. How will we recognise the moment when assistance becomes influence, and influence becomes control? That moment will not announce itself. It will accumulate quietly in habits of thinking and feeling. Staying awake will depend on the choices we make long before the threshold appears.

Maintaining the Human Core

In April 1996, in a hall at the Cape Town City Council, Archbishop Desmond Tutu opened the first public hearings of South Africa's Truth and Reconciliation Commission. Reporters recorded the room falling into a taut, almost reverent silence as the testimonies began: mothers describing sons who had vanished, former police officers confessing to crimes once hidden by official secrecy. No dataset could capture the tremor in a witness's breath or the weight of Tutu's tears as he paused the session to steady himself. The Commission relied on documents, forensic reports, and legal evidence, but its authority emerged from something that refused quantification: an insistence that truth required human presence. Five words encapsulate that moment. *Grief cannot be automated.*

That hearing retains its resonance because it revealed a truth about truth itself. Even when facts are meticulously recorded—dates logged, injuries catalogued, orders traced—meaning must still be drawn through human interpretation, empathy, and moral judgement. Digital systems can structure information. They cannot feel its ache. As we stand amid proliferating algorithmic infrastructures, the Commission offers a motif that threads through this section: *the irreplaceability of the human core.* It is a reminder that the wisdom shaping democratic life, ethical standards, and collective memory arises not from pattern recognition but from lived experience and moral reflection.

To maintain the human core, we must first recognise what is uniquely human about judgement. Consider the behaviour of clinicians working with AI-augmented triage systems in Manchester's Salford Royal Hospital in 2020. The software prioritised incoming emergency cases by analysing symptoms and vital signs. Yet nurses regularly overrode the machine when they sensed something the system could not register: a parent's panic, a child's laboured hesitation, or the faint slackening in a stroke patient's gaze. Those judgements were not inefficiencies; they were expressions of embodied expertise. The implication is immediate. Even where machines measure physiological metrics with precision, humans contribute interpretive nuance that anchors care in compassion.

The first major claim, then, is that ethical governance of technology depends on nurturing the kinds of insight that resist quantification. This becomes clearer when we examine specific examples. In 2021, the European Data Protection Supervisor criticised the adoption of predictive policing tools in several EU member states, arguing that these systems risked reinforcing existing inequities. The behaviour under scrutiny was simple: officers were dispatched more frequently to areas flagged as "high-risk", which happened to be neighbourhoods already subjected to disproportionate surveillance. The implication is that data does not merely describe a pattern; it can solidify it. Maintaining the human core means refusing the passivity of accepting patterns at face value and insisting on contextual interpretation.

A second example reveals what happens when human values guide the redesign of digital systems. In 2019, the Wikimedia Foundation altered its editing interface to highlight "knowledge gaps", encouraging contributions from women, scholars from the Global South, and indigenous communities. The behaviour change was visible: editors sought sources in multiple languages, checked cultural representation, and questioned editorial assumptions. Here again, the implication is clear. Diversity of human experience deepens informational integrity. No algorithm could have identified which histories remain untold without the interpretive labour of people who perceive the world through plural lenses.

A credible limitation must also be acknowledged. Humans are not consistently wise, kind, or attentive. Bias, fatigue, and personal history colour interpretation. One might point to newsroom failures, such as the 2003 reporting errors around the Iraq War, where journalists across respected outlets accepted claims about weapons programmes that later proved unfounded. Human intuition faltered. This limitation does not weaken the argument for maintaining the human core; it sharpens it. It is precisely because humans are fallible that we must engage consciously with technology, rather than retreat from responsibility. An algorithm cannot replace wisdom, but it can amplify our mistakes if we abdicate judgement.

At the heart of this section lies a quiet motif: *the pause before response*. When individuals pause—before sharing a fragment of rumour, before accepting a machine's verdict, before reacting to a provocation—they enact the essence of the human core. The pause is behavioural, measurable in seconds, yet dense with meaning. It signals reflection, humility, and a willingness to let values, not impulses, shape action. This motif reappears as we consider how people navigate digital influence. Maintaining humanity is not an abstraction; it is a practice enacted one decision at a time.

Let us turn to another major claim: preserving the human core requires active cultivation of values, not passive reliance on systems that encode other people's assumptions. Psychologists such as Daniel Kahneman and the late Amos

Tversky demonstrated that humans often rely on heuristics—mental shortcuts that simplify judgement. In digital settings, these shortcuts become especially potent because platforms are engineered for speed. The behaviour is familiar: users scroll rapidly, react quickly, and often treat the first interpretation offered—whether by a friend, a feed, or a machine—as the most plausible one. The implication is that values wither under conditions of haste. Reinvigorating them requires structured opportunities for slow thinking.

Slow thinking is reinforced by traditions that pre-date computation by centuries. In the Benedictine monasteries of 6th-century Italy, monks practised *lectio divina,* a structured reading method involving slow reflection on a text. The aim was not comprehension alone but moral formation. Today, digital literacy educators in Denmark have adapted similar principles, encouraging students to annotate emotional shifts while reading online articles. They measure improvement by comparing early annotations with later ones, noting increased attention to tone, motive, and rhetorical framing. The human core is strengthened not by rejecting technology but by training interpretive muscles that prevent emotional manipulation from bypassing critical judgement.

The question of agency also returns. If algorithms shape the choices presented to us, what sustains autonomy? Autonomy is not a static state. It is a dynamic ability to recognise influence and respond with deliberation. Behaviour again reveals the truth. When citizens in

Reykjavik participated in the city's open consultation platform, Better Reykjavík, they rated proposals, suggested improvements, and revised their own submissions after reading others' perspectives. The process made influence visible. Participants could see which ideas gained momentum and why. The implication is encouraging: when influence is made transparent, the human core is fortified rather than diminished.

Yet another limitation must be confronted. There are contexts in which human judgement fails under pressure. High-intensity domains such as aviation or nuclear safety rely on automation because human error can be catastrophic. For example, after the 1979 partial meltdown at Three Mile Island, investigators noted that operator misinterpretation of instrument readings worsened the situation. Automated safeguards helped prevent further escalation. How, then, do we reconcile these cases with the argument for the human core? The answer lies not in rejecting automation but in clarifying its role. Machines can prevent immediate disaster by adhering to strict rules. They cannot guide societies toward fairness, dignity, or moral progress. The reconciliation is practical: automation can handle emergencies; humans must handle meaning.

The next major claim brings us to humanity's relational dimension. Wisdom grows in dialogue, not isolation. Technology often fragments dialogue into microbursts—likes, retweets, algorithmic recommendations—each one accelerating emotional reaction while reducing reflective exchange. Reclaiming the human core therefore requires collective as well as individual practices. Two examples demonstrate this. In 2021, New Zealand's Broadcasting Standards Authority encouraged public engagement through moderated online forums discussing misinformation. Participants compared sources, challenged assumptions, and reflected on their own interpretive habits. The behaviour that emerged—curiosity rather than defensiveness—strengthened democratic resilience. Meanwhile, in South Korea's citizen assemblies on digital ethics, participants used consensus-building software to visualise agreements and disagreements. They could see where values converged, enabling respectful debate instead of polarisation. These models show that when people come together to examine truth claims, their collective judgement attains a depth no automated system can replicate.

As this section progresses, the motif of *the pause before response* recurs. The pause is not simply a technique; it is a symbol of mindfulness, a reminder that action should follow reflection rather than impulse. It signals that the human core is maintained not by perfect wisdom but by deliberate attention to the forces shaping perception. When individuals cultivate this disposition, they resist becoming extensions of their own digital environments.

What, then, anchors the human core across contexts as varied as healthcare, justice, education, and public discourse? The anchor is the capacity to care. Care is more than emotion; it is a commitment expressed in behaviour:

listening closely, revising opinions, acknowledging another's dignity, refusing to treat people as variables in a model. Algorithms can process inputs. They cannot care. They cannot grieve, apologise, forgive, or imagine the future through the lens of empathy. These acts form the infrastructure of human wisdom.

A final question remains, one that threads together every claim in this section. How do we protect the human core in a world where automated systems grow increasingly confident and increasingly persuasive? The question resists easy resolution. It must remain open because its answer will be shaped by decisions still unfolding—in parliaments, in classrooms, in living rooms, in the quiet pause before someone decides whether a machine's suggestion deserves trust.

The unresolved tension is deliberate. What safeguard will you choose when efficiency tempts you to relinquish reflection? The answer will not be produced by an algorithm.

About the Author

Yunis Al-Raqib is a researcher and commentator who delves into the intersection of emerging technologies and everyday human experience. Growing up at the crossroads of different cultures, he witnessed how cultural narratives and beliefs are molded by evolving digital ecosystems. His work advocates for transparency and ethical reflection in AI-driven societies, with a focus on ensuring that human values are never overshadowed by technological conveniences. By sharing stories and insights from various communities, he encourages readers to question the surface-level neutrality of algorithms. His ultimate goal is to equip individuals across generations with the perspective and curiosity needed to navigate a world where data dictates much of what we perceive as true.

www.ingramcontent.com/pod-product-compliance
Lightning Source LLC
Chambersburg PA
CBHW031336230926
51848CB00002B/257
9789374597866